D0639454

The Power of
the Social Brain

The Power of the Social Brain

Teaching, Learning, and Interdependent Thinking

EDITED BY

Arthur L. Costa
Pat Wilson O'Leary

Foreword by Jerry Jennings

Teachers College, Columbia University
New York and London

Published by Teachers College Press, 1234 Amsterdam Avenue, New York, NY 10027

Copyright © 2013 by Teachers College, Columbia University

All rights reserved. No part of this publication may be reproduced or transmitted in any form or by any means, electronic or mechanical, including photocopy, or any information storage and retrieval system, without permission from the publisher.

Library of Congress Cataloging-in-Publication Data

The power of the social brain : teaching, learning, and interdependent thinking / edited by Arthur L. Costa, Pat Wilson O'Leary ; foreword by Jerry Jennings.
       pages cm
   Includes index.
   ISBN 978-0-8077-5414-6 (pbk. : alk. paper) — ISBN 978-0-8077-5415-3 (hardcover : alk. paper)
      1. Learning, Psychology of. 2. Thought and thinking-—Study and teaching. 3. Adult learning. 4. Professional learning communities. I. Costa, Arthur L., editor of compilation. II. O'Leary, Pat Wilson, 1948–
   LB1060.2.P6792 2013
   370.15--dc23   2012046937

ISBN 978-0-8077-5414-6 (paper)
ISBN 978-0-8077-5415-3 (hardcover)

Printed on acid-free paper
Manufactured in the United States of America

20   19   18   17   16   15   14   13   8   7   6   5   4   3   2   1

We dedicate this book to Pat's granddaughter, Neve Jayne O'Leary, and Art's great granddaughter, Annabelle Brynn Wilsey, who, as the concepts in this book become fully implemented, will grow up in an increasingly empathic, compassionate, and thought-full world.

Contents

Foreword
Thinking Together

Life is full of differences: different priorities, customs, and thinking
Living and/or working together is full of challenges: We can think through
    them or not
Thinking interdependently means we invest in the idea that good can
    come from diversity of thought
We need to connect: mind-to-mind
Connecting mind-to-mind will serve the common good
Connecting mind-to-mind is not going to just happen
Connecting mind-to-mind requires developing new processes
We must be intentional about connecting mind-to-mind

When people are good at thinking together, good things happen. There is a great need for adults to become more intentional and successful as interdependent thinkers and catalysts for helping students and others to gain these skills.

The focus of this book is first to illuminate the value of interdependent thinking among adult learners who work in service of the common good. Second, it is to explore facilitation approaches that support adults and children as they intentionally pursue the practice of interdependent thinking.

THE GLOBAL CHALLENGE

The challenges faced by individuals in families, workplaces, communities, regions, countries, and all across the globe beg for people to collaborate and to think interactively. Man didn't get to the moon through the thinking of one person—it took the collective thinking of many people to accomplish this goal. Interdependent thinking is the best response to the complex challenges we face. Block (2008) explains, "Community offers [the] promise of belonging and calls for us to acknowledge our interdependence. To belong is to act as an investor, owner, and creator of this place" (p. 3).

The complexity of the world can lead adults to respond to problems in ways that are almost devoid of interdependent thinking—in spite of the potential good that can come from collaboration as a "co-creator." Kegan and Lahey (2009) explain, "When we experience the world as 'too complex' we are not just experiencing the complexity of the world. We are experiencing a mismatch between the world's complexity and our own at this moment. There are only two logical ways to mend this mismatch: reduce the world's complexity or increase our own" (p. 12).

Kegan and Lahey conclude that, despite the challenge of developing interdependent thinking skills, it is not impossible. In the interest of more effectively addressing the many challenges in the world, it is clearly worth increasing our own complexity by becoming thinkers who are good at thinking with others.

The promise of people thinking interdependently through contentious problem-solving situations is that such efforts ultimately can achieve significant positive outcomes for society and/or the individual. When we engage in interdependent thinking, we can all influence and be part of positive change. We all will not get our way or be the "argument winner." But if we invest in the concepts of thinking together with an open mind, a willingness to understand how others think and feel, and a desire to reflect and rethink throughout the process of coming to an actionable decision, we can accomplish much together.

Block (2008) asks the question, "How are we going to be when we gather together?"(p. 10). This is a crucial question. My answer is that we need to intentionally develop abilities for thinking interdependently. We must actively deploy these skills to effectively work, listen, and think with one another. It is our shared responsibility to engage one another with the goal of producing positive change for the future.

FACILITATION SKILLS

There are many hurdles for those engaged in intentionally improving as an interdependent thinker. Individuals intent on independence, faced with the fact that others think differently about a given problem, often engage in aggressive or avoidant techniques. These techniques vary and can include holding onto past thinking, refusing to interact with other thinkers, labeling other thinkers as the enemy, and jumping to conclusions. The stability of a person's status-quo thinking is often very attractive. It can be challenging to move into the instability and tentativeness of shared thinking. Patterson et al. (2008) explain that unpleasant endeavors "require a motivation that can come only from within. People stimulate this internal motivation by investing themselves in an activity. That is, they make the activity an issue of personal significance. They set high standards of who they'll be, high enough to create a worthy challenge, and then they work hard to become that very person" (p. 93). Being internally motivated to grow and develop as a person who thinks well with others is a value for the person and for the common good.

Some individuals and like-minded groups of individuals can and do become walled silos of thought. Often adults in one specialty or with one point of view are certain that individuals who hold different worldviews won't be willing to connect openly and think together without tensions erupting or without having the discussants fall back into unproductive "winner" and "loser" arguments.

Many others make no attempt even to politely associate with those who think differently. Those committed to having their thoughts become the winning thoughts harbor hostility toward those who think differently. The other extreme is to be polite and settle for superficial interactions.

When preschoolers play, they mostly engage in a separated style of side-by-side interactions often called "parallel play." Sadly, many adults are willing to settle for the separateness of polite or not-so-polite "parallel thinking." One reason for this is that when an individual effectively engages in thinking with others who think differently, he may experience a sense of disequilibrium. This happens because he is exploring very different thoughts than those most familiar to him.

An individual needs considerable motivation to put him- or herself in a position of disequilibrium. Crosby and Bryson (2005) describe the "desired outcome of leadership for the common good as a regime of mutual gain, a system of policies, programs, laws, rules and norms that yields widespread benefits at reasonable cost and taps people's deepest interest in their own well-being and that of others" (p. 360). For interdependent thinkers, a focus on the common good is essential.

Adults and children benefit from appropriate support and coaching when engaged in the kind of new learning that thinking interdependently requires. The description of the needs of adult learners, offered by Malcolm Knowles, Edward F. Holton III, and Richard A. Swanson (2005), can be seen to be helpful to students as well.

- a need to know the "why, what, and how" of things
- an autonomous and self-directing self-concept
- the resource of prior experiences and influences on their mental models
- a readiness to learn when information is connected to their life and the learning is developmental

- an orientation to learning that is problem centered and contextual
- a motivation to learn for both intrinsic values and personal payoff

When those interested in helping others to grow and develop as collaborative thinkers consider the content of Knowles's work, it is clear that development of interdependent thinkers will require the initiated and sustained facilitation of adaptive learning.

THE IMPERATIVE OF ACTIVE LISTENING

Increasing one's ability to listen and listen well is an additional imperative for those who want to think together. *Active listening* is the label of the set of skills that, when learned and put into practice, will help adults improve understandings of the ideas and perspectives of others. Hoppe (2006) explains that "active listening involves six skills: paying attention, holding judgment, reflecting, clarifying, summarizing, and sharing. Each skill contributes to the active listening mindset, and each skill includes various techniques or behaviors" (p. 12). Thus, as individuals endeavor to get better at thinking together, they face the necessity of getting much better at listening with a sincere intent to strive to understand the incoming message. Those not interested in understanding often tend to listen only long enough to know which argument they want to employ against the thinking of the speaker. That kind of listening will not lead toward interdependent thought. However, as a person becomes more and more skilled she very likely will be able to listen her way into actually beginning difficult conversations. Listening can help people to stick with the process of learning from and impact the learning of those who think differently.

The complexity of teaching children as they learn to be successful at thinking interdependently is amplified by the fact that there are not a lot of observable models of adults in our daily lives who look at things differently—talking, listening, and jointly thinking through differences to actionable conclusions.

CONCLUSION

Thinking interdependently is a set of behaviors that can be taught, coached, and learned. The benefits of individuals assimilating these skills are significant to families, places of work, communities, and beyond.

Tomorrow belongs to those who can collaborate and create in concert
Tomorrow's promise is complex and thus requires interdependent thinkers
Those who listen and think together will realize tomorrow's opportunities

—Jerry Jennings

REFERENCES

Block, P. (2008). *Community: The structure of belonging.* San Francisco: Berrett-Koehler.

Crosby, B. C., & Bryson, J. M. (2005). *Leadership for the common good* (2nd ed.). San Francisco: Jossey-Bass.

Hoppe, M. H. (2006). *Active listening: Improve your ability to listen and lead.* Greensboro, NC: Center for Creative Leadership.

Kegan, R., & Lahey, L. L. (2009). *Immunity to change.* Boston: Harvard Business Press.

Knowles, M. S., Holton, III, E. F., & Swanson, R. A. (2005). *The adult learner* (6th ed.). Burlington, MA: Elsevier Butterworth Heinemann.

Patterson, K., Grenny, J., Maxfield, D., McMillan, R., & Switzler, A. (2008). *Influencer: The power to change anything.* New York: McGraw-Hill.

Preface

Independent Thinking

Arthur L. Costa & Pat Wilson O'Leary

If you want to go quick, go alone.
If you want to go far, go with others.

—African proverb

After 32 years of conversation, in which time we have worked together and on parallel paths, we remain committed to the combined effort of Habits of Mind and cooperative learning. Representing work in education, business, family life, brain research, community projects, music, and architecture, this collection is a sample of high-level, interdependent thinking. This book is written by individuals who are living out this way of thinking and teaching others to do the same. The group of authors share our vision of a world in which children learn how to think and work together. This book is a model of our message.

Cooperation has been a consistent message from researchers like David and Roger Johnson, Robert Slavin, and Spencer Kagan since the 1970s. Books have been written and thousands of workshops conducted to help teachers organize cooperative learning to increase student achievement and student social skills. We have known for years that educational researchers have encouraged teachers and leaders in schools to move from their individual and competitive work to collaborative efforts that create a common school-improvement vision and plan. Professional learning communities (PLC) are a model for the 21st-century school system. However, bringing interdependent thinking practices to school systems has not been easy. Woodrow Wilson is quoted as saying, "It is easier to move a cemetery than change a school system."

We have been in classrooms where students sit together and work quietly without fighting. The problem is that they may not be working from a common effort, and they aren't always thinking together. We recall observing team meetings where the loudest voices got the most attention while the other members played bobble-head dolls, nodding their head to whatever decision would end the meeting the most quickly. Later, team members complained that nothing had improved or that they hadn't agreed to the latest actions. Such group situations may be described as "traditional" groupwork or even "pseudo-cooperative" groups. To the untrained eye and ear, some of it looks good, but nothing substantive may be happening. Change will not take place. Team members will continue to work individually or competitively.

We have observed exemplary learning situations where a teacher or leader facilitates dialogue so that children or adults listen with empathy, paraphrase to hear the correct message and feeling, and ask questions to probe deeper. New ideas and learning are created for everyone involved. Participants know and use the Habits of Mind (Costa & Kallick, 2008). When we observe groups with a common appreciation of diverse opinions and experiences, we see civil disagreements and hear honest questions. People learn through active participation, not head nodding. Facilitating these high-performing, collaborative groups that think together is our goal for children and adults.

What we believe is the missing piece of the collaborative puzzle is "interdependent thinking." In previous writing (Costa & O'Leary, 1992) we called it co-cognition. Simply working collaboratively is not enough. We also must learn to grow the thinking that we do together. This book adds the cognitive dimension to cooperative learning. We hope to help individuals monitor and improve their thinking while contributing to and learning in groups. Our goal is to help educators apply these strategies of successful groupwork in classrooms and professional educational learning communities.

THINKING INTERDEPENDENTLY: THE CONFLICT WITHIN US

Humans in our Western culture have two very basic needs:

1. *To assert oneself as an individual: to seek status, identity, power, and fulfillment.* We strive for autonomy. There are times when we prefer solitude. We want to be alone to look inward, to think and reflect on our personal situation. Extreme isolation, however, is unhealthy. Dr. James Lynch, author of *A Cry Unheard* (2000), draws on decades of extensive medical and sociological research to conclude that every citizen living in the world's technologically advanced nations faces the potential of suffering debilitating and deadly health threats caused by "communicative disease" as well as communicable disease.

2. *To share experiences with others: reciprocity, intimacy, relationships, connectedness—the "snuggle to survive."* We strive to become one with the larger system and community of which we are a part. Forming relationships, as illuminated by Pat Wolfe in the introductory chapter that follows, is a survival mechanism. Humans cannot exist in isolation. They thrive, create, solve problems, and learn in harmony with others.

We believe that an educated, interdependent thinker is one who becomes increasingly aware of this internal conflict and knows how to manage it with flexibility—being alert to both environmental and internal cues that inform his or her knowing when and how to act autonomously, as well as when and how to act interdependently. This book is dedicated to that educational outcome and process.

OPERATIONAL DEFINITIONS

When we see and hear students and adults working and playing together, we may interpret that they are collaborating through their actions. Thinking interdependently, however, cannot be inferred from actions alone because it is covert; it takes place inside the head. It consists of the decisions we make, the internal dialogues we have, the beliefs we hold, our perceptions of others and ourselves, our inclinations, our dispositions, and the mental models by which we filter and understand our world.

We, and other *cognitive educators*, believe that what we observe people doing overtly is a product of these inner thought processes, and to improve overt behavior, we must surface, alter, enhance, and refine those inner perceptions to help learners become aware of and modify their decisions, beliefs, values, and paradigms.

People who think interdependently:

- know that they benefit from working collaboratively—all of us are more efficient than any one of us;
- are altruistic—they are inclined to lend their energies to benefit the larger good;
- value consensus, while holding their own values and actions in abeyance;
- seek collegiality;
- value, seek, and draw on the resources of others;
- regard conflict as valuable and can manage group differences in productive ways;

- experience a sense of interconnectedness, unity, and commitment to common goals and shared values; and
- enlarge their conception from "me" to "us"—understanding that as we transcend the self and become part of the whole, we do not lose our individuality but rather our egocentricity.

We want this book to provide content that is intellectually challenging with examples of interdependent thinking that cross life experiences. We want each chapter to represent authentic, applied combinations of theory and practice. Thanks to the many authors who accepted our invitation, we believe that we have achieved our purposes.

If you are reading this book, you likely share our beliefs or are concerned enough with the state of the world that you are looking for solutions. Without hubris, we hope that this book fills a gap. We wish that each and every chapter buoys your hopes, challenges your thinking, and gives you tools for polishing your own habits of interdependent thinking, enabling you to support the development of the same in students and in others with whom you live and work. It is easy to see that this is what the world needs now.

SUGGESTIONS FOR USING THIS BOOK

While you may wish to read this book from beginning to end, you probably will select chapters or parts to meet your individual and group interests. It also works well to use the book as a basis for group study, having each group member volunteer to read one chapter and then present his or her interpretation of the reading to the rest of the group. The following discussion may include finding themes and patterns, relating the content of the chapter to the group's setting or situation, drawing implications for improved practice, and experimentation with strategies for group or classroom implementation. The book is organized as follows.

Preface and Introduction

We start with how this book adds a *metacognitive* dimension to the wealth of work in cooperative learning accumulated and applied over the years. Thinking and acting together is introduced not only as a needed skill to live productively in our uncertain, problem-filled future but also as a human survival mechanism found and developed in hard-wired structures of the human brain.

Part I

Interdependent thinking is illuminated in a variety of settings: the arts, the sports industry, the community, and schools. The chapters in this part illustrate that the need to think interdependently is basic to solving problems in a wide range of settings. No one person can solve complex problems alone.

Part II

Facilitating groups and professional learning communities to think and solve problems together is the subject of the next section. Many strategies are suggested for leaders who wish to maximize the mindfulness and pro-ductivity of effective groups.

Part III

Included here are contributions from experienced classroom teachers and many instructional strategies intended to teach young people to think and work interdependently at home and at school.

At the end of each part, reflective questions are provided to help guide readers' thinking or to stimulate conversation in a book study with col-leagues. We suggest that readers, as they read each part, jot notes to record thoughts for continued consideration or for discussion with other readers, and add some of their own reflective questions to ours.

Our focus is on how groups think together, what some of the disposi-tions of effective group thought are, what strategies might be employed to develop those dispositions, and how those dispositions are applied in real-life settings, whether in classrooms, professional learning communi-ties, or other groups.

REFERENCES

Costa, A. L., & Kallick, B. (2008). *Learning and leading with habits of mind: 16 essential characteristics for success.* Alexandria, VA: Association for Supervi-sion and Curriculum Development.

Costa, A. L., & O'Leary, P. W. (1992). *Co-cognition: The cooperative development of the intellect.* In N. Davidson & T. Worsham (Eds.), *Enhancing thinking through cooperative learning* (pp. 41–65). New York: Teachers College Press.

Lynch, J. (2000). *A cry unheard.* Baltimore, MD: Bancroft Press.

Acknowledgments

We wish to thank all the authors who have contributed to this book. Their rich experience in working with groups to build interdependent communities, their skillfulness in communicating their knowledge, and their dedication to the topic of enhancing interdependent thinking are greatly admired.

We also wish to thank those who have contributed their editorial polish to this text: Cat Jones, Carole Cooper, as well as John Bylander and the other editors from Teachers College Press.

We greatly appreciate Jean Ward, acquisitions editor for Teachers College Press, who not only had faith in us but also had the patience to sustain her encouragement over time.

And we wish to thank our spouses, Art O'Leary and Nancy Costa, for putting up with the many hours we seemed more interested in computer screens than in them, for allowing us the many phone conversations we had rather than conversing with them, and for the hours of meetings when we could have been spending time with them. We appreciate the time they gave us to pursue this dream.

Together, as a team, we are all striving to make the world a more thought-full place.

—Arthur L. Costa, Granite Bay, California
Pat Wilson O'Leary, Portage, Michigan

Thinking Interdependently—
A Human Survival Mechanism

Pat Wolfe

> To keep your resolve, surround yourself with those who want you to succeed. The brain cannot do its job of protecting the body without contact with other people.
>
> —Robert Ornstein & David Sobel, *The Healing Brain*

The conception of the thinker as alone rather than embedded within a human community has been a fundamental characteristic of Western science and philosophy for many years. This belief has changed radically as our knowledge and understanding of the brain have grown. This introductory chapter proposes to explain how working and thinking interdependently (in groups) is not only a desirable process but the key to our survival as a species.

NEUROPLASTICITY

The past 3 decades have produced a prodigious body of research about the structure and function of the human brain. Probably the most amazing information to come out of this research is that the brain is changed as it interacts with and is influenced by the environment. This concept is referred to as *neuroplasticity*. It wasn't too many years ago that it was believed that the brain you are born with is the brain you are stuck with; that your genes are the main determinants of who you are and the environment plays a rather insignificant role. We now know that this is far from true; the environment, by means of the brain's plasticity, plays a vital role in who we become. One example of this plasticity can be seen in the brains of persons born without sight. It was supposed that the brain cells designed to process vision in a

The Power of the Social Brain, edited by Arthur L. Costa and Pat Wilson O'Leary. Copyright © 2013 by Teachers College, Columbia University. All rights reserved. Prior to photocopying items for classroom use, please contact the Copyright Clearance Center, Customer Service, 222 Rosewood Dr., Danvers, MA 01923, USA, tel. (978) 750-8400, www.copyright.com.

blind person would atrophy since they were not activated. Instead, it was discovered that the visual cells actually change their function and become cells that process auditory and tactile input. Numerous additional research findings validate the fact that the environment plays a major role in the sculpting of the brain.

An understanding of plasticity has led to an increased understanding of how the human brain has evolved and developed over millions of years. At the outset, it is critical to understand that the main purpose of the brain is survival. We have brains in order to keep the individual and the species alive. Those traits and behaviors which increase the probability of survival are selected and passed on to the next generation. A fast runner had a better chance of escaping from a saber-toothed tiger and living to produce progeny. The same is true of many other skills or traits. For example, good hunters or gatherers had a better chance of survival, and if they worked together with others, their chances were even better. Humans are relatively weak, with no fur or armor to protect them. Being a weak lone individual competing for scarce resources would certainly be a disadvantage. But you could double your strength by establishing cooperative agreements with some of your neighbors. Being a member of a group would then make survival more likely when resources were limited. It is easy to see how eventually the brains of our ancestors began to change from purely survival brains into social brains. Most scientists now agree that our social brains have been shaped by natural selection because being social enhances survival (Cozolino, 2006).

Further evidence to support the concept of the social brain comes from studies of very young children. In his book *Why We Cooperate*, Michael Tomasello (2009) makes a strong case for an innate capacity that children have for empathy and cooperation. He states that at an astonishingly early age, children begin to help one another and to share information. It appears that we are born ready to cooperate.

Given the brain's plasticity, it is not surprising that it appears that living in larger and more complex social groups has resulted in larger brain regions. The development and increasing complexity of social life changed not only behaviors but the anatomy and circuitry of the brain as well. Daniel Goleman (2005), in his book *Emotional Intelligence*, explains that earlier thinking on what allowed humans to develop such large and intelligent brains focused on our ability to hold and make tools. In recent decades more proponents have been drawn to the brain's role in the social life of the species—its role in survival and in raising children who survive into parenting age.

The brain regions that have undergone the most change are those capable of the emotion, reason, and intellect necessary to form relationships and work collaboratively with others. (Size typically is considered an indicator of processing capacity.) This has been corroborated by research in the comparative anatomy of humans and other primates. For example, the amygdala, a brain region necessary for emotion and social interactions, demonstrates the impact of the environment on the brain. A 2011 study by researchers (Bickert et al.) determined that humans with larger and more complex social networks had larger amygdala volume. The neocortex (the outer layer of cells covering the brain) is another area that expanded as humans became more involved in larger social groups (Cozolino, 2006). Various parts of the neocortex are designated for language, thinking abstractly, problem solving, and interpreting social information, areas necessary for success in navigating our increasingly complex social environment. In primate studies, it has been found that the more members of a band in a species, the larger the neocortex relative to the rest of the brain (Sawaguchi & Kudo, 1990). However, the social brain (with its proportionately larger neocortex) became the most highly evolved in humans who developed the highest degree of social prowess.

MIRROR NEURONS

Another group of neural structures called *mirror neurons* appear to play an important role in the workings of the social brain. These neurons reflect an action we observe in someone else, causing us to mimic the action or have the impulse to do so (Goleman, 2006). For example, when you observe someone yawning, it often causes you to yawn. The same is true of smiling. These hard-wired mirror neurons also allow us to "read" the feelings of others and resonate with those feelings. Our minds are not independent, separate, and isolated, but are continually interacting with the minds of others. Psychiatrist Daniel Stern (2004) believes that as these mirror neurons bridge brains, they create a pathway that allows us to engage in powerful interaction.

A deficit of the social brain, whether genetic or the result of brain trauma or surgery, often results in the inability to form relationships or have a productive social life. This can be observed in autistic individuals, who often are not equipped with the skills to read the feelings of others and have difficulty empathizing or socializing with them. The well-known case of Phineas Gage is a tragic example of the loss of social skills that occurs with damage to the frontal cortex. While Gage was working with explosives on a railroad crew, a steel rod accidently exploded through his frontal lobe. Amazingly, he survived but his personality changed. He previously had been well liked and had worked well with the rest of the crew. After

Phineas Gage: Neuroscience's Most Famous Patient

An accident with a tamping iron made Phineas Gage history's most famous brain-injury survivor (Twomey, 2010). To find out more about Phineas Gage, go to http://en.wikipedia.org/wiki/Phineas_Gage. Image courtesy of Jack and Beverly Wilgus.

the accident, he no longer related appropriately to others, lost his job, and died destitute and alone.

We have seen that certain behaviors increase the probability of survival. But what causes us to repeat these behaviors? Is it the knowledge that if we run faster we have a higher probability of escaping the wild beast, or are other factors involved? Knowledge alone is probably not enough of a reinforcer. Consider that most of us know that exercise and eating healthy foods are productive behaviors, but often that is not enough of an impetus to change our habits. Something else must be at play.

That "something else" is a hard-wired group of structures deep in the brain that rewards us for behaviors that increase our chances of survival. This primitive neurological system is referred to as the *reward pathway*, the *pleasure center*, or the *natural reinforcement center*. This system is composed of two main structures, the nucleus accumbens (NA) and the ventral tegmental area (VTA). As with all other brain systems, the neurons (brain cells) within these structures communicate with electrical and chemical signals at junctures called synapses. Electrical impulses (action potentials) cause neurons to release chemicals (neurotransmitters) into the synapse. The result is that the neuron receiving the chemical is activated.

DOPAMINE: THE FEEL-GOOD NEUROTRANSMITTER

There are several neurotransmitters released by the NA and VTA, but dopamine appears to be the primary activator of the pleasure center. Because the NA and VTA have projections to the conscious part of the cortex, we are able to be aware of the pleasurable sensation that dopamine produces. Dopamine says, "That feels good; do it again." You probably have unknowingly experienced this effect. Think about how a delicious meal produced a pleasurable feeling or how you felt when someone smiled at you or complimented you on a job well done, or when you finally solved a difficult problem. You can thank dopamine! Why are you rewarded by these behaviors? It is because they increase your chances of survival. Is eating pleasurable? Yes, because if we didn't eat, the species would die out. Have you heard of "runner's high"? The effect is a dopamine reward for being a fast runner, another survival benefit. As we have seen, working well with others increases your chances of survival. Therefore, being complimented or smiled at, and collaboratively solving a problem can cause the activation of the reward pathway and increase the probability that you will engage in these behaviors again.

SURVIVAL AND SOCIAL COOPERATION

Validation of the neural basis for social cooperation comes from neuroscientists at Emory University. They found in their research that the act of helping another person triggers activity in the reward pathway, producing the same sort of pleasure as gratifying a personal desire (Rilling et al., 2002).

As mentioned at the start of this chapter, we are beginning to understand that thinking interdependently (with another person or group of persons) is more than just another strategy to use in classrooms; it has survival benefits as well. In addition, it appears that thinking interdependently increases student understanding and retention of concepts. For example, if I have just read or heard information new to me, I may think I understand it. However, when I am asked to teach it to a partner or discuss it with a group of my peers, several things may occur. I may find I didn't understand as well as I thought and through group interaction I may get my misconceptions corrected. Or perhaps I will come to a better understanding when I hear others' perceptions of the information. An added benefit is I will literally strengthen the synapses between brain cells holding the memory of the discussion, thereby increasing the probability of retaining the information.

SURVIVAL AND THE SCHOOL'S ROLE

Traditional educational methods generally have not focused on cooperation and collaboration. Individual accomplishment and competition with others for grades are often the norm. As the understanding of the importance of working with others has increased, schools are beginning to look for ways to help students develop needed social skills. One process that is gaining momentum is social emotional learning (SEL). Its main goal is learning life skills such as how to recognize one's emotions and manage one's feelings, developing sympathy and empathy for others, maintaining positive relationships, and working constructively and ethically in a group. In our increasingly complex and interrelated society, these skills are becoming more essential. Certainly, learning to think interdependently fits well within the SEL process.

Another process or strategy for groupwork that includes interdependent thinking is cooperative learning. Studies of this method regularly report an increase in the engagement and active participation of students, which in turn increases student motivation, time on task, and retention of information. (See Chapter 13 by Judy Willis in this book.) It also improves cognitive reasoning and the ability to see from others' perspectives (Munro, O'Brien, & Payton, 2006). Without the opportunity to work in groups, it is doubtful that these skills will develop to their fullest capacity.

REFERENCES

Bickert, K. C., Wright, C. L, Dautoff, R. J, Dickerson, B. C., & Barett, L.F. (2011). Amygdala volume and social network size in humans. *Nature Neuroscience, 14,* 163–164.

Cozolino, L. (2006). The social brain. *Psychotherapy in Australia, 12,* 16–21.

Goleman, D. (2005). *Emotional intelligence.* New York: Random House.

Goleman, D. (2006). *Social intelligence.* New York: Random House.

Munro, S., O'Brien, M. U., & Payton, J. W. (2006). *Common ground: Teaching kids the benefits of working together.* Retrieved from http://www.edutopia.org/common-ground

Ornstein, R., & Sobel, D. (2009). *The healing brain.* Los Altos, CA: Institute for the Study of Human Knowledge.

Rilling, J. K., Gutman, D. A., Zeh, T. R., Pagnoni, G., Berns, G. S., & Kilts, C. D. (2002). A neural basis for social cooperation. *Neuron, 35,* 395–405.

Sawaguchi, T., & Kudo, H. (1990). Neocortical development and social structure in primates. *Primates, 31*, 283–289.

Stern, D. (2004). *The present moment in psychotherapy and everyday life*. New York: Norton.

Tomasello, M. (2009). *Why we cooperate*. Boston: MIT Press.

Twomey, S. (2010, January). Phineas Gage: Neuroscience's most famous patient. *Smithsonian*. Retrieved from www.smithsonianmag.com/history-archaeology/Phineas-Gage-Neurosciences-Most-Famous-Patient.html

Interdependent Thinking in Life Settings

We now live in a world that's becoming a system of systems. . . . Given that, we believe that for effective action there's got to be collaboration across organizations, not just within one specific organization.

—Tim Espy, leader for strategy and transformation at IBM, quoted in *Forbes*

The first part of this book contains a collection of chapters by authors from a variety of professions, careers, and walks of life. Each describes his or her experiences in and strategies for working in interdependent ways. The intent of including these chapters is to illuminate how interdependent thinking is basic to the success of endeavors in business, industry, the arts, schools, sports, and the community. Increasingly our world depends on individuals and organizations that can plan, think, and work together in reciprocity with others. Our international problems, coupled with rapidly changing technology, have become so complex that no one person can solve them. It takes teamwork, communication, flexibility, listening, and building on one another's creative ideas—on a global scale. It demands having the humility of being a continuous learner and remaining open to the consideration of others' contributions.

As you read each successive chapter, you may wish to search for each author's message about thinking interdependently in that particular setting: What themes, patterns, or threads emerge repeatedly and link all the chapters together? What implications might you derive from these linkages for your classroom, business, home, or organization? You and your colleagues also might divide up the chapters, each reading one and then discussing it (interdependently) to find those linkages and connections.

CHAPTER 1

Creating and Influencing Momentum

The Challenges and Power of Adults Thinking Interdependently

Jerry Jennings

When eight adult professionals got together and decided to take a serious look at the future of passenger rail transportation in Michigan, where less than 1% of the state's total transportation budget goes to passenger rail, the average observer could be forgiven for wondering, what are they thinking? Could there really be a future for this type of travel in the home state of Ford, Chrysler, and General Motors?

Of course, these were no ordinary folks making idle chat. They were participants in the Great Lakes Leadership Academy (GLLA), a leadership development program created through the efforts of the W.K. Kellogg Foundation, the Michigan State University College of Agriculture and Natural Resources, MSU Extension, and MSU AgBioResearch. The eight were part of a total cohort of 24 adults who spent 45 days learning together during 2009 and 2010.

The mission of the Great Lakes Leadership Academy is to promote positive change, economic vitality, and resource conservation, and to enhance the quality of life in Michigan by encouraging leadership for the common good. Those who created GLLA concluded there was a critical need for leadership development that would focus on the issues and challenges associated with helping leaders from diverse constituencies transcend self-interest and create workable solutions for the common good.

GLLA participants are private or public workers or owners who represent the professions associated with communities, food systems, agriculture,

The Power of the Social Brain, edited by Arthur L. Costa and Pat Wilson O'Leary. Copyright © 2013 by Teachers College, Columbia University. All rights reserved. Prior to photocopying items for classroom use, please contact the Copyright Clearance Center, Customer Service, 222 Rosewood Dr., Danvers, MA 01923, USA, tel. (978) 750-8400, www.copyright.com.

natural resources, environmental, and manufacturing sectors in Michigan. They are a diverse group of leaders who have demonstrated commitment to their community.

GLLA strives to develop individuals to *advance their abilities to lead with others* in the interest of the common good. The curriculum focuses on:

- exposing participants to emerging issues;
- analyzing the impact of our major themes on society;
- creating a forum where diverse perspectives are encouraged;
- infusing the program with the experience and wisdom of Michigan leaders;
- developing broader perspectives by exposing participants to societal, economic, and cultural differences on the community, state, national, tribal, and global levels; and
- providing for ongoing networking, training, and support of GLLA alumni.

Subgroups of GLLA members form issue teams to study a specific issue and then present a program to the rest of the cohort regarding that topic. Issue teams focus on topics that affect natural resources, agriculture, environmental, business, and/or manufacturing sectors of Michigan, such as food systems, land use, energy, youth development, or water. Issue teams are given no direction or structure, but simply a goal of producing a one-and-a-half-day session for others to learn from.

GLLA faculty coaches don't direct the teams nor do they do anything to organize the teams' effort or outcomes. Coaches do encourage members to think together and to find ways to work through challenges by supporting thinking together across differences and by encouraging the group to appreciate their individual and collective judgment and knowledge.

In the world of real-life stories, some are full of drama or noble sacrifice. Others have suspense or a fall from grace. This is a story of a journey, a journey revealing the power of adults thinking interdependently.

Let's recall the context. Michigan is the home of Ford, General Motors, and Chrysler. We are the auto state. Hoping to develop an interest in exploring transportation options other than repairing and/or expanding the roads and bridges is a rather bold move given the past and current structure of the state. Yet, because we asked people to dream about what might be possible, things are changing in Michigan. This is a story of possibility that came to life by engaging people in thinking together.

The rails issue team was made up of an environmental planner for a council of governments, a university academic, a manager in the Food and Dairy Division of the State Department of Agriculture, an owner/operator of a large-production vegetable farm, a program associate for a major foundation in southeastern Michigan, a religious social justice chair and civic organizer from Detroit, a county extension director for a major university, and a deputy policy director of a statewide environmental nonprofit.

This diverse group came together with different prior knowledge around a topic of rail transportation. They had very different levels of interest in and commitment to the future of passenger rail transportation. In many ways the knowledge, dispositions, and interests represented in this team reflect those of any task force for a given project in a work setting or in the community.

But something was different. This group of people had been learning together about being predisposed to appreciating what might be possible, actively listening to others, seeking to understand the thinking of others, seeing themselves as "a work in progress," being intentionally present and engaged, focusing on general desired outcomes or solutions (as opposed to being highly focused on having their own ideas embraced by others), thinking together in small or large groups, being open to new ideas and ways of looking at issues, cooperating for the common good, and collaborating.

As this team began to look, with openness, at the concept and history of rail transportation in Michigan, they discovered these facts:

- There was a rich history of passenger train travel in Michigan during the first part of the 1900s.
- Small towns had train depots and were connected to one another as trains moved between larger cities.
- People were riding these trains and goods were being transported.
- An elaborate rail system existed in the state.
- Michigan was a state where "cars and roads rule"—that thinking seriously about rail transportation in this state at this time was not something that seemed to carry much momentum.
- There was an 8-mile Woodward light rail project in Detroit and there was an additional potential of federally subsidized high-speed rail lines between Chicago and Detroit that would require $38 million of Michigan support to become a reality. (The Michigan Department of Transportation apparently, and quietly, had come to the conclusion that very little would be happening with rail in Michigan.)
- Currently, high-speed rail options were being implemented in Spain, Japan, and China. European countries, such as France, had already implemented high-speed rail. The U.S. federal government was supporting rail initiatives with the incentive of money that could be applied for by states and regions around the country.
- The efficiency of high-speed rail and the accessibility it potentially would allow for travel to and from work, and for entertainment

or vacationing, was substantial, especially as we look to the future cost of fuel for personal vehicles.

- The complex economic realities of Michigan potentially could be influenced for the better by adding the dramatic improvement of rail transportation into a comprehensive plan for the state's future. Improving and increasing rail transportation would serve the common good of Michigan citizens.

The work of the rails issue team was not smooth. It was messy work. Not to say that working as a group trying to collaborate and benefit from one another's strengths is ever easy. It is not.

The team studied, interviewed, discussed, listened to one another, thought out loud, accessed data, heard from experts, read extensively, and visited sites. The members learned about the possibilities of a Michigan that included rail transportation. They also argued, became passive, entered into minor conflict, had some commitment follow-through issues, avoided conflict, and avoided ownership of the challenge.

Tension was present. One thing was surfacing—the team was becoming convinced that it wanted to influence the members of the larger cohort favorably toward the potential of rail transportation in Michigan for the common good. Broad as this general agreement was, it kept the group moving along on its journey.

Members wrestled with how to use their day-and-a-half session to make the greatest impact on the thinking of the other members of the Academy. Should they try to increase the members' knowledge about the history of passenger rail transportation in Michigan or about the high-speed systems in Spain, Japan, and/or China? Should they put forth a well-thought-out, desired plan for rail passenger travel in Michigan and try to sell it? Should they focus on one project like the Woodward light rail project and work to gain support for that? It was a struggle for the group. They looked at things from different perspectives and with varying levels of interest. They were struggling with what they might do. Experts could be lined up to make speeches and/or teach lessons, books and articles could be assigned, and videos could be presented. A bibliography of wonderful resources could be created. After talking, listening, learning, and thinking together (thinking interdependently), the team decided to present the session in a way that would actively engage all cohort members. This was a consensus decision that everyone supported. When our issue teams formed, we had established as one of the ground rules that we would make decisions through consensus. Consensus doesn't mean each member is willing to be the leader for the agreed-upon idea; however, for a true consensus to exist, each member truly has to support the idea.

Engagement was the key the team members were looking for. When this decision was made, the tension seemed to end and excitement among the team members began to develop. They came up with the following plan:

- Create a session that would engage the cohort members in "thinking about" this issue rather than the traditional kind of "learning about" this issue.
- Start their one-and-a-half days by having the whole cohort ride a passenger train together from Jackson, Michigan, to Kalamazoo so these adults could experience the current reality of rail transportation in Michigan.
- Ask their fellow GLLA members to reflect, in journals the team provided them, on the experience of riding the rails, the experience of being in the train stations in both Jackson and Kalamazoo, and about the February walks from the train station to the hotel and the public library.
- One expert would speak for approximately 1 hour, explaining and showing pictures of high-speed rail plans in America and the reality of high-speed rail as it is being experienced in Japan, Spain, and China.
- Put large maps of Michigan in front of small groups of four or five GLLA members and staff and ask them to dream together in these small groups about where they would want rail transportation to exist in the future for Michigan.
- Ask the individual small groups to think interdependently about where rail transportation should exist in Michigan.
- Engage everyone in the room in thinking about and framing a positive future for Michigan with realistically accessible rail transportation opportunities.
- Have each of the small groups report to the whole cohort about their specific dreams for the future of rail transportation in Michigan.
- Reflect on their learning while walking back to the train station and boarding a train to Jackson.

As a result of the experience, the rest of the cohort was ready to clearly see the potential value of a Michigan that included high-speed rail in its future. No state policy battles were won in this day and a half. However, as a result of the GLLA rails issue team session, one of the team members led similar condensed sessions around the state under the title of Michigan by Rail. Sixteen public forums were held in the summer and fall of 2009 across state from Traverse City to Royal Oak and from New Buffalo to Flint.

Eleven hundred citizens participated and produced 100 maps. Members of the rails issue team and other GLLA members assisted with some of these events in various cities. Over 400 comments from citizens attending these sessions were shared with the Michigan Department of Transportation. The journey started by the rails issue team was having an impact on the state.

Interest in this rails issue and in the general issue of transportation in Michigan was stirring, in part as a result of the Michigan by Rail public forums. As a result of interest from the 16 forums around the state, Trans4M, a broad-based coalition of partners and supporters including nonprofits, businesses, policymakers, environmental groups, planners, academic institutions, and others was created. Trans4M, which formally began in November 2010, is leading the discussion and actions for transportation into the future for Michigan. Trans4M is an architect and product of a growing consensus: Strategic investments in public transit and non-motorized options, combined with maintaining existing road infrastructure, can revive our urban centers, reconnect people to opportunity, and reduce our environmental footprint. A member of the rails issue team is a leader of this coalition, and a member of the coalition is one of the GLLA cohort that took the train ride to Kalamazoo and helped create a map of her dream for Michigan's future rail lines.

In the fall of 2011, both the Michigan Senate and House passed legislation to support Michigan's contribution, to be combined with the federal funds, to make high-speed rail between Chicago and Detroit a reality.

Who knows whether this would have happened, in this time frame or at all, if the GLLA rails issue team hadn't thought together, and if one of those issue team members hadn't invited more and more people to join in the thinking.

CHAPTER 2

Efficient Thinking with Architectural Teams

Peter Saucerman

The design and execution of buildings is one of the oldest and most complex undertakings of human society. From the great Pyramids of Giza to Chartres Cathedral; from the earliest skyscrapers to modern theaters, societies have sought to demonstrate their power, wealth, and technological achievements through impressive public buildings.

The evolution of planning, design, and construction of monumental buildings presents visible evidence of the power of collective thinking. The complexity of buildings has increased exponentially over the centuries, while the time required to design and erect them has shrunk dramatically. As buildings have become larger and more complicated, the creative approach to design has necessarily evolved—from linear to interactive and finally to interdependent thinking. To frame this evolution in creative thinking, here are three historical examples from three ages.

LINEAR THINKING IN DESIGN:
THE GREAT PYRAMID AT GIZA (3600 BCE)

The pyramids of Egypt are among the earliest and most recognizable monuments produced by humankind. For over 3,500 years the Great Pyramid (of Cheops) held the record as the tallest man-made structure in the world. This construction marvel put the ancient world on notice that Egypt was a wealthy, powerful, and technically advanced people. Although we may never know the exact organizational and engineering processes that produced this monument, the principal technologies were simple: quarrying, shaping, transporting, and erecting stones—very large ones—to create a striking memorial.

The Power of the Social Brain, edited by Arthur L. Costa and Pat Wilson O'Leary. Copyright © 2013 by Teachers College, Columbia University. All rights reserved. Prior to photocopying items for classroom use, please contact the Copyright Clearance Center, Customer Service, 222 Rosewood Dr., Danvers, MA 01923, USA, tel. (978) 750-8400, www.copyright.com.

The Pyramids of Giza

It is a pure geometric design with very simple detailing—no cornices, carvings, or embellishment; just smooth stone finishes on a solid mound edifice. Tens of thousands of laborers were required for construction, operating with a consistent vision of the outcome. The precise techniques used are still debated by scholars, and we remain in awe of this early building achievement.

SPECIALIZATION AND THE MASTER ARCHITECT: CHARTRES CATHEDRAL (13TH CENTURY CE)

By the Middle Ages the Christian church had become the dominant political and social force in Europe. The principal physical evidence of the power and influence of the church lies in the immense cathedrals constructed in this period. As Europe awoke from the Dark Ages, building technologies rapidly improved, at least for the largest ecumenical projects. Craftsmen's guilds emerged and flourished, creating separate technologies for various building components—stone, metal, wood, glazing, and the like. The guilds were exclusive and secretive organizations, protecting and refining their tools and methods to maintain commercial advantage for their members. Masonry, iron working, carpentry, glazing, roofing, and other specialized trades evolved, decentralizing the construction process and introducing new materials and techniques. The building process sped up and it took decades rather than centuries to complete a monument. Chartres cathedral in France is notable for having been constructed in a mere 57 years, between 1193 and 1250—a lightning pace by medieval standards.

Chartres Cathedral

With multiple tradesmen in separate specialties, a master builder was charged with overseeing the project in all its separate elements. His role was to maintain the overall project vision and ensure the design remained coordinated—windows and doors fit their openings, rafters landed upon solid stone seats, roofing drained water away from building interiors. While there would be growing interaction among the specialists, the creative design process remained largely linear: the vision of the church leaders, laid out by the master builder and constructed by tradesmen under his direction. We can still see the impressive results of these medieval enterprises in grand cathedrals throughout Europe.

INDUSTRIAL AGE: SKYSCRAPERS AND INTERACTIVE DESIGN (19TH–20TH CENTURIES)

With the blossoming of the Industrial Age in 19th-century America, architectural design evolved from the master builder, linear design hierarchy to larger groups of specialists working as interactive design teams. The architect maintained overall project design authority, but relied increasingly on expertise and input from specialists such as civil, mechanical, and structural engineers. New technologies, including elevators (essential for the birth of the skyscraper), electric lights, and telephone systems, brought more specialists to the design team.

The separation between the "art" of architecture and the "craft" of construction was complete with the emergence of the general contractor. This was now a separate business entity, further narrowing the architect's direct responsibilities while increasing his collaborators. The architect managed his design team while his counterpart, the contractor, managed the specialized tradespeople who actually would construct, using the architect's drawings.

The Flatiron building in New York City was an early product of this interactive approach. Constructed in 1902 and nicknamed for its iconic shape, it was designed by Daniel H. Burnham, the esteemed architect and creator of the 1893 Chicago World's Fair. Chicago was at the leading edge of light-frame steel construction and Burnham was its most famous architect. The Fuller Company, a leading Chicago-based builder of high-rise steel structures, teamed with Burnham to bring their expertise to New York, an emerging market for skyscrapers.

The Flatiron Building Under Construction, 1902

Figure 2.1. Traditional Design–Construction Interaction

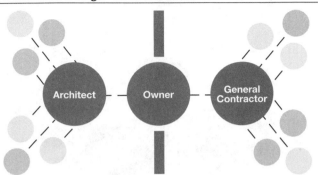

A tripartite relationship became the contractual norm for design and construction in the 20th century and it shaped the thinking process (see Figure 2.1). In broad terms: The architect has a contract with the owner to create a building design. The general contractor has a separate contract with the owner to erect the building described by the architect's plans. The architect and contractor do not have a contractual relationship with each other—each acts as a separate agent of the owner. Since they did not share in the creative thinking that shaped the building design, the architect and contractor sometimes find themselves in a tug of war trying to influence the owner.

This separation between the architect and contractor can be stifling to their collaboration, as each has his or her own turf to defend. It can result in delays as work stops for the two parties to wrestle over design changes. It can lead to litigation as one party sues the other to lay blame for cost overruns, delays, or deficiencies. Building has become big business, and many fortunes are won or lost over real estate deals. Rigid contractual terms often keep parties separated, stifling creative relationships. But new, interdependent, creative alignments are emerging.

21ST CENTURY:
NEW WAYS OF THINKING, NEW WAYS OF BUILDING

By the close of the 20th century, segregated/linear thinking traditions in design and construction began giving way to new organizational models (see Figure 2.2). Sophisticated owners such as hospitals and universities began seeking cohesive teams to both design and construct their buildings. This approach promotes true teamwork and interdependent thinking. The architect and contractor are both in for the long haul; they have common, overarching goals and each has a voice in the creative process from the very

Figure 2.2: Interdependent Design-Construction Interaction

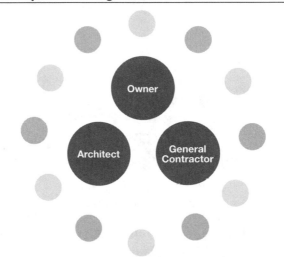

beginning. Moreover, all the specialty consultants and tradespeople are a part of the creative conversation from the outset.

New ways of thinking are permeating the design and build realms, as evidenced by the comparative chart from the Design Build Institute of America (Figure 2.3). The design team (architects) can obtain immediate feedback on design choices from the building team (contractor). For instance, certain material prices may be spiking due to international demand or short supply; the contractor may propose systems or materials known to be readily available, better quality, or better value. The architect then evaluates the suitability of the alternatives, adjusting design concepts as necessary. This interactive feedback is invaluable and enriching to the design process.

Figure 2.3. Design Thinking

Segregated Services Mentality	Interdependent Services Mentality
What's wrong?	What works?
Who's to blame?	What are our responsibilities?
How can I prove I'm right?	What are the facts?
How can I protect my turf?	What's the big picture?
How can I be in control?	What are our choices?
How could I lose?	What is useful?
How could I get hurt?	What can we learn?
Why is (this person) so clueless, frustrating?	What is (everyone) feeling, needing?
Why bother?	What is possible?

Material manufacturers also can readily become part of the creative process. Manufacturers must test and license their products to very specific industry and government-mandated performance standards. Architects often push the limits of performance, imagining new and innovative ways to use building materials. If they sense a market for new sales, manufacturers may respond by exploring the possibilities of their materials in novel situations. Truly interactive design teams will invite manufacturers to work with them to create new applications or materials, improving function and quality along the way.

APPLE FLAGSHIP STORE, FIFTH AVENUE, NEW YORK

When Apple Computer decided to venture into retail sales, CEO Steve Jobs insisted that the physical architecture for each store be as simple, elegant, and unique as the Apple products they would sell. He assembled a team of architects, engineers, designers, and constructors to create something special. Mr. Jobs had a reputation for interpreting the statement, "It can't be done," as an invitation and a challenge. For this flagship location, he envisioned a crystalline glass cube with a simple Apple logo suspended in the center. It soon became clear to his design team that this was a starkly literal statement: a glass cube. No steel supports, concrete floor, or wood bracing would be tolerated; a pure glass building was the design goal.

This was new design territory, and the design team had to broaden its ranks. Glass manufacturers were brought into the circle and challenged to

The Apple Flagship Store

deliver new products that could meet demanding specifications. New fasteners were developed; glazing fabricators and erectors consulted; heating and cooling systems modified; lighting systems customized. A full complement of designers and fabricators were drawn to work closely together under complete secrecy to create a structure that would be striking, dramatic, and beautiful. Although there was one strong leader and vision, the full team was required to work interdependently to achieve this technological marvel. The results were singular enough to warrant original patents on parts and techniques created.

HAND, CAD, AND BIM DRAWINGS

Computer-based design is changing the way we think about and create buildings. As handmade architectural drawings largely have given way to computer-aided design (CAD) drawings, so CAD is now giving way to building information modeling (BIM). Two-dimensional drawing is being supplanted by three-dimensional "virtual buildings" created entirely on computer platforms. Every bolt, plate, door, window, post, and beam is rendered faithfully, to exact scale, in the computer model. Rather than multiple disconnected drawings, prepared in isolation and coordinated at the eleventh hour, all team members contribute continuously and in real time to layers or elements of a single amalgamated building model.

A single pencil sketch may start the conceptual design idea. From there, a small team might explore simple cardboard or Styrofoam models. A larger team soon begins translating the creative concept into a digital architectural model using BIM software. Complex shapes can be modeled in the computer in three-dimensional forms and shared with erectors or fabricators, who can comment and contribute based on their knowledge of the limits and possibilities of their materials. Curving or tapered structural beams, glass, wood panels, or other materials can be modeled, tested, and fabricated directly from these computer drawings, a feat that was never possible in the pre-computer world. Structural integrity, weather-tightness, costs, and quantities for materials and systems can be accurately projected early in the design process, preserving budgets and allowing testing of multiple alternatives.

General contractors have been early adopters of BIM technology and are often as proficient as architects or engineers in using digital files. They can access the electronic files concurrently with the designers, interacting with the design model, placing material orders with fabricators, and contributing to design refinements. As more and more fabrication is accomplished by computer-driven machines, fabricators can produce assemblies that

One of Frank O. Gehry's Earliest Sketches of the Disney Concert Hall

Courtesy of Frank O. Gehry

exactly match the architect's creative vision. Buildings with a complexity that scarcely could be imagined a generation ago can now be erected with reliability and confidence.

The era of the architect drafting at his table in the wee hours and handing finished "blueprints" to the contractor is largely history. It has been replaced by a new medium: collaborative digital files, accessible to multiple team members, constantly revised and improved by interdependent thinking.

GEHRY TECHNOLOGIES AND INTERDEPENDENT THINKING

The architect Frank O. Gehry, designer of the Guggenheim Museum Bilbao and the Disney Concert Hall, has refined a system that marries computer technology with old-fashioned analog creativity to meet building industry challenges. For more than 2 decades he has amazed and delighted the architectural world by crafting technologically complex structures that remain true to the sculptural, sometimes whimsical sketches of their original concepts. A Gehry-designed building appears both technologically advanced and exquisitely handcrafted. To accomplish this marriage of analog design ideas with precise execution, Gehry Technologies (GT) has refined proprietary modeling software that can be shared by designers, manufacturers, and contractors alike. The ability for these disparate groups to work together on a common design solution leads to dramatically new designs, often exceeding what any one group could create on its own. Gehry Technologies has become a free-standing entity separate from Mr. Gehry's traditional

The Disney Concert Hall Under Construction in Los Angeles

architectural practice, available as a consulting resource to architects around the world. This is a remarkable turn of events, a major architect consulting freely with other architects to share his technological advantage.

Gehry Technologies was called in to advise on the construction of the Beijing National Stadium, built for the 2008 Olympic Games. GT provided a series of project-specific design development workshops for the project teams, building on previous work done with co-designer Arup Sport. The team built a parametric model of the stadium roof in Digital Project, beginning from wireframe roof geometry, and subsequently adding a suite of

Completed Disney Concert Hall

Photo by Carol M. Highsmith

Bird's Nest Stadium

adaptable user components to build the box girder and connector element assemblies. The team then assessed different methods for curving the steel geometry in 3-D space and compared resulting effects in detail. To meet value engineering requirements, the GT team subsequently reused the 3-D Digital Project model to simplify the stadium roof structure and reduce steel quantities. Parametric modeling in Digital Project enabled basic redesign in a matter of weeks, and the stadium was completed on time.

In the fall of 2011, Mr. Gehry announced "a strategic alliance of the world's most distinguished architects and designers [brought together] to transform the building industry and the practice of design." The alliance

Lou Ruvo Brain Institute, Frank O. Gehry, Architect

© Kurt Gittings

included a dozen of the world's most renowned architects, engineers, and designers, all accomplished in their own right. Mr. Gehry stated, "I am dedicated to giving architects better control of the process so they can deliver the fruits of their imagination, which is what our clients expect. I have gathered a group of my friends together who believe in this mission as much as I do and who can help me find the solutions that will ultimately lead to better buildings throughout the world." This commitment to open collaboration and sharing of technologies is one of the most exciting recent developments in the field of design (Gehry Technologies, 2011).

THINKING INTERDEPENDENTLY, THINKING ENVIRONMENTALLY

Sustainable design is an overarching goal for buildings today, and the design process often starts with an interactive *eco-charrette*. The term *charrette* comes from the 18th-century Ecole des Beaux Arts, a leading design school in Paris. A *charrette* was the rolling cart that moved slowly through the studio, picking up student projects at deadline. A ringing bell as the cart approached was the signal to students to scribble furiously, getting those last, intense thoughts down before submission. In modern lexicon, the term has evolved to mean a fast-paced and intensive design meeting, bringing multiple partners together to brainstorm ideas for achieving a common goal. In an *eco-charrette*, all design and construction team members, as well as project owners, come together for this brainstorming session. Architects, engineers, general contractors, material suppliers, window fabricators, and others sit down together face to face to discuss the environmental features and impacts of the project. Overall goals are established for energy use, for building materials, and for mitigation of environmental impacts. Broad design parameters are discussed and laid out for all to see—site location, seasonal sun paths, weather patterns, and building parameters (number of floors, operating hours, etc.). An open discussion among all participants helps to set goals, prioritize design decisions, and surface innovative ideas for consideration. Each specialist is an expert in his or her realm, with limited knowledge of associated disciplines. Open and frank discussion helps all team members simultaneously to better understand the complex building they are designing, and to better understand the ramifications of their design ideas for other systems or areas of the building. Here is one possible exchange:

> Concrete guy: What if we thicken the west wall concrete by 4 inches to increase thermal mass?
> Structural engineer: That will increase structural weight, meaning bigger footings, but it also might reduce steel bracing for the

structure. Steel is more expensive than concrete right now, so that's a plus for the budget.

Glass guy: Deeper wall openings means more shading of the glass—okay in the summer, but we should study how this works for winter.

Mechanical engineer: We'll need natural convection or fans to distribute thermal mass effects through the building.

The architect retains an overall coordinating role, but direct interaction and interdependent thinking among all team members creates a synergy that is a real benefit to the design process. The synergy between members often leads to competitive solutions that exceed expectations and break new design ground. This is interdependent thinking at its best.

SUMMARY

Architectural design, once the realm of elite, autocratic masters, is constantly evolving. The circle of interdependent thinkers contributing to design and construction is growing ever wider, while the lines separating disciplines are dissolving. Moving to more interactive and less adversarial contract models encourages owners, architects, and contractors to communicate frankly, candidly, and creatively, recognizing that the success of one is interrelated with success for all.

Computer-aided design and modeling systems allow increased collaboration between designers and constructors, where multiple entities can contribute simultaneously to a "virtual building" that is better and more successful because of that collaboration. Renowned design practitioners are now sharing their technical prowess widely in the design community, resulting in better buildings throughout the world.

Sustainable buildings require a holistic approach in which the owner's goals, the architect's concepts, and the contractor's methods all lead in the same direction: to reduce energy use, zero out waste, and integrate healthy building products. The interdependent thinking fostered in *eco-charrettes* helps accomplish these goals.

REFERENCE

Gehry Technologies. (2011, October 18). *Architectural leaders join Frank Gehry to form strategic alliance dedicated to transforming the building industry through technology.* Retrieved from http://www.gehrytech.com/news/content/architectural-leaders-join-frank-gehry-form-strategic-alliance-dedicated-transforming

CHAPTER 3

Thinking Together in Industry

James Heath

With the words, "Congratulations, Jim!" I officially became the president for the Instruments Division of Stryker Corporation, a medical device company. I now had the responsibility of leading and caring for 2,500 employees. I also had a new team of somewhat skeptical executives who were wondering if I could live up to the role I just received.

UNDERSTANDING THE ROLE

It was imperative to reflect on my new position and determine my priorities. I needed a clear vision for my role to get my team and ultimately the entire organization to line up behind me. I needed to create an environment of success for customers and our Instruments associates. My 7 years as a college football coach at Ohio State, New Mexico State, and Kalamazoo College taught me that clarity of purpose and alignment were essential for team success. I learned that talent alone was not enough to ensure success. These players needed a goal, direction, and coaching just as much as those I had coached at the high school level. I carried these lessons with me into business and they have served me well.

First, integrity had to be at the core of everything we did as a business. Second, I needed to drive a culture of trust and accountability. Third, I had to make sure that we hired the best talent and put them in positions where they could flourish. We would continue the culture that rewarded perseverance and teamwork. Stryker Instruments also would be a place where family came before business and we would keep the atmosphere fun. If we could establish this environment, we would pave the way for continued success in the market.

The Power of the Social Brain, edited by Arthur L. Costa and Pat Wilson O'Leary. Copyright © 2013 by Teachers College, Columbia University. All rights reserved. Prior to photocopying items for classroom use, please contact the Copyright Clearance Center, Customer Service, 222 Rosewood Dr., Danvers, MA 01923, USA, tel. (978) 750-8400, www.copyright.com.

CREATING AN ENVIRONMENT FOR INTERDEPENDENT THINKING

Virtually everything we do at Stryker—marketing, product development, and manufacturing—is dependent upon strong teams. In our division, the leader of each team selects people with the competence, relationship skills, and diversity of thought to create a framework for building on others' ideas, combining efforts, and creating new modes of operation. The leader models and fosters an atmosphere of trust where interdependent thinking is encouraged and leads to successful outcomes. The leader encourages such skills as listening for understanding, paraphrasing, and dialogue. Such conversations result in effective conflict resolution and creative solutions. For instance, to improve inventory management, our supply chain team, in forming its strategy, will consult with individuals from operations, materials management, and top suppliers. The collective inputs from each of these groups can be contentious based on their needs and timelines. However, an environment built on trust and interdependent thinking that leads to challenging and purposeful dialogue allows the supply chain team to produce outstanding results for the division and significantly improved customer satisfaction levels (faster delivery, fewer errors, and reduction in freight costs).

Supervisors in our Integrated Manufacturing Unit hold daily huddles with their teams around a rotating information kiosk. Each kiosk has the daily, weekly, and monthly production goals for the team. The kiosk also reflects the outputs for related products, current issues, training schedules, and team recognition. The supervisor facilitates the discussion, but the huddles are run by the team members. The team discusses problems, new production methods, scrap reduction, and bottlenecks. Through interdependent thinking, the team can resolve most issues without the assistance of the supervisor. If team members need additional assistance, they often will confer with members from other Integrated Manufacturing cells to discuss how to develop the best solution. This teamwork and interdependent thinking has resulted in record production levels with minimal defects. The engagement level of the Integrated Manufacturing Unit associates is excellent due to their ability to work interdependently.

BUILDING TRUST

Trust is an essential element for building an engaged work environment. It begins with solid relationships across the organization. As with other foundational aspects of the business, trust begins at the top of the organization with the Senior Leadership Team.

The Senior Leadership Team (SLT) is committed to honest and open discussion on all topics. Members of the SLT must challenge convention, contribute in all meetings, and offer solutions to problems. We believe in a culture of candor in every engagement, and that healthy debate, without fear of reprisal, improves the quality of our decisions. Healthy debate challenges conventional thinking and allows difficult issues to be brought to the table. We encourage questions like, "What would happen if . . . ?" "What if we changed . . . ?" The culture of questioning has spread across the Instruments Division. Managers and supervisors become facilitators in meetings and allow their teams to make decisions. They take an active role when the debate gets derailed or other agendas begin to surface. The manager's responsibility is to paraphrase points of view, restate the critical issues, and assist the group in reaching consensus. The manager also will intervene when there is an impasse and a decision needs to be made quickly. Healthy debate, without fear of reprisal, improves the quality of our decisions at Stryker Instruments.

At Stryker Instruments we have a way to measure trust, candor, and employee engagement through the Q12 employee survey, which was developed by the Gallup Organization for companies to measure and assess employee engagement. The survey has been used in a wide range of industries. It is based on study of productive workgroups and individuals for more than 30 years (Buckingham & Coffman, 1999). The Q12 survey is based on a 5-point scale, with 5 denoting Strongly Agree and 1, Strongly Disagree, with the following statements:

1. I know what is expected of me at work.
2. I have the materials and equipment I need to do my job right.
3. At work, I have the opportunity to do what I do best every day.
4. In the last 7 days, I have received recognition or praise for doing good work.
5. My supervisor, or someone at work, seems to care about me as a person.
6. There is someone who encourages my development.
7. At work, my opinions seem to count.
8. The mission/purpose of my company makes me feel my job is important.
9. My associates (fellow employees) are committed to doing quality work.
10. I have a best friend at work.
11. In the last 6 months, someone at work has talked to me about my progress.
12. This year, I have had the opportunities at work to learn and grow.

The closer an overall Q12 score is to 5, the higher the employee engagement level, which creates a more trusting workplace. The Q12 also reveals strengths and opportunities by business segment, as well as for the division. In addition to the Q12, we include some division-specific questions.

The Q12 results are compiled and given to each unit manager in the form of a scorecard. A feedback session is held for each unit in the division with all the team members, the manager, and a facilitator. These sessions are honest, candid, and constructive. An action/improvement plan is developed for each team, which is utilized throughout the year. Interdependent thinking helps in forming the Q12 action plan and helps foster future collaboration.

The Q12 process is one of the most significant factors in establishing a healthy culture at Stryker Instruments. This process also builds a trusting environment, which is essential for interdependent thinking.

CLARITY OF PURPOSE—HANDLING CRISIS

In 2009 we were wrestling with the economic downturn and how to drive growth during this difficult period. In addition, the management team had to find ways to cut costs across the division. We also received notice that the FDA would audit our Kalamazoo facility in May. With all the distractions and headwinds facing us, the leadership team needed to get out in front of the organization and show how we move the organization forward. Our audit highlighted a number of gaps in our manufacturing and quality systems, which called for immediate action.

I huddled the SLT to discuss the best plan for the multiple issues we were facing. We had to quickly address our quality issues and make sure we took care of our customers. Clarity of purpose encouraged excellent interdependent thinking with the SLT team. We restructured the division around the customer and quality. We formed the Customer Excellence Team and placed a veteran leader who had broad industry experience and outstanding leadership skills in charge of the team. Our most skilled people were moved into key leadership positions and given wide latitude to pick their teams. We focused solely on areas that impacted customer care and quality of projects.

Our Instruments associates realized we were in a period of transition and high challenge, but trusted that we would prevail because of our culture and commitment to improvement. Teamwork and creative thinking were more important than ever. Our Customer Excellence (CE) leaders conducted associate round tables across the division. The CE leaders sought diversity of thought by selecting associates from a variety of departments who were regarded as leaders among their peers and willing to voice their opinion in a group setting. The purpose of these sessions was to solicit employee ideas on process improvements. It was also a good forum to communicate the vision for the division during this period. This form of communication greatly increased the engagement level of all our employees and fostered ownership of the problem. We had to instill a high sense of urgency because we had objectives to meet and an imminent reaudit by the FDA. Interdependent thinking helped us move through unchartered areas and change our culture.

Through our round tables we learned that we needed more experience in our highly technical testing areas. As a result we began hiring people out of the automobile industry, who had long-established expertise in these critical testing areas. The round table discussions also set in motion our Project Management Office for scrutinizing and resourcing our divisional projects. These were mind-changing suggestions that altered our practices to achieve better results.

In September 2010, the FDA returned to the Instruments Division. The results reflected the hard work and new focus we had employed for the past 16 months, and we received a positive assessment. Clarity of purpose, teamwork, and creative thinking also moved the organization to be on an impressive growth trajectory.

THE RIGHT GOALS—THE BALANCED BUSINESS PLAN

Building the right culture and promoting trust in the organization help create an environment for interdependent thinking, which leads to better decision making. It follows that the right environment will lead to achieving goals.

SUMMARY

Coming into a new leadership role in a complex organization is a daunting proposition. It requires building an environment for success and the right culture for employees. One person cannot do this properly. It demands a great team that will collaborate effectively. At Stryker the team agreed to dispense with titles, chain of command, and politics to create an atmosphere of trust and engagement. We encouraged every SLT member to challenge "the norm" and one another, which fostered interdependent thinking. That model carried through the rest of the organization to other Instruments managers.

Stryker Instruments dealt with economic downturns in addition to a number of other significant business challenges. A great team, a strong culture, and a creative approach to every issue allowed the Instruments team to successfully navigate through the tough times. Interdependent thinking helped during the rough patches and will continue to assist us to succeed in the future.

REFERENCE

Buckingham, M., & Coffman, C. (1999). *First, break all the rules: What the world's greatest managers do differently.* New York: Simon & Schuster.

CHAPTER 4

Knowing the Score

Thinking Interdependently in the Orchestra

Virginia V. Baker, Elizabeth Baker, & William Baker

Thinking interdependently as a musician is an interesting, complicated process. On the one hand, one would think that it is a given for any musician because almost all music is the product of two or more people coming together to produce a musical rendition. Yet, in order to become an accomplished performer, one must spend the long practice hours, over an extended period of time, to develop the technique and facility on the instrument to produce a musically pleasing and technically proficient performance. So one notes these two competing forces: (1) the need to spend long hours alone and with intense individual perseverance expending the effort to become an accomplished player, and (2) playing with others, learning to blend in and to be part of a whole producing a performance beyond the contributions of each individual. In order to gain entrance into a major symphony or chamber group, one must be well schooled in the solo and orchestral literature and have complete mastery of the instrument. One also must be able to adapt, instantaneously, to the directions of the conductor or music director. In short, the individual must be highly independent (able to produce beautiful music by oneself) as well as highly interdependent (able to adapt to the group and produce a coherent whole). This dichotomy is consistently present throughout a musician's professional career.

THINKING INTERDEPENDENTLY WITH OTHER MUSICIANS

It is an exhilarating experience to participate in concerts where the results are the product of a total groupthink. Many years ago Virginia had the opportunity to play with a select group of musicians, who accompanied

The Power of the Social Brain, edited by Arthur L. Costa and Pat Wilson O'Leary. Copyright © 2013 by Teachers College, Columbia University. All rights reserved. Prior to photocopying items for classroom use, please contact the Copyright Clearance Center, Customer Service, 222 Rosewood Dr., Danvers, MA 01923, USA, tel. (978) 750-8400, www.copyright.com.

Gregor Piatigorsky, cellist, and Jascha Heifetz, violinist, in southern California where these two internationally renowned artists played with the orchestra without a conductor. Michael Tilson Thomas assisted with organizing the rehearsal, but the final dress rehearsal and performance were accomplished without the aid of a conductor. Virginia explains that she had to play with many ears and eyes, on the music, on herself, on her stand partners, on the soloists, on the concertmaster, and on the whole of the orchestra. It was a wonderful and yet terrifying experience, demanding the utmost concentration and collaboration among all 80 or so musicians in the orchestra and the soloists as Piatigorsky played Schelomo by Bloch, Heifetz played the Brahms Violin Concerto, and the two of them played the Brahms Double Concerto. She also remembers playing with a small chamber orchestra that rehearsed and played without a conductor. In this case, the concertmaster was the leader of the group, but all the members had to attend to one another with great concentration throughout rehearsals and in performances.

Negative experiences also can teach the importance of working together collaboratively. During Elizabeth's student days at the summer Taos Music School, which focused on chamber music, the different instrumental combinations had to prepare a new program every 9 days, so there was a lot of pressure during rehearsal. She was playing in a piano quartet where she and the cellist were out of sync, viewing the piece in two different ways. The coach stopped them after a while and said, "You're not playing together. I'm leaving and you need to work things out!" He then left them to settle their differences, which they did after some talk and further rehearsal. The experience was important for Elizabeth's growth as a musician, for from it she learned the necessity of listening and adapting to others to produce a musical whole.

Throughout their professional lives, musicians experience times when their orchestras play together as a harmonious whole, almost as one person. When this happens, and it does not happen in all cases, it is a marvelous experience.

CONDITIONS THAT PROMOTE
OR HINDER INTERDEPENDENT PLAYING

The Acoustical Properties of the Hall

It seems an obvious point, but if musicians can't hear their fellow musicians, they can't play together very well. When the San Francisco Symphony moved into the new Davies Symphony Hall in 1980, the musicians soon discovered that they could scarcely hear one another, even when sitting in close proximity. Over the first few years of the hall's existence, this phenomenon became more and more troublesome. After some time, the management decided to close the hall for a season, perform in another venue, and reconfigure the inside of the hall. The result was more than satisfying. Violists sitting toward the back of their section could hear the violins on the opposite side of the stage. Everyone could hear one another more clearly and reliably. Playing together became not only possible but also pleasurable. Likewise, when the Los Angeles Philharmonic moved into its new hall, Walt Disney Concert Hall, the musicians experienced a major revelation: They could hear one another clearly. Hearing across the stage in their former hall had been more problematic. What this means in school settings is that the acoustical properties of the rooms or stages in which students perform are a significant factor in helping or hindering students' ability to hear one another. If they can't hear one another well, they can't learn much about playing interdependently.

Bloopers and Train Wrecks

Every orchestra that performs has experienced something go awry. A player makes an entrance too soon. A section comes in a beat late. The conductor has a lapse of memory, bringing a section in too soon or too late. When this happens, the musicians think, "Train wreck!" Eyes, ears, and attention are heightened. Everyone usually focuses on the concertmaster or a section principal to come together and re-rail the train wreck. Once Virginia's orchestra was playing a Mahler symphony with a well-known but older conductor. At a particular point in the piece, there was a long pause. The conductor hesitated, seemingly experiencing a loss of memory. Everyone held their breath as well as their instruments when the principal violist took the initiative and brought the section in, enabling the orchestra to move on and continue to complete the performance. In another instance, at a particular point in a piece the conductor seemed to go into another world; what he was doing with his hands and body was not in sync with what was on the page. After rehearsal everyone agreed to hone in on the concertmaster, or first violin, if the conductor strayed, staying together through this passage until the conductor came back in focus. At a concert of the San Francisco Symphony, it became clear as the concert progressed that something was going on within the orchestra. There was electricity in the air. After the concert, one of the musicians reported privately: "We couldn't follow the conductor so we all agreed to focus on each other, and particularly the concertmaster, in order to get through the concert together." When the conductor is the principal instigator of the blooper or train wreck, it is more important than ever that the musicians are able to think together and communicate their thinking through their contingency planning and their instruments.

The orchestra is an entity unto itself: a self-renewing, self-directing body. All are professionals wanting to put on a stellar performance. When something goes awry, they band together and truly become an interdependent entity.

How Conductors' Leadership Promotes Interdependence

Despite instances like those where the musicians need to overcome a lapse by the conductor, in most cases the conductor of an orchestra is a major actor in giving direction and in forming the character and interpretation of a piece. The direction conductors give, orally and bodily, helps the musicians to know what and how to play. Some conductors are very clear and precise in giving these directions. Some are less so. In either case, they contribute to the orchestra members' interdependency. When clear and precise orchestra members know what to do, playing together becomes second nature. When less clear and precise, orchestra members (as we have seen) band together in order to produce a quality rendition.

Conductors vary in their rendition of a piece. Some will conduct a piece with the same interpretation from concert to concert. Others will modify their interpretation from concert to concert. Virginia remembers playing Strauss's "Alpine Symphony" with a well-known conductor. The orchestra had completed the four rehearsals they usually had for each concert. The "Alpine Symphony" was familiar, part of the standard repertoire, and the musicians were well prepared for the concert. In the first concert the conductor began to cue different directions with his baton as well as his body. This quickly alerted the musicians that something different was transpiring from what they had rehearsed. These changes continued throughout the piece, causing the musicians to become more and more alert, finishing the piece successfully. The next evening as the conductor began the piece the musicians were expecting some of the same interpretations that had been given the night before. Not to be. He shifted stance and changed again. This went on throughout the second, third, and fourth concert. Virginia says that each night began with the thought, "What new adventure are we going to have tonight?" The anticipation was high; everyone was alert, prepared to follow the conductor. This did seem to promote interdependency among the orchestra.

The present music director of the Los Angeles Philharmonic provides leadership that seems to promote collaboration and cooperation. While he is very clear about what he wants in a given section or piece, he gives the impression that he believes that playing in the orchestra is a communal act—that we're all in it together! One of his comments is, "I hear you with my eyes!", which encourages everyone to be together.

Another conversation that Elizabeth had with a colleague regarding interdependent playing in an orchestra seems related to the importance of the conductor in providing focus. Her colleague mentioned that he thought that in order to be a good follower there had to be strong leadership demonstrated by the conductor. His comment was, "For me to play well with everyone, I have to be strongly directed." We think the best conductors and section leaders do this in an authoritative rather than authoritarian way.

Under-Rehearsed Conditions

From time to time, orchestras are faced with a limited time frame for rehearsal. This often happens during summer seasons but can happen during a winter season, too. When an orchestra has only one rehearsal and then a concert, there is a greater possibility for experiencing a train wreck. When this condition occurs, orchestra members can be under quite a bit of stress, sometimes leading to mistakes and at other times inviting a banding together to achieve a quality performance.

Tours

When orchestras go on national tours or foreign tours to Europe, Asia, or South America, they usually go with a small repertoire of two or three concerts. These concerts have been played in their home halls prior to the tour, and as they arrive in the various cities of the tour, they often have 30-minute rehearsals to test out the acoustics of the hall. The orchestra is fully prepared and can play at its best. This, along with the fact that they are playing before an unfamiliar audience, invites them to be on their best behavior and their performances are usually well done.

How Orchestra Members Promote Interdependence

Knowing the music and being totally prepared is a critical priority to being able to play interactively with others. To interact with others one needs to know one's own part well. Particularly in the small configuration of chamber music, knowing the part well, almost to the point of having it memorized, frees the musician to interact with the other musicians in the group. In instances like these, the interdependent thinking is not verbalized but the musical choices of each musician are responsive to the choices and cues of fellow musicians.

Within an orchestra, members attend to and listen to many different individuals and groups. First of all is the self and how one is performing; then there are stand partners, then the whole section and the section leader, as well as the whole orchestra and of course, last but not least, the conductor. One has to have attention and ears focused on all these players in order to fulfill the responsibilities of an orchestra member. While monitoring one's own playing, a musician is fitting the individual performance to the nonverbal but equally thoughtful contributions of fellow musicians in order to create together a beautiful whole.

Playing only in an orchestra can lead to a player's deterioration. For this reasons many orchestral musicians seek out opportunities to play chamber works. When playing in a small chamber group—a trio, quartet, quintet, or even a small chamber orchestra—individuals must play at the top of their game. It helps them to keep on honing their skills and makes them a better, more productive orchestral player.

A Final Observation

It seems to us that the symphony orchestra is a fine example of interdependency in action. A symphony orchestra is an entity comprised of 100 or more highly skilled individuals who have developed their visual, verbal and nonverbal communication skills, as well as their musical and technical skills, which enable them to produce an articulated whole—a harmonious interpretation of a particular musical score—no mean feat. Both Virginia and Elizabeth say that being in an orchestra, on stage, with all that magnificent sound swirling around you as one is performing a Mozart, Brahms, Beethoven, Mahler, or Adams piece is a unique and ever exciting collaborative experience—well worth the time, effort, and practice expended to make it happen.

CHAPTER 5

Thinking as a Team

Mark Jones

This chapter is about thinking, working, and playing together as a team rather than as a collection of individuals—a valued capacity not only on the football field but also in life.

SUCCESS THROUGH TEAMWORK

Teamwork does not start at the beginning of the season. The building of the team starts at the end of the previous season, after the last game, and centers on football conditioning class. Most of the next year's varsity team is in the class. The athletes create an unselfish team attitude by working extremely hard in the class.

Coaches start identifying potential new leaders for the team from members of the conditioning class. The athletes projected as captains for the next year normally are students who will be starting for their 3rd year. Leadership can take many forms and aspects. The captains do not necessarily have to be the best athletes, but someone whom the students admire, someone who can motivate them. Sometimes the leaders are powerful personalities who can tell a group of players who are not putting in a full effort to "toe the line." Sometimes the leaders could be quieter types who lead by example in the classroom and on the field. Other times they could be people who are really excitable and project that excitement onto others.

In athletics, as in music, much of the thinking within and across a team is nonverbal. One year, the team did not have a returning quarterback for the new season. One player was a very talented scholarship athlete who generally played as a defensive back, but the team needed a quarterback so he was drafted for the job. He had to learn a new and complicated position.

The Power of the Social Brain, edited by Arthur L. Costa and Pat Wilson O'Leary. Copyright © 2013 by Teachers College, Columbia University. All rights reserved. Prior to photocopying items for classroom use, please contact the Copyright Clearance Center, Customer Service, 222 Rosewood Dr., Danvers, MA 01923, USA, tel. (978) 750-8400, www.copyright.com.

He did not really want to play quarterback, and definitely would not play that position in college, but he stepped up and did not complain. He got a lot of attention for it, took it in stride, and remained humble about the attention. The other athletes could have been jealous about his talent and attention, but because he unselfishly learned a position he did not choose to take, he gained stature on the team. He possibly hurt his chances for a larger scholarship. He was rarely rested during the game, having to play both offense and defense. Because he unselfishly sacrificed for the team, he possibly gained stature with the college coaches anyway.

Building teamwork and the success it brings is like putting together the pieces of a puzzle. If every puzzle piece is put in the right place, success will result. If every person does his own job, and is unselfish, success will result. If someone tries to do another person's job, it creates a hole in the offense or defense, and the goal—whether scoring a touchdown, or stopping the offense from moving the ball—can be unsuccessful.

There are many impediments to success: Someone gets beaten by improper technique, does not have enough strength, did not understand the job, did not study the playbook, got fooled during the play. The bottom line is that the successful player and good teammate will be smart, thoughtful, *and* athletically excellent on the field.

To be successful, football players must spend study time learning complex concepts, principles, and philosophies. The concepts they learn have to be recognized immediately during the play so they can be acted on. Players have to learn terminology, secondary coverages, and how to run their routes based on where the defense is aligned. Beyond knowing the plays, however, there is a great amount of trust and teamwork that must take place in order for the receivers to be in sync with the quarterback.

As part of building trust and teamwork on the football team, the players have to be taught to make decisions on their own in response to what their teammates are doing, as well as what the opponents are doing. Our team uses a "no-huddle" offense much of the time. Using this offensive philosophy, the quarterback gets signals from the sideline, or has a series of plays that he will run. Then, he gives signals to the team as they are at the line of scrimmage, and the players have to make choices on what to do depending on how the defense lines up. The team members must trust that their teammates are going to make the correct decisions as well. This trust is built during study periods and a lot of repetitions in practice. Mistakes are understandable, and the players have to accept the fact that not all of the players are going to make the correct decisions all of the time. If everyone made the correct decisions all of the time, each play should lead to a touchdown, and this is not realistic. The players make fewer mistakes as time goes on because of more studying and practice together.

Teamwork consistently involves athletes monitoring one another. An athlete does not want to let the team down, or be criticized by teammates. During film study or in competition, anyone can see when a teammate makes a mistake and help him out. This constructive criticism can come from any player, or one of the leaders. This acts as a motivator to learn the system and make good decisions in play.

REFLECTION ON PRACTICE

One way to build interdependent thinking and the disposition to be coached is to experience group coaching during practice and after a game. During practice the players study game films so they can analyze their performance from the previous game and the tendencies of the players and team that they will play in the next game. It is difficult for the coaches to guide them from the sidelines, because the plays happen so fast, and the other team is constantly making adjustments. Coaches have to trust that players will make the right decisions on the field, based on their learning from game debriefs.

A common technique to increase a player's reflection and analysis is by debriefing films of a recently played game. The coach may guide thoughtful discussions by inviting small group, pairs, or trios to engage with the film using prompts such as these:

1. Identify the good plays and the bad plays. Reach consensus.
2. Explain your analysis of each play, specifically describing what made the play good or bad.
3. Consider what went on in the players' heads as the plays were made. If you are on the video, explain what you were thinking and why. Describe what you would do differently next time in similar circumstances.
4. Brainstorm suggested fixes for the bad plays.
5. Discuss pros and cons of each suggested fix. Reach consensus.
6. Visualize yourself and the rest of the team running the improved plays.
7. Randomly select players to explain group responses.

After the game, before the films are shown, ask players to recall how the suggestions of the other team members guided their thoughts and actions on the field.

Sometimes the other team starts to make plays that were not anticipated by the coaching staff, and therefore not practiced by the team the week before. A team leader should be able to come to the sidelines during a time-out or a change-over of downs, and tell the coach about something he sees that was not expected. The coaches, with the leader, at that point should make some adjustments to counteract what the athlete sees, and the leader should give new coaching instructions to the players on the field. In a team whose members trust one another, and trust their leaders, these types of adjustments should be effective.

Competition among players can produce excitement and build teamwork. Team-building activities can be competitive games that build togetherness. Games like tug of war, passing the medicine ball, and weight-lifting competitions are encouraged as a way for team members to do their best to promote the best efforts of others. This is the physical corollary of individuals in groups supporting best efforts as they think together to solve problems or even to understand those problems better. Sometimes psychological activities such as "trust falls," when one person closes his or her eyes and falls backward, expecting another player to catch him or her, can be a team-building activity as well. This mirrors openness in interdependent thinking, where individuals learn to trust others' thinking and not always rely on their own.

CONCLUSION

Success depends upon players' willingness to perform their role at the right time and in the right way. In part that comes about by the leadership of the coach in having an organized practice and being able to deliver the message properly to the athletes. The athletes also need to know their expectations. They have to be convinced that team play, not individual play, is what we strive for. Finally, a good coach, and a good team, must be interested in and concerned about the players as people. There are far more important aspects of sports than winning and losing, like learning to help one another work through obstacles, critique one another respectfully, be willing to take on more work for the sake of the team effort, listen with an open mind, and put the team effort above personal glory.

Reflecting on Part I

The first part of this book included a collection of chapters illustrating interdependent thinking in a variety of settings. The limitations of space determined how many settings could be illustrated. You, however, can find more examples and are encouraged to do so. As you encounter friends or colleagues and meet people, inquire about situations in which they work, play, or participate that depend upon interdependent thinking.

GUIDING QUESTIONS

1. Which chapter (life situation) in Part I touched your head and/or your heart? Why? Did you connect with a certain chapter because you have experienced similar situations or because you want to have similar experiences?
2. As you name and describe the patterns you noticed in these life settings, how do they compare and contrast with others debriefing this part of the book?
3. As you describe the cultural conditions that foster interdependent thinking, as represented in these life situations, in which settings do you live and work with similar conditions? What would have to be added or changed to create these conditions?
4. If you are an interdependent thinker, list the things you say and do in a group setting that a competitive or individual thinker does not do. How do you think that list has changed or will change as a result of reading this book?
5. What commitments will you make to improve your own capacities for interdependent thought and action?

PART II

Facilitation Strategies for Interdependent Thinking

> Every organization needs leaders who can help people regain their capacity, energy, and desire to contribute. And this is only accomplished when people work together in community, not in isolation.
>
> —Meg Wheatley, as quoted in *Strategy + Business*

The second part of this book is about facilitating others to develop personal and group capacities and processes of interdependent thought and action. Contributions from eminent leaders in the field of group development draw upon both research and their own experiences to provide numerous insights into what leaders need to know and do to compose groups and enhance their collaborative thought. They provide numerous practical strategies for engaging individuals to think, work, and grow together. Group leaders who wish not only to make their meetings more productive but also to become increasingly more thoughtful will profit from helping group members become conscious of and reflect on their own and the group's thinking that contributed to the meeting's success.

Probably the main recurring theme linking these chapters together is individuals' capacity to listen deeply, nonjudgmentally, and empathically—detecting and valuing one another's differing styles, culture, values, and perceptions.

You are invited not only to learn from the expertise of these authors but to anticipate situations in your setting in which to apply the numerous concepts and strategies that might make your group meetings and organizational systems even more thought-full.

CHAPTER 6

A Virtual Continuum for Thinking Interdependently

Bena Kallick & Marie Alcock

Trees in Alaska

In Alaska, when the soil is frozen for more than 2 years, a condition called "permafrost" takes place. Seeds fall in the soil but, due to the lack of depth for roots to take hold, the growth of trees is stunted. Note how these Alaskan trees grow like some ideas do in the social media—as small, episodic events that come in bursts and are quickly stunted.

On the other hand, in Colorado, aspens multiply continuously because they have a strongly networked root system. Considering the aspens as an analogy, we might say that when the roots of our thinking are not allowed to be sufficiently deep, thinking is stunted; when the roots of our thinking are richly networked but with no particular sense of direction, they multiply without particular care about how distracted or on the surface they remain.

The Power of the Social Brain, edited by Arthur L. Costa and Pat Wilson O'Leary. Copyright © 2013 by Teachers College, Columbia University. All rights reserved. Prior to photocopying items for classroom use, please contact the Copyright Clearance Center, Customer Service, 222 Rosewood Dr., Danvers, MA 01923, USA, tel. (978) 750-8400, www.copyright.com.

Aspen Trees in Colorado

To continue our analogy, Neptune grass forms "meadows" from shallow water to a depth of 150 ft (45 m) in the clearest waters. It grows on both rock and sand, and has a tough, fibrous base and persistent stems that grow both horizontally and vertically. These build up into a structure known as "matte," which can be several yards high and thousands of years old. These analogies suggest that if our thinking interdependently forms a community, it can sustain itself by growing from shallow to greater depth, inclusive of multiple cultures that develop across time and space.

With a clear understanding of the purpose of the community, thinking interdependently can be supported in an online network by individuals who have decidedly different ideas and questions. The evolution of such thinking can be rich and innovative, and provide an opportunity to dialogue in ways that are often not possible when face to face.

When we engage with thinking in online communities—thinking through digital exchange rather than a face-to-face exchange—we are, by definition, engaging in a social exchange even though we may be at a great physical remove from our co-thinkers. In some instances, we are limited to the permafrost concept—short bursts of communication with

Neptune Grass

no requirement for response. However, we may read the burst and wish to explore it further. In that instance, we may move from Twitter, for example, to Facebook, where we learn more about the person who has been communicating and know more about the context and the point of view that is expressed. We may be networking with friends of the friend—expanding the network as with the aspens. Finally, we may find that we are moving from shallow to deeply rooted conversations and ex- plorations of ideas. Now we are behaving more like the ocean sea grass, seeking more depth to our thinking interdependently. We may want to join a discussion group or forum. We may want to join an online course. We, the participants of a network, are getting beyond the commonplaces of our daily lives and are extending, engaging, and debating about more important ideas.

Technology has brought us the opportunity to think interdependently, collaboratively, in groups that can be scattered and asynchronous, and, with practice, it can help us to think big. However, we must learn how to do so. Vygotsky (1978) refers to the social construction of knowledge—the idea that people learn through dialogue, discussion, building on one another's ideas. And, following the thinking of Vygotsky, constructivist theorists added that teaching students to experience these processes "help[s] learners to internalize and reshape, or transform, new information. Transformation occurs through the creation of new understandings (Jackson 1986, Gardner 1991b) that result from the emergence of new cognitive structures" (Brooks & Brooks, 1999, p. 16). The work of these theorists has transformed the international practices of teachers in their classrooms and has led to the term *social learning* when using networks for the purpose of truly thinking interdependently.

How do individuals interact effectively in these social learning networks? What is it about interdependent thinking that attracts individuals and rewards them for participating in these virtual networks? Although a critical ingredient in these situations is the role of facilitator, we have chosen to focus on the user as facilitator of his or her own learning by focusing on the purpose for the interaction such as feedback or commentary. A most important step to successful interaction in a virtual community is self-knowledge—who am I as a learner and user of technology?

A VIRTUAL CONTINUUM

Although many people design this sort of continuum on the basis of generational categories, they often limit a true description of behaviors and attributes. In the continuum described here, we focus on how the user's interest is engaged with social learning networks or professional learning networks.

This continuum is designed to help a user identify the purpose for engagement (what situation are you trying to address?), the user's best learning style to meet that purpose (what technologies do you prefer to use?), and then, based on the purpose of engagement and the choice of technologies, the implications for how the user might progress as a learner.

This continuum offers a tool for self-assessment, as well as consciousness raising, before entering a network. As participants become more familiar with what they want from a network, they might know more about what they expect from others, and what they would need to expect from themselves. Thinking interdependently, if it is to be of influence to all who participate, requires reciprocity, credibility, and honesty.

THE CONTINUUM IN ACTION

As a member of a social learning network, one needs to be more self-directed than in face-to-face settings. One needs to decide when to participate and when not to. One has to make choices about interactions.

For example, in the continuum, we recognize as independent those people who choose to be "bystanders," only observing the interactions of others. Their purpose is to learn more about the topic being discussed and explore the breadth of points of view. This is most helpful to someone focused on building her own thinking and someone not ready to contribute or participate openly for either academic or emotional reasons. This type of thinking is also powerful for testing innovation and sprouting foundling ideas that are outside the box and need nurturing before being opened to broad contribution or critique.

There are some learners we refer to in the continuum as "sharers" who participate in a limited capacity by posting their own thinking and then look for feedback on their work. The purpose here is to "field test" their solution and get feedback for refining their work. At this point, the person is open to feedback but reserves the right to heed or reject the feedback, as it is her final product that is being shared. This kind of thinking is powerful for checking the validity of ideas or the perception of an idea by a greater audience.

Finally, there are some who choose to participate by engaging in "interdependent" thinking sessions. The purpose here is to generate product, feedback, and discussion openly with no personal ownership of the thinking. This is most helpful when the solution to a problem might need the combined knowledge, perspectives, and thinking of a diverse group.

A self-directed user of networks should identify his purpose and then seek the tools and atmospheres that support that purpose. For example, a bystander might not feel comfortable in an environment that requires interdependent thinking, and a sharer may not be open to changing her idea based on feedback from the group. An interdependent thinker may be seen as "over-contributing" or "disagreeable" by a sharer who just wanted some feedback; a bystander may be seen as "noncontributing" by an interdependent thinker. If the purpose is not clear and overtly stated by participants, then the group or virtual network may become unsuccessful.

The continuum is designed intentionally to show a range of possible engagements rather than a sequence. For example, it is possible that a person might have a really good, innovative idea and prefer to observe what is going on in a network without revealing his thinking. It could be that the idea is not well formulated and that observing how others think serves as a catalyst for further thinking. However, to move to interdependent thinking would be premature. This individual is still feeling possessive of the thinking and does not want feedback or interaction. At some point, after listening in on the interactions of others, the user moves into the conversation. Sharing the thoughts leads to more thoughts. Soon the individual finds that the feedback he is receiving is profitable and shapes his thinking further. Meanwhile, another individual is wide open for interaction. She wants to hear from many others in a live engagement—one that moves back and forth with simultaneous thinking and reflecting. This person may want to maintain that engagement for some time, learning as she is going. A time may come when she will want to consolidate her thinking. Perhaps she

Figure 6.1. Thinking Interdependently Virtually: A Continuum

Situational Questions	Types of Thinking		
	Independent	*Shared*	*Interdependent*
What will best serve my communication needs?	Email, journaling, note taking, online database tools, online publications, private websites, videos, online Q & A tools	Video conferencing (large webinars), texting, blogs, email, posted videos, topic-specific discussion forums, online networking tools	Wikis, real-time networking tools, IM, face-to-face, cell phones, video conferencing (small webinars), online meeting tools
How will I participate best and what is my commitment to the group's thinking?	Observe interactions, learn from interactions, and think independently about the use of or reaction to such interactions; minimal commitment to the group's thinking	Post drafts of thinking with choice about whether to receive and make use of feedback; greater sense of responsibility to the group's thinking	Live or real-time interactions to clarify thinking and possibly take action on ideas; group participation is required in order for successful interdependent thinking
In what ways will the Habits of Mind serve my work?	Needs to think independently before joining a group; listens with understanding but does not join; not ready to take a risk on his or her thinking; might be creating, innovating, or imagining, and does not want to receive feedback yet	Is thinking about thinking and becomes more aware of a desire to interact with others about ideas; eager for feedback but does not want it to be continuous and ongoing	Is thinking with the intention of interaction; communicating with clarity and precision, realizing that the thinking will be continuous and ongoing in relation to others in the conversation; thinking flexibly as group moves quickly
What will my feedback look like?	Contributions of information can be built upon or shared to develop a new body of knowledge; voted forums without text feedback	Comments or thoughts are given directly and the user can take them or not; these might be blog comments or video comments, but they are textual	Feedback is live and often in the form of new ideas built upon originals; the feedback creates new product open to feedback in return
How will I assess success best?	The process has engendered high-quality thinking	The process has proved to engender more new ideas and thinking than when working alone; feedback has influenced thinking	The process has developed a sense of teamwork; the thinking is of high quality and the "muscle of the mind" has been exercised in a new way

sets up a forum or a discussion as a subset of the original group and is more interested in sharing ideas without feeling the need to respond to all that is happening in the network, as shown in the virtual continuum in Figure 6.1.

BUILDING COMMUNITIES FOR THINKING

The continuum provides a series of possible situations in which thinking is engaged as it moves from more independence to more interdependence. The ebb and flow of communication, and communication needs, build multiple bonds among people as relationships develop based on the exchange of ideas. The Internet, as vast as it is, allows for us to build multiple communities for thinking, engaging, joining, and departing. Whereas we are more limited when we require people to be in a common physical space, we are able to move regularly in a virtual space.

In a sense, the joining of, departing from, and expanding of ideas greatly resemble the way children play with blocks. Let us meet Alison, who has never played with blocks before. She sees a group of children playing and there she meets Louis. Louis is busy building a city with his friends using blocks. Alison observes Louis; she is learning and thinking about the blocks and how they work. She decides to try building her own tower mirroring the technique used by Louis and the others. Alison thinks she can make a stronger tower and tries a different way. Louis looks over and says, "No, no, we do it this way!" Alison pulls away and hides her tower. She wants to work alone right now. She is not ready for contribution or critique yet.

Louis returns to his group and they are working together building all aspects of the city. The children in this group have different ideas, often building, rebuilding, and removing parts to make it work. Some put block upon block in pairs and design and refine simultaneously. Others work but point and suggest as they go along, and change direction based on comments even before their structure is complete. Louis is from an urban area and decides to add a bus station; while he is doing that, Kathy joins and adds three bus stops. Louis looks up, smiles at the growth, encourages Kathy to add more, and begins making another tower.

Alison looks over and sees that Louis is making a tower and it keeps falling down. She feels confident her new design for a tower might work so she joins Louis and says, "What do you think of what I built?" Louis smiles and assimilates Alison's idea and says, "Great, but it might need a tunnel for the buses." Alison thinks this is neat and lets Louis change the tower. Alison practiced independent, shared, and interdependent thinking in the same LEGO block session.

A CITY IN PERIL

Alison sees the bus station and says, "We can add a garden to the top of this building here!" Louis is unsure of the garden idea and asks, "Why?" The future of the city is now dependent on how well Alison and Louis navigate this interdependent thinking. This kind of ebb and flow of thinking mirrors what makes virtual networks so powerful but also can lead to confusion when participants shift purpose. In the same way that the builders wonder whether the city is about tall buildings or a pretty living environment, so do the participants in a virtual environment question whether they are all talking about the same issue or have moved to diversified purposes.

Without effective cues or protocols, a seeded network quickly may become stunted. If Alison's answer to Louis is clear and focused on making a better block city, then the interdependent thinking will continue. If Louis rejects Alison's idea without giving feedback about the purpose, Alison might disengage from the process. Based on this interaction, the entire play group may build a strong and pretty city, or disband into smaller groups making different purposed cities. This is the way interdependent networks function. We have found that there is a balance, and those who are able to sustain their ideas, build the most complex and innovative structures. So it is with thinking interdependently. Ideas flourish through the varied means of exchange, which means that each person who enters ultimately must become a "player".

MAKING A COMMITMENT AND GETTING IN THE HABIT

For many who are not familiar with social learning networks, there is a critical learning curve. At first it appears to be just another group to join. However, as we begin to participate, we understand how to use the group for learning, not merely socializing. Key to becoming a more skillful user is to develop the habits and disciplines for interdependent thinking.

To become more skillful as an interdependent thinker, one must:

- remain open to deepening one's thinking through the influence of others' ideas; and
- evaluate the credibility of sources of information and sort fact from opinion.

In our culture, we stress independence and self-sufficiency. We are often reluctant to be clear about what we want from others. However, in order for the virtual community to work, we will have to state what we need:

- a small-group discussion on an issue
- feedback from members of the network based on work or ideas we are considering
- a problem-solving group to share ideas
- specific examples of practice, including multimedia
- the opportunity to observe exchanges of ideas without committing to participation

Networks work because all people engage. Each must make a commitment to doing the work of thinking interdependently. Therefore, we must believe that what we will learn from this network will be greater than what we would learn if we were working independently. We need to be in the habit of checking in on the group—observing what is happening, contributing new ideas, responding to questions that are raised. In fact, in order to be a positive and contributing group member, we need to develop some habits of mind such as the following:

- Listening with understanding and empathy and managing impulsivity—when working virtually, these two are closely associated. It is so tempting to respond quickly to whatever is being said rather than paying attention to what we know from what is written and what we need to know.
- Questioning and problem posing—learn how to ask questions that will provoke deeper thinking and pose problems that tap into the uncertainties we all experience.
- Responding with wonderment and awe—genuinely respond to work with admiration, excitement, and ways that we will apply, or what we have learned from, the work of others.

FACILITATING THINKING: PROMPTING THE GROUP INTERACTION

We have all had the experience of being in successful groups—ones that we feel are so productive that we look forward to the next meeting. On the other hand, we also have been captive to groups that do not work—ones that are not well structured or designed to elevate our thinking. Facilitation is a key to successful groupwork. And facilitation, as we have learned over the past few years, can be done in a variety of ways. For example, many groups use a protocol for facilitation. The protocol works as a guide for interaction and can be used for thinking virtually (see McDonald et al., 2012).

COACHING POINTS

The group members might agree to the following parameters:

- Ask clarifying questions when you are uncertain about what entry into the discussion means; don't assume.
- Be certain that the others in the group are looking for feedback before providing it; again, don't assume.
- Provide constructive feedback that is in keeping with what the other person is asking. Make certain that you are coaching for better thinking and not replacing the other person's thinking.
- Raise questions as frequently as you respond to what others are saying.
- Respond promptly, without letting time lapse in the discussion. So in a virtual classroom, don't let a week go by. On a conference call, do not change the subject or ignore a clarifying question.

There are other situations in which a facilitator is appointed, such as a teacher for a course, a leader of an organization, an assigned mentor, or coach. In this instance, we have learned to prompt interdependent thinking with suggestions such as the following:

- Post and play (post an issue or an idea and invite people to play with it—to generate new ideas, brainstorm, problem solve).
- Try, say why, reply (try something out, say why you chose to do this particular activity, get others to reply to your thinking).
- Read and respond (read text and respond; enter discussion using strategies for encouraging interaction around text).
- Live and learn (apply to your practice and learn from it; engage with others on what you are learning).
- Take stock (reflect on your practice by making journal entries— what are you learning, what insights are you gaining, how might you change based on what you are learning?).
- Go global! (join the global community—enlarge your thinking in a community of practice).

OTHER MEDIA FORMS

Regardless of what prompts or serves as a catalyst for the user, all media tools have the ability to be used for any kind of thinking on the continuum.

For example, blogs can be used for independent thinking if users sign up for an account and begin posting their thoughts in a diary format. They are writing to a public audience but are not open to feedback because the purpose is to share their perspective or observations. Feedback for this might be encouragement from the audience but have no impact on their thinking. However, blogs can be used for shared thinking as well, as when people post ideas and look for comments back. They are looking for feedback so they can refine their own thinking. Finally, consider the use of a blog format in an online classroom. Here the facilitator may post a question and ask the group to generate an academic discussion that results in a solution that ideally works for all members. All participants will commit to the purpose and, using the blog format of post and comment, will explore options, give feedback, and refine the solution until all members suggest that it will work. So, here we see that the tool is flexible and can be used for all kinds of thinking if the purpose, participants, and product are all clear.

CONCLUSION

The Internet, which gives us access to many new platforms and tools, continues to intrigue us while, at the same time, it presents a dilemma. When should we play with new ideas and perhaps leave some of the ones we started with stunted in their growth? When should we recognize the need to get the work done and not become too distracted by the many directions that the network has taken, much like the aspens? What will enhance the capacity to learn globally so that, as with the ocean sea grass, there is the option to move from shallow to deep? What will cause a paralysis of too much information? When will we structure time to learn? How do we keep up with the rapidly changing technological environment?

We have tried in this chapter to provide some suggestions for how to use the tools offered by technology to your best advantage by considering three main points:

- How clear are you about your purpose for thinking interdependently?
- What do you know about yourself as a learner?
- What do you know about the tools that are available and how much do you need to learn in order to maximize your thinking?

We often say, "Thank you for sharing—but too much information." The questions and suggestions raised in this chapter focus on making both the sharing and the selection of information more meaningful. We are only beginning to realize the power of the social media as a rich opportunity for thinking interdependently.

NOTE

Thanks to Bruce Wellman and Laura Lipton for their collaboration in developing these strategies. They promote social learning through their virtual learning path for school leaders, "Collaborative Groups at Work" produced by Eduplanet 21 (www.Eduplanet21.com.)

REFERENCES

Brooks, J. G., & Brooks, M. G. (1999). *In search of understanding: The case for constructivist classrooms*. Alexandria, VA: ASCD.

McDonald, J. P., Zydney, J. M., Dichter, A., & McDonald, E. C. (2012). *Going online with protocols: New tools for teaching and learning*. New York: Teachers College Press.

Vygotsky, L. S. (1978). *Mind in society: The development of higher psychological processes*. Cambridge, MA: Harvard University Press.

CHAPTER 7

Creating Communities of Thought
Skills, Tasks, and Practices

Laura Lipton & Bruce Wellman

Thinking together is not a new idea. What is new is the increasing complexity within which groups work as information flows more quickly, demanding more immediate attention than ever before. Transient organizational affiliations add to this complexity as employees move among and between roles, teams, and employers. As a result, groups need to continually create and re-create themselves, stimulated by provocative questions and rich resources. Developing these communities of thought requires explicit structures, well-honed tools, and attention to the emotional and cognitive resources needed for thinking interdependently.

This chapter poses five questions about thinking interdependently. We describe ways in which thoughtful groups balance task and relationship skills to achieve desired outcomes, and present five principles of practice and related tools for shaping collective thinking.

WHAT IS A COMMUNITY OF THOUGHT?

A [community of thought embraces a] process through which parties who see different aspects of a problem can constructively explore their differences and search for solutions that go beyond their own limited vision of what is possible.

—Barbara Gray, *Collaborating:*
Finding Common Ground for Multiparty Problems

The words *community, common, communicate,* and *communicable* all stem from the same root. In community we have common understandings,

The Power of the Social Brain, edited by Arthur L. Costa and Pat Wilson O'Leary. Copyright © 2013 by Teachers College, Columbia University. All rights reserved. Prior to photocopying items for classroom use, please contact the Copyright Clearance Center, Customer Service, 222 Rosewood Dr., Danvers, MA 01923, USA, tel. (978) 750-8400, www.copyright.com.

common values, and common expectations. We communicate to produce and sustain these, and communicably transmit them within and without the group.

To be a community of thought means to think interdependently. This complex exchange requires both cognitive and emotional energy and cognitive and emotional risk. A community of thought shares an intellectual and emotional commons. Like the village greens of old, groups gain sustenance and energy from shared pastures. These energy sources include systematic experimentation and complex problem solving. When groups meet, physically or virtually, they create and re-create this commons.

Collective thinking draws on the resources of individuals to produce ideas and insights, and to support and extend the production of ideas and insights of others. This rich and deep collaboration comes with emotional challenges: I might not know; I have to think in public; I might be wrong; I might be judged by others.

WHY COMMUNITIES OF THOUGHT?

There is an established method for accomplishing this aliveness
that values all voices in the room, uses the small group even in large
gatherings, and recognizes that accountability grows out of co-creation.

—Peter Block, *Community: The Structure of Belonging*

Rich, meaningful collaboration is both complex and challenging. Three compelling reasons for meeting these demands include:

1. ***The lone genius is a myth.*** Regardless of whether the field is physics, biology, or linguistics, teams of researchers, not individuals, make scientific breakthroughs. Significant studies are no longer produced by a lone genius like Einstein or Darwin. In fact, papers with at least 100 citations, or "home run" papers, are more than six times as likely to come from teams of scientists (Lehrer, 2012). The group is the unit of work. Insight and innovation emerge from interdependent thinking.
2. ***The most interesting mysteries lie at the intersection of minds.*** Novel solutions are necessary to address increasingly complex problems. For example, the study of sustainable agriculture combines the fields of biology, agronomy, sociology, and climatology in a multidisciplinary response to world hunger. Overwhelming problems are too messy for individuals to solve

independently. The collective imagination is more expansive than any individual vision. The cross-fertilization of divergent minds generates possibilities beyond the limits of isolated thinkers.

3. ***Accountability grows out of co-creation.*** Collaborative construction of understanding around data, problems, and plans inspires commitment to action. A greater degree of participation in the genesis of decisions produces a greater likelihood of follow-through. Given the challenges of multiple demands and conflicting priorities, individuals need to make choices about use of their time, attention, and energy. When group membership is valued, the values of the group prevail. Identity as a group member increases accountability to the group and the group's goals. Our goals become my goals.

WHAT MAKES THINKING INTERDEPENDENT?

A strong community helps people develop a sense of true self, for only in community can the self exercise and fulfill its nature: giving and taking, listening and speaking, being and doing.

—Parker Palmer, *A Hidden Wholeness:
The Journey Toward an Undivided Life*

Relational skills help group members get tasks done. Successful task completion enhances group skills when structured reflection is part of the process. This interdependence is a value, an outcome, and a resource that supports collective thinking.

Communities of thought experience three types of interdependence: between group members, between the group and its environment, and between relationship and task. These dynamics require both cognitive and emotional energy.

Managing the emotional energy in groups requires personal monitoring of internal states, the effects of those states on the ways information and feedback are presented, and the effects of these contributions on the group's emotions and thinking.

Managing cognitive energy is related to managing feelings, as emotions and cognition biologically entwine. This discipline requires impulse control for knowing when and when not to edit idea production, ways to get oneself and others unstuck when idea production stalls, and knowing when and how to critique work in progress. Thought-provoking questions, confidence in working with data, and frequent pauses, both individually and collectively, fuel cognitive energy in groups.

The output and interactions of group thought shape the ways in which relational skills and task skills intersect. The following descriptions characterize groups that are fluent with relational and task skills.

Relational Skills

Skillful group members understand themselves, one another, and what it means to be part of a high-performing group. In these groups, members:

- cultivate an emotional and cognitive container to support thinking (They apply structures and strategies to shape productive interactions, and build inclusive communities of practice. Psychological safety supports cognitive complexity.);
- identify with the group, relying on processes and one another (Groupwork requires cognitive and emotional risks. Surviving this leap increases trust and confidence. Risk taking expands trust, fostering greater risk taking.);
- are emotionally flexible, knowing when to self-assert and when to integrate personal thinking and work style preferences with the preferences of others (Differences are encouraged, not discredited.);
- display more curiosity than judgment as they listen and respond to one another (A spirit of inquiry shapes groupwork.);
- disagree with and respond to ideas, not to individuals (Ideas, not personalities, focus conversations.); and
- balance participation, spending as much energy on listening to others as on putting their own ideas on the table (Therefore, *my* view is not *the* view).

Task Skills

Productive group members are clear about tasks, outcomes, and expectations. These groups focus both on task completion and expanding their capacity for doing more complex, collaborative work. In these groups, members:

- clearly define their tasks and success criteria for products, performances, and decisions (Goals and processes are possibilities, not boundaries.);
- uphold high standards and persevere by monitoring and adjusting processes, timelines, and roles to achieve desired outcomes (Poking and prodding expand expectations.);

- see thinking as a collective production (They treat personal ideas as contributions to the cognitive kitty and not as private property. *My* idea becomes *our* idea.);
- intentionally design their work (They tap structures and strategies to co-construct ideas, perspectives, and plans. Tasks are opportunities to learn.);
- seek external resources when they reach the boundaries of what they know and don't know (They are not limited by their own knowledge and skills. Looking out, not in, avoids the trap of self-sealing logic.); and
- thrive by working on the edge of current capabilities and what is familiar (Exploration energizes and hones the thinking as group members create new approaches and ideas—invention, not convention, drives the work).

HOW ARE CAPACITIES FOR INTERDEPENDENT THINKING DEVELOPED?

If it is a credible process (that is, it has both integrity and a fair chance of producing results) and an open process (that is, the dialogue is both honest and receptive to different points of view), then people will invest the energy—the enormous expenditure of energy necessary to make collaboration succeed. Creating and nurturing this open and credible process is extraordinarily important for those who are initiating collaboration.

—David Chrislip & Carl Larson, *Collaborative Leadership: How Citizens and Civic Leaders Can Make a Difference*

Collective thinking flourishes when process meets purpose at the center of a group's work. Well-engineered processes merge task and relationship by rallying the necessary emotional resources for collaborative engagement. Stimulating and productive interactions invigorate groups socially, emotionally, and cognitively, increasing capacities for increasingly stimulating and productive work.

STRUCTURING INTERDEPENDENT THINKING

Process design includes multiple options related to two essential considerations: (1) group size, composition, and length of time working together; and (2) interaction patterns, materials, and use of space. These design choices focus energy, balance participation, and, most important, produce a psychologically safe forum for participants to contribute ideas and to engage with the contributions of others. Effective design choices increase a group's capacity to address hard-to-talk-about topics and shape thoughtful dialogue and productive discussion.

FIVE PRINCIPLES OF PRACTICE FOR
SHAPING COLLECTIVE THINKING

Groupwork may be informal, but it should never be casual. Shared principles and processes drive purposeful designs for collective thinking.

1. Balance the Energy

Thinking in groups requires and produces mental and emotional energy. Thoughtful groups purposefully balance this energy by structuring group size and composition, physical space, and use of time. For example, starting a process in pairs offers think and speak time for each participant and increases the psychological safety when merging with the larger group. Organizing seating arrangements for both side-by-side and face-to-face interaction, or to focus all the energy on a chart or slide, are key design choices. Pacing for both internal and external processing by using collective pauses, journal entries, and protocols such as round-robin; and thinking and writing before sharing balance individual and collective resources.

2. Structure for Success

Thoughtful groups assess the emotional and cognitive demands of a task and adjust the degree of structure accordingly. Consideration for different style preferences, varied processing speeds, volatility of the topic, and stress factors related to time of day/year all influence design decisions regarding tightness or looseness of structure. For example, varying group size; specifying roles, such as facilitator, recorder, process monitor; using a public timer; utilizing visual directions; and establishing clearly defined protocols are all ways of structuring for success.

As an example, consider a group that is exploring a controversial topic. The group elects to stimulate individual thinking by responding to a stem, such as, "One critical factor related to this topic is . . ." Partners share their thinking, pair with another set of partners to widen the conversation, and prioritize concerns. They use active public charting to create their priority list and for sharing with the larger group. A public timer keeps groups focused and time efficient.

3. Be Explicit

You can't be too explicit. Transparency and clarity establish trust and confidence in process and in the group. Labeling the intentions behind communications, surfacing and inquiring into assumptions, and sharing rationales reveal inner thought. Clearly naming expectations, sequencing cognitive processes, applying well-defined protocols, and identifying and structuring particular modes of discourse, such as dialogue or decision making, move the group forward cohesively.

One example of a tool for focusing and sequencing cognitive processes is the strategy Generate, Sort, Synthesize (Lipton & Wellman, 2011). This protocol begins with group members generating associations to a topic; sharing their items; sorting, categorizing, and labeling them during structured discourse regarding their thinking; and finally crafting a group synthesizing statement.

4. Create a Third Point

A third point is an artifact in the room that provides a visual focal point for the conversation, rather than a focus on any individual speaker (Grinder, 1997). This emotional distance from the topic focuses and fuels collective thinking. Examples of third points include charts or slides displaying questions, data sets, and visual images. Other possibilities include problem scenarios, student work samples, and professional articles. Active public charting is a powerful form of a third point for focusing and capturing thinking in process and ultimately creating a product owned by the whole group.

5. Make Text or Media the Expert

The infusion of external resources enriches the knowledge base and expands perspectives. Presenting text or media as the expert frees group members to argue with the text and not one another. Providing provocative material with well-structured protocols creates a safe place for the cognitive clashes that spark high-powered collective thinking.

For example, any paired reading strategy balances energy, focuses attention, and opens space for exchange of diverse perspectives. One such protocol is Read and Inquire: Partners segment the text, read individually to a chosen stop point, and ask questions of the text and each other.

HOW ARE COMMUNITIES OF THOUGHT SUSTAINED?

Because questions are intrinsically related to action, they spark and direct attention, perception, energy, and effort, and so are at the heart of the evolving forms that our lives assume.

—Marilee Goldberg, *The Art of the Question*

In an increasingly complex and interconnected world, no one works in isolation. Physical privacy does not mean working without the benefit of others' thinking. Virtual connections, cyber resources, social and intellectual networking all define the difference between being alone and working alone. When, how, and with whom we participate shapes the possibilities of our lives. Participation fuses with purpose when catalytic questions energize the cognitive reaction.

Purpose, process, and reflection are the essential components of provocative and thoughtful inquiry. The challenge of the questions that we ask ourselves, and how we ask those questions, make the difference between committees and communities.

We offer the following formulation:

Purpose + Participation + Catalytic Questions =
A Sustainable Community of Thought

REFERENCES

Block, P. (2008). *Community: The structure of belonging*. San Francisco: Berrett-Koehler.

Chrislip, D. D., & Larson, C. E. (1994). *Collaborative leadership: How citizens and civic leaders can make a difference*. San Francisco: Jossey-Bass.

Goldberg, M. C. (1998). *The art of the question*. New York: Wiley.

Gray, B. (1989). *Collaborating: Finding common ground for multiparty problems*. San Francisco: Jossey-Bass.

Grinder, M. (1997). *The science of nonverbal communication*. Battleground, WA: Michael Grinder & Associates.

Lehrer, J. (2012, January 30). Groupthink: The brainstorming myth. *The New Yorker, LXXXVII*, 22–27.

Lipton, L., & Wellman, B. (2011). *Groups at work: Strategies and structures for professional learning*. Sherman, CT: MiraVia, LLC.

Palmer, P. (2004). *A hidden wholeness: The journey toward an undivided life*. New York: Wiley.

CHAPTER 8

Creating Interdependent Thinking Among School Staff

William A. Sommers & Shirley M. Hord

Learning is a consequence of thinking.

—David Perkins, *Smart Schools*

The road of experience from the singular and isolated teacher to that of educators interacting, learning, and working in a community with colleagues to learn how to increase their effectiveness, has been long and challenging. Professional learning communities are more myth than reality if teachers operate independently and in isolation from each other (Hord, 1997). Working productively in such groups requires the ability to justify ideas and to test the feasibility of solutions on others. It also requires the openness and willing spirits of individuals to accept feedback from their critical colleagues. Listening, consensus seeking, discarding one's own idea to work with another's, empathy, compassion, group leadership, supporting group efforts, and altruism are all behaviors that describe cooperative and collaborative human beings, and are mandates for engaging in interdependent thinking (Costa & Kallick, 2008). How to move school staffs encased in their egg-crate classrooms to circles of interactive problem solving and reciprocity is the challenge (Olsen & Sommers, 2010). This is a long highway, and, of course, the journey is not yet complete.

In the late 1990s, professional development and research focused attention on a new strategy—professional learning communities (PLCs)—where educators (teachers and principals) gathered to identify poor student-learning performance and to consider what to do about it.

Learning teams or learning communities became the innovation du jour. Every school and district wanted to be sure that they were "doing it," although many had no idea what doing it meant. When queried, some

The Power of the Social Brain, edited by Arthur L. Costa and Pat Wilson O'Leary. Copyright © 2013 by Teachers College, Columbia University. All rights reserved. Prior to photocopying items for classroom use, please contact the Copyright Clearance Center, Customer Service, 222 Rosewood Dr., Danvers, MA 01923, USA, tel. (978) 750-8400, www.copyright.com.

learning communities said that their grade-level team met together. Others said that they met to work collaboratively. Still others noted that they met to work on school improvement. However, the advent and implementation of PLCs was a distinct turning point for how teachers and their principals learn and work together, addressing without interruption their goals for their students' increased learning success. We now look into the work of an elementary school learning community, and at a high school, to ascertain how these two examples reflect professional learning communities and demands for interdependent thinking.

AT TWO SCHOOL SITES

We use two schools as exemplars that illustrate the creation of the PLC and subsequently the development and imperative of interdependent thinking of the PLC staff.

Prairie Hill Elementary School

In one small community of 10,000, 38% are Anglo/Caucasian and 59% are Hispanic. The students reflect the population groups of the town, as does the teaching staff. Raymondo Castro is principal at Prairie Hill, a K–5 school that employs 32 teachers, 17 aides, and the usual support staff, with the addition of Julia Johnson, a mentor teacher who supports instruction for all teachers. Principal Castro and Julia Johnson have worked persistently and patiently with their staff for more than a year to develop grade-level PLCs (Hord & Sommers, 2008). Castro and Johnson assess the PLCs. Although there is some typical variation in how the grade-level PLCs operate, most could be said to work in this way.

The teachers at each grade level, including two aides, meet every week on a rotating basis in the classroom of one of the teachers. The district has organized a master schedule for all the schools so that on Wednesday, at 1:30 P.M., all students depart from the schools, leaving the professional staff two-and-a-half hours of professional learning time. Thus, the PLCs have *supportive physical conditions,* one of the research-based descriptors of a successful PLC (Hord, 2004).

Principal Castro arranged for an ice cream sundae event for the staff at the beginning of the school year, and has engaged a committee to create a way to give attention to each staff person's birthday, because he knows the research on social capital builds collective trust. He also visits regularly with each teacher to gain an understanding of their personal/professional goals regarding teaching. In addition, he has subscribed to several quality professional journals, with copies for each grade-level team, and inquires of the teachers what they are finding of interest in the text. In these two ways—social and professional—he is supporting the development of respect and regard for one another, *relational conditions* (a second descriptor of effective PLCs).

Initially encouraging the teachers and meeting with them in their PLCs for some months, Castro has relinquished the reins to Mentor Teacher Johnson to monitor and support the work of the communities. Both Castro and Johnson encourage and support the communities' members to self-organize, set their norms, develop their group policies, and grow in leadership skills. Sharing the leadership power, authority, and decision making allows the group to develop their leadership skills (another descriptor of PLCs—*sharing and supporting leadership*, an important factor in increasing the professionalism of the teacher).

Johnson has been instrumental in developing all teachers' skills in reading, understanding, and using data—using multiple sources of student data. Teachers have transferred their data knowledge and skills learned in their community to their classrooms, where monitoring and assessment have become a routine part of their classroom practice.

Importantly, PLC members use their data to inform them of the next content for their adult learning, learning that focuses on the deficiencies of their students, indicated by data (here is the soul of PLC, *intentional and collegial learning*). To sharpen members' PLC skills, Johnson visits the meetings, offers her support, and monitors the communities' operations. She also has taught the members to visit one another's classrooms, observe, take notes, and share feedback on the observations (*peers supporting peers, a fifth attribute or descriptor of a PLC*).

These five dimensions of PLCs are executed within the frame of *a shared vision* of what the new learning looks like and sounds like when it has been implemented with a high degree of fidelity. This shared vision constitutes the sixth research-based dimension of a PLC.

However, the PLC members have not yet engaged meaningfully in considering an array of concepts and instructional strategies. Nor have they been conducting conversations that generate creative ideas through trusting interactions, planning, and working toward shared goals (Hord, Roussin, & Sommers, 2010). What to do?

Principal Castro, in a district meeting supporting the leadership skills of the principals for creating effective communities of professional learners, listened intently to the high school principal who was reporting about PLC developments at her school.

Westside High School

Davilla Acosta came to Westside 3 years earlier as principal. Although the school had a strong history in academics and co-curricular activities, test scores had become static and in decline in some areas. A learning culture was nonexistent, although professional learning communities were part of the structure of the school, but more in name than in practice. Until Acosta arrived, the department heads met and made decisions about who taught what subjects, how much budget was allocated to departments, and the perfunctory school improvement goals. These decisions were necessary but insufficient to move toward a school of continuous learning.

With encouragement from the principal, the department heads distributed their decision-making authority to include all staff in each department's PLC. Simultaneously, Acosta persisted in the notion of a school vision, advancing the idea that a shared picture must be created of what the school should be: what visitors should see students doing, how students would be engaged, and what should transpire in the professional communities of learners that would reflect each individual's knowledge, instructional skills, creative instincts, and those habits of mind that depict educators as true professionals.

Davilla knew that in order to examine data and to answer tough questions, each educator would need to trust his or her colleagues and be viewed as trustworthy. Developing trust among individuals who work independently would be a challenging job. First, she persuaded the PLCs to organize and schedule several after-school informal activities involving problem solving and teamwork. One of these was a scavenger hunt in which the teams read cleverly devised notes (prepared by the art and journalism teachers) that led the groups around all the school's academic departments and the teachers' workroom. These activities were designed so that all persons could participate without feeling unprepared or unskilled. More important, the activities required the teams to meet and devise a group plan, and to trust one another for help in reaching the goal. Davilla knew the research on trust and its importance as a foundation for free and uninhibited interaction among groups.

This simple social activity was followed by a professional challenge to the teams: Review each team member's array of activities for teaching a single concept (determined by the team), search the literature to find additional means by which to teach the concept effectively, and interview an expert in their school, in other schools in the district, at central office, at the intermediate service center, or at the local university. The team then organized and synthesized all the possibilities that they found. The final steps were to determine one approach to use with students, to co-create a lesson plan to which all team members contributed, and then try it in their classrooms.

Meanwhile, the assistant principal, designated as the "curriculum and instruction" coordinator, convened a large group learning session with all teachers. His teaching goal was to enable teachers to define several types of conversations (dialogue and discussion), to identify the purpose for each type of conversation (Garmston & Wellman, 1999), and to specify the conversation mode to be used in each team's efforts to share ideas and make plans.

Significant amounts of time, attention, and energy were invested in reviewing types of student data and how each type contributed to a robust picture of the students' learning success, as well as to identifying areas, indicated by the data, where students were not performing well.

You may ask, what did Principal Castro learn from the report of Principal Acosta? Quite a bit, as it happens. He has asked Davilla Acosta if he might bring a representative from each of his school's grade-level teams to visit with the department heads of the high school—all of whom serve as the chairs of their respective PLCs.

INTERDEPENDENT THINKING BY THE STAFF

Engaging teachers and principals in regular and frequent meetings demands that time become worthwhile. We suggest the following steps to change how time is spent and to keep the focus on learning with school staff members:

1. Have regularly scheduled and facilitated PLC meetings, with the staff setting agendas and understanding the purpose of PLCs.
2. Prepare staff to become skillful data users.
3. Build trust among group members.
4. Expand staff's conversation structures and skills.
5. Start conversations in pairs or trios when introducing participants to interdependent thinking.
6. At the end of the meeting, take time to reflect on the learning, decisions made, and skills developed by PLC members.

A construct that is helpful to us in guiding groups to develop interdependent thinking is IRGA:

Introduction—present an issue or problem;
Reaction—stimulate reaction through sharing data, an incident, or a story;
Generation—solicit ideas to address or solve the problem/issue, directing the ideas to be built on one another; or accept all ideas, then assess each to determine whether they have added to and enriched the earlier ideas, retaining those that have and deleting those that are unrelated or not linked;

Adaptation—change practice, based on the resulting and agreed-upon interdependent thinking solution.

The facilitator maintains these steps or structure for use in initiating and developing interdependent thinking practice in a group. At the conclusion of the activity, the facilitator guides the group in analyzing what it did to reach the end product.

Until the group has adopted interdependent thinking as a routine process and has learned to clearly and candidly articulate its emerging ideas that link, build, and enrich colleagues' thoughts and ideas, the facilitator's ongoing role is encouraging, calling attention to, applauding, and critiquing the group's work. The facilitator consistently engages the group in these same actions, until the group members assume these activities themselves and exercise them independently of the facilitator.

We believe that the professional learning community is the most powerful structure/strategy and context in which continuous educator learning and school improvement can occur. In 1988, Suzanne Bailey, a professional development consultant, said, "We don't have school improvement without people development." The PLC is the incubator for the development of its members' interdependent thinking and professional development.

REFERENCES

Costa, A. L., & Kallick, B. (2008). *Learning and leading with habits of mind: 16 essential characteristics for success*. Alexandria, VA: Association for Supervision and Curriculum Development.

Garmston, R. J., & Wellman, B. M. (1999). *The adaptive school: A source book for developing collaborative groups*. Norwood, MA: Christopher-Gordon.

Hord, S. M. (1997). *Professional learning communities: Communities of continuous inquiry and improvement*. Austin, TX: Southwest Educatioal Development Laboratories.

Hord, S. M. (Ed.). (2004). *Learning together, leading together: Changing schools through professional learning communities*. New York: Teachers College Press.

Hord, S. M., Roussin, J. L., & Sommers, W. A. (2010). *Guiding professional learning communities: Inspiration, challenge, surprise, and meaning*. Thousand Oaks, CA: Corwin Press.

Hord, S. M., & Sommers, W. A. (2008). *Leading professional learning communities: Voices from research and practice*. Thousand Oaks, CA: Corwin Press.

Olsen, W. R., & Sommers, W. A. (2010). *The trainer's companion to habits of mind*. Retrieved from http://habitsofmind.corecommerce.com

Perkins, D. (1995). *Smart schools: Better thinking and learning for every child*. New York: Free Press.

CHAPTER 9

Developing Smart Groups

Robert J. Garmston

Effective groups are not born; they are developed. Interdependent people working together to achieve common goals can result in innovation, goal achievement, group member satisfaction, and maximum achievement in minimum amounts of time. They enjoy healthy and productive connections with the broader communities of which they are part, and have continuous drives for improvement in the way they work and the results they achieve. Learning about how to be increasingly effective is inextricably linked to their achievements. This chapter provides leaders with research knowledge and strategies intended to maximize groups' capacities for thinking and working productively together.

FORMING SMARTER GROUPS: THREE PREMISES

Woolley and colleagues (2010) ask three questions. Is there such a thing as *collective intelligence*? If so, does it make a difference in a group's effectiveness? And is it possible to raise the IQ of working groups? A short answer is that groups can have a collective wisdom far beyond the intelligence of individual members (Gherardi & Nicolini, 2002; Woolley et al., 2010).

1. Collective Intelligence Is Real

To know whether collective intelligence exists, it may be helpful to be specific about what it is. Thomas W. Malone (2006), director of the MIT Center for Collective Intelligence, defines it succinctly: "Collective intelligence is groups of individuals doing things collectively that seem intelligent."

Anita Woolley, a researcher at Carnegie Mellon who has made it a primary aspect of her research, describes collective intelligence as a "factor that explains a group's performance on a wide variety of tasks" (Woolley

The Power of the Social Brain, edited by Arthur L. Costa and Pat Wilson O'Leary. Copyright © 2013 by Teachers College, Columbia University. All rights reserved. Prior to photocopying items for classroom use, please contact the Copyright Clearance Center, Customer Service, 222 Rosewood Dr., Danvers, MA 01923, USA, tel. (978) 750-8400, www.copyright.com.

et al., 2010, p. 686). The group's collective ability to perform on one set of tasks is predictive of its results on others. This is similar to findings with individual intelligence.

Woolley et al. (2010) conducted two studies in which they gave subjects standard intelligence tests and then assigned the subjects randomly to teams. They asked the teams to complete several tasks—including brainstorming, decision making, and visual puzzles—and to solve one complex problem. Then the teams were rated on how well they performed the tasks. The researchers found substantial evidence for the existence of collective intelligence. Collective intelligence is real, and it is measurable.

2. Groups Are Living Things

The group has a personality of its own that is more than or different from those of the individuals within it. It is its own social network. Human beings are social animals. We operate better with others than we do independently of others. Christakis and Fowler write, "Social networks can manifest a kind of intelligence that augments or complements individual intelligence, the way an ant colony is 'intelligent' even though individual ants are not" (2009, p. 26). In a similar fashion, birds work together as they flock by following three simple principles: maintain velocity similar to that of birds in the vicinity, maintain close physical proximity to the rest of the flock, and whenever possible move toward the perceived center of the flock.

3. Group Intelligence Depends on Group Process

Woolley and colleagues (2010) suggest that what makes great groups is not that the members are all really smart but that they listen to one another, share criticism constructively, and have open minds. They're not autocratic. Groups whose members work well together produce better results, and working well is enhanced by strong commitment to a shared process. There are many approaches to team building that can help groups develop greater collaborative and collective intelligence.

THREE ATTRIBUTES OF SMART GROUPS

Researchers (Woolley et al., 2010) find three individual-level features that correlate in a statistically significant way to collective intelligence:

1. The greater the social sensitivity of group members, the smarter the group.

2. The more turn taking within the group, the better the group performs.
3. The more women in the group, the higher the group IQ.

Woolley and her colleagues surmised that groups with more women are smarter because women tend to be more socially sensitive than men. Thus, the gender factor is real but indirect—that is, it is mediated by the property of social sensitivity.

In another classic experiment (Lafferty & Pond, as cited in Loden, 1985), group intelligence was measured by presenting small groups of executives with a hypothetical wilderness survival problem. All-female teams arrived at better solutions (as judged by wilderness experts) than all-male teams. The women's collective problem-solving capabilities were enhanced by their collaborative style, while the men's efforts to assert their own solutions led them to get in one another's way. The difference in collective intelligence did not occur because the individual women were smarter than the individual men, but rather because of a difference in gender-related group dynamics.

While social movements and changes since the mid-1970s might or might not result in different results today in terms of the style of men's and women's participation in groups, the important point is that collaboration trumped assertiveness as a productive path to group results.

Others emphasize creating collaboration to build collective intelligence. Tapscott and Williams (2008) promote four elements to develop collective intelligence: openness, peering (allowing members to adapt and build on one another's ideas), sharing ideas, and acting globally to access ideas.

DEVELOPING SMARTER GROUPS

Group development is not linear. On the contrary, studies have shown that groups operate much as dynamic, nonlinear systems and thus growth is affected by tiny events whose significance accrues in nonlinear ways. Groups evolve over time, as do dynamic systems like the weather or the stock market. Within the dynamic dimensions of group life, group achievement and progress interact with setting, history, mental models, degrees of authority, cognitive styles, knowledge, skills, personalities, leadership, and the resolution of tensions related to individual needs as contrasted with group needs. These variables add up differently during a school year and from year to year, and are more like calculus than arithmetic (Wellman, personal communication, June 2009).

Given the reality that group development is dynamic, not linear, following are some strategies for skillful leaders to employ in working toward developing smarter groups that embrace positivity, inquiry, and effective collaboration.

1. Given the Opportunity, Construct Diverse Groups

Collective intelligence increases as groups creatively include diverse relevant viewpoints, people, and information in collective deliberations. Groups that integrate the diverse gifts of their members enhance their collective intelligence.

Interestingly, research on what constitutes a diverse group has found that the difference in group IQ comes not from diversity in individual intelligence or gender, nor from racial, ethnic, or cultural backgrounds. It is differences in class backgrounds and life experiences that create better working groups (Hong & Page, 2009). For example, having all members of a group from middle-class backgrounds, whatever race they may be, does not create the divergent perspectives that bring a group new ideas.

Mental diversity trumps ability. Diverse groups of problem solvers outperformed groups of the brightest individuals because diverse members bring different problem-solving skills to the table. Hong and Page (2009) define diversity as cognitive differences in perspective (different ways of representing situations and problems); interpretation (putting things into different categories and classifications); heuristics (different ways of generating solutions); or ways of approaching problems, as in analyzing a situation or looking for themes.

When members of a group have diverse sets of mental tools, the process of group decision making is less likely to get stuck on less-than-optimal solutions, and more likely to result in superior ways of doing things.

2. Include Members with Higher Social Sensitivity

Social sensitivity can be measured. One measure of social sensitivity, developed by Simon Baron-Cohen, a professor of developmental psychopathology at the University of Cambridge, is the "reading the mind in the eyes" test. Google has numerous results that allow users to take the test online and receive instant feedback. One such site is http://glennrowe.net/BaronCohen/Faces/EyesTest.aspx

3. Develop Skills in the Ways Groups Talk

The group's ability to create a connectedness among its members and be open to creativity, to respect and honor the individual parts while expecting a higher outcome from the whole, is essential to the ability of the group to work well. It has been said that in smart groups, members are like tuning forks. What sets off a vibration in one creates a resonance in the rest. Groups whose members align their efforts rather than pursue their own agendas for individual status are able to create higher collective intelligence and produce better outcomes. The norms of collaboration (outlined in Figure 9.1 in an appendix at the end of this chapter) were originally formulated by Baker, Costa, and Shalit (1997). Since then the norms have undergone three revisions by Garmston and Wellman (2009) and have been used extensively in the adaptive schools work. The most current revision appears in Garmston and von Frank (2011). the norms outlined in Figure 9.1 suggest that groups focus on developing certain key communicative skills. (For further information on these norms, visit www.adaptiveschools.com.)

4. Positivity in the Workplace

Workplaces often are labeled as positive or negative. Lucky are those workplaces labeled positive; they are positively reinforcing systems. Those labeled negative are notoriously difficult to recalibrate because they are negatively reinforcing. Simply stated negativity begets negativity (Zimmerman, personal communication, 2009).

Negativity, especially continuous negativity, leads to stress. Continued stress in organizations leads to a reduction in the *ability to think* positively and with creativity. That is, the more stress, the less capable a group is of responding effectively to the stressors. Rather than becoming creative and adaptive, they retreat.

Transforming the day-to-day interactions in a team to be more positive than negative is a means to achieving a productive balance between the team's focus on itself and on its environment, between seeking understanding and asserting authentic beliefs and opinions. This shift in the pattern of discourse, in turn, leads to measurable success for the organization.

Positivity and negativity have been examined in many earlier studies (Fredrickson, 1998). Some of the observations and inferences from these findings are as follows:

- Positivity generates expansive emotional spaces that open possibilities for action, whereas negativity creates restricted emotional spaces that close possibilities for action.
- Depending on the emotional space we are in, certain actions are possible and others are not—some possibilities open for us, others close.
- In a state of enthusiasm, our horizon of possible actions is widened.
- Fear narrows the space of what is possible.
- Emotional spaces not only contain the actions that are possible, but also modulate the way in which we carry out those actions (Echeverría, 1994).
- Positive emotions broaden thought/action repertoires and build durable physical, intellectual, and social resources.

- At the organizational level, the work of Stacey (1996) has shown that it is the nonlinear interplay between positive and negative feedback processes that characterizes an organization's capacity to deal with increasingly complex environments.

In groups, the amount of positivity influences the amount of inquiry and the ratio at which people talk about others rather than themselves. The more positivity in a group, the higher the achievement on measurable goals.

5. Reflect on Experience

Smart groups see encounters as learning opportunities. They use both formal and informal means of assessing what is working and what needs refinement. Some groups mature. Some mature along a continuum from novice toward expert performance. But not all groups make this journey.

Experience is not enough for growth. Reflection is essential because humans don't learn from experience; they learn from reflecting on experience. We have heard the statement, "He taught school 30 years," only to be countered with, "No. He taught school 1 year 30 times." When groups reflect, they recall what occurred, relate this to attained outcomes, compare the outcomes with what was they hoped to achieve, examine causal factors leading to what was achieved, and note what they are learning that can be applied not only to the next group session but in long-term thinking about the group's work. These cognitive processes engage the affective-emotional dimension of human experiences and energize positive movement in human growth and development (Feuerstein, Feuerstein, & Falik, 2010). While this might sound complicated, its execution is simple, sometimes stimulated by the open question, "How did it go today?" or a slightly more formal process of brainstorming and recording what went well and what wishes group members have for a more productive meeting.

Reflection, it turns out, is the key to growth. A dilemma dogs each group. In practically every meeting, working groups have more tasks than time. While it seems logical to invest all available meeting time in working, doing so results in negligible learning about how to work most effectively and little likelihood the group will progress to the next stages of maturity. This universal truth holds: Any group too busy to reflect about its work is too busy to improve. Effective teams are conscious of what makes them effective. They possess knowledge about being a productive group.

CONCLUSION

Some groups mature; others do not. Smart groups are developed, not born. Groups are nonlinear systems in which tiny events cause major disturbances. A paraphrase can change the tenor of group behavior. Inquiry becomes an important factor in group success. Diversity in background and in cognitive style helps groups to be more effective in their deliberations. Such seemingly simple strategies as turn taking, when they become norms, contribute to the collective intelligence of groups.

Leaders are well advised to invest in the kind of group development activities in which groups are encouraged to self-reflect, learn from their experiences, and modify their practices. Reflection, not repetition, is the key to growth.

REFERENCES

Baker, W., Costa, A. L., & Shalit, S. (1997) The norms of collaboration: Attaining communicative competence. In A. L. Costa and R. M. Liebmann (Eds.), *The process centered school: Sustaining a renaissance community* (pp. 119–142). Thousand Oaks, CA: Corwin Press.

Christakis, N., & Fowler, J. (2009). *Connected: The surprising power of our social networks and how they shape our lives.* New York: Little, Brown.

Echeverría, R. (1994). *Ontologa del lenguaje* [Ontology of language]. Santiago de Chile: Dolmen Ediciones.

Feuerstein, R., Feuerstein, R. S., & Falik, L. H. (2010). *Beyond smarter: Mediated learning and the brain's capacity for change.* New York: Teachers College Press.

Fredrickson, B. L. (1998).What good are positive emotions? *Review of General Psychology, 2*(3), 300–319.

Garmston, R. J., & von Frank, V. (2011). *Unlocking group potential for improving schools.* Thousand Oaks, CA: Corwin.

Garmston, R. J., & Wellman, B. (2009). *The adaptive school: A sourcebook for developing collaborative groups* (2nd ed.). Norwood, MA. Christopher-Gordon.

Gherardi, S., & Nicolini, D. (2002). Learning in a constellation of interconnected practices: Canon or dissonance? *Journal of Management Studies, 39*(4), 419–436.

Hong, L., & Page, S. (2009). Interpreted and generated signals. *Journal of Economic Theory, 144*(5), 2174–2196.

Loden, M. (1985). *Feminine leadership: Or how to succeed in business without being one of the boys.* New York: Times Books.

Malone, T. W. (2006, October 13). *Transcript of remarks at the launch of the MIT Center for Collective Intelligence.* Retrieved from http://cci.mit.edu/about/MaloneLaunchRemarks.html

Rowe, M. B. (1974). Relation of wait-time and rewards to the development of language, logic, and fate control: Part II—Rewards. *Journal of Research in Science Teaching, 11*(4), 291–308.

Stacey, R. D. (1996). *Strategic management and organizational dynamics* (2nd ed.). London: Pitman.

Tapscott, D., & Williams, A. D. (2008). *Wikinomics: How mass collaboration changes everything.* New York: Penguin.

Woolley, A., Chabris, C., Pentland, A., Hashmi, N., & Malone, T. W. (2010). Evidence for a collective intelligence factor in the performance of human groups. *Science, 330*(6004), 686–688.

Figure 9.1. Seven Norms of Collaboration

Pausing	There is vast research on the positive effects of teacher pausing and silence on student thinking. The "wait time" research of Mary Budd Rowe (1974) has been replicated around the world. By inference, the same applies to adults. Thinking takes time. High-level thinking takes even longer. This research indicates that it takes from 3 to 5 seconds for most human brains to process high-level thoughts. Pausing before responding or asking a question allows time for thinking and enhances dialogue, discussion, and decision making.
Paraphrasing	Use a paraphrase starter that feels comfortable. Begin with "So . . . ," "As you are (verb)ing . . . ," or "You're thinking . . . ," and follow the starter with a paraphrase to help others hear and understand one another as they formulate decisions. Paraphrasing is one of the most valuable and least used communication tools in meetings. Groups that develop consciousness about paraphrasing and give members permission to use this reflective tool become clearer and more cohesive about their work. One caution: Don't use the phrase, "I hear you saying," as a starter. That phrase, beginning with "I," is about the listener, not the speaker, and often evokes a negative reaction. This form of paraphrasing was taught in the 1960s when it was thought paraphrasing was a language skill. It is not. It is a listening skill.
Posing questions	Two intentions of posing questions are to explore and specify thinking. Pose questions to explore perceptions, assumptions, and interpretations, and to invite others to inquire into their own thinking. One recommended practice is to inquire into others' ideas before advocating for one's own ideas. Effective inquiry follows a pattern of pause and paraphrase before posing a question. Humans have a finely tuned threat mechanism, so offer well-formed questions with a slightly melodic voice rather than in a monotone, and construct questions in plural forms using exploratory language such as *some, might, seems, possible*. For example, What might be some purposes of X?
	At times, we question in order to specify thinking. Our brains delete details from streams of data and distort incoming and outgoing messages to fit our own deeply embedded models of reality. This human trait causes difficulties in communication. Conversations go haywire when the various parties make different assumptions about the meanings of words and concepts, and neglect to verify or correct their assumptions. Successfully defining and generating solutions in order to solve problems requires specificity. Using gentle, open-ended probes or inquiries such as "Please say more . . . ," or "I'm curious about . . . ," or "I'd like to hear more about . . . ," or "Then, are you saying . . . ?" increases the clarity and precision of the group's thinking.
	Five categories of vague speech are worth probing to clarify thinking and communication: • Vague nouns and pronouns as in *they* or *students*. Press for specificity by asking, who specifically? • Vague verbs, such as *understand* or *improve*. Ask what these terms mean. • Comparators, such as *better* or *larger*. The issue is, better than what or larger than what? You must ask to get clarity. • Rule words, such as *must* or *can't*. What is behind these rules? What are the conditions that make a must or a can't? Asking questions about rule words may result in learning that the rule was imagined and not real. • Universal quantifiers, such as *everybody* or *all the time*. Check to see whether it really is everybody (even your neighbor?) or all the time.

Providing data Providing data, both qualitative and quantitative, in a variety of forms allows group members to develop collective understanding from their work. Data have no meaning except that which we make; shared meaning comes from collaboratively organizing, analyzing, and interpreting data. Effective groups collect and select relevant data for their work, develop and use data displays, and use data to make decisions. Groups follow agreed-upon protocols and work to invite and sustain others' thinking through pausing, paraphrasing, and posing questions.

Placing ideas on the table Ideas are the heart of groupwork. In order to be effective, they must be released to the group. For example, a group member might say, "Here is an idea we might consider. One possible approach to this issue might be. . . ." When individuals indicate ownership of an idea ("I think . . ."), the other group members tend to interact with the speaker based on their feelings for and relationship to the speaker rather than to the idea presented. This is especially true when the speaker has role or knowledge authority related to the topic at hand. To have an idea be received in the spirit in which the speaker intends, the speaker should label those intentions by saying, "This is one idea," or "Here is a thought," or "This is not a proposal; I am just thinking out loud."

Knowing when to pull ideas off the table is equally important. For example, say, "I think this idea is blocking us; let's set it aside and move on to other possibilities." In this case, continued advocacy of the idea is not influencing other group members' thinking. This is a signal to pull back and reconsider approaches.

Paying attention to self and others Attention is the essence of social sensitivity and a key factor in collective intelligence. Meaningful dialogue and discussion are facilitated when each group member is conscious of both self and others. Skilled group members are aware of what they are saying, how they are saying it, and how others are receiving and responding to their ideas. This includes paying attention to both physical and verbal cues in oneself and others. Since the greatest part of communication occurs nonverbally, group members need to be conscious of the total communication package. Nonverbals include posture, gesture, proximity, muscle tension, facial expression, and the pitch, pace, volume, and inflection in their voices.

Presuming positive intentions Positive presuppositions reduce the possibility that the listener will perceive threats or challenges in a paraphrase or question. Instead of asking, "Does anybody here know why these kids aren't learning?" the skilled group member might say, "Given our shared concern about student achievement, I'd like to examine our assumptions about what might be causing gaps in learning." The first question is likely to trigger defensiveness. The second approach most likely will lead to speculation, exploration, and collective understanding. This is especially true when a speaker has strong emotions about a topic, and even more important when the respondent initially disagrees with the speaker.

Assuming that others' intentions are positive promotes and facilitates meaningful dialogue and eliminates unintentional putdowns. Making positive intentions in one's speech explicit is one manifestation of this norm. This is an operating stance that group members must take if dialogue and discussion are to flourish; it is also a linguistic act for speakers to frame their paraphrases and inquiries within positive presuppositions.

CHAPTER 10

Working Smarter, Not Harder

Building Interdependent Communities of Practice

Diane P. Zimmerman

The meeting was boring; the presentation droned. Participants glanced at watches, fidgeted, nodded off. Suddenly, the facilitator stepped to the front and said, "We only have about an hour left and I am not sure these aspiring administrators are getting all their questions answered. Let's take a break, and when we come back, we will jot down some of their questions and make sure they get answers." Ten minutes later participants were back and asking questions, while the facilitator captured them. The transformed audience became interested and engaged, having forgotten now about time that was previously dragging.

For me, that afternoon proved to be a valuable learning experience—I had just had a glimpse of interdependent facilitation and I was hooked.

How had this facilitator managed to turn the meeting around? How had he done it in such a way that no one was offended? What had happened to re-energize the group? I wanted to be able to replicate this experience. It engendered a commitment to make meetings meaningful, to foster learning-centered, interdependent interactions to develop powerful communities that learn and improve their practice together.

When groups work well together, their learning becomes emergent and is greater than the sum of the parts. While *professional learning communities* (PLCs) and *communities of practice* will be referenced, this chapter describes a hybrid model of interdependent communities, one that is tenacious about getting better at the craft of teaching and learning. When groups become collective learners, my friend Bill Baker would say we have achieved *congia*

The Power of the Social Brain, edited by Arthur L. Costa and Pat Wilson O'Leary. Copyright © 2013 by Teachers College, Columbia University. All rights reserved. Prior to photocopying items for classroom use, please contact the Copyright Clearance Center, Customer Service, 222 Rosewood Dr., Danvers, MA 01923, USA, tel. (978) 750-8400, www.copyright.com.

la maraderie, a clever weaving together of camaraderie and conglomerate to describe ideas generated by emergent groups.[1]

Most teachers say that they have participated in PLCs. While credit necessarily must go to Senge (1990), Hord (1997), and DuFour and Eaker (1998) for creating a wide audience for PLCs, in many instances the process becomes streamlined and simplified, failing to lead to a true community of practice. Communities of practice, by definition, must move to actual practices. Learning communities do not always move to practice; they stay in the realm of ideas and concepts. Since teaching is a practice-based art, communities should become practice-based, with the measure of success being the creation of emergent knowledge that improves the practices of teaching and learning.

PROFESSIONAL LEARNING COMMUNITIES

DuFour and colleagues (2006) stressed the need for teachers to collaborate about changes in practice and framed three questions: (1) What do we want each student to learn? (2) How will we know when each student has learned it? (3) How will we respond when a student experiences difficulty in learning? Armed with these questions, many leaders have charged ahead, identifying standards considered to have the most leverage and then working to create common assessments. In some cases, schools work on rubrics; in other cases, they design multiple-choice tests with the goal of ultimately studying student work. Because collaborative time in schools is limited, teachers report that they often run out of time and usually do not get to that last and most important question: How will we respond when a student experiences difficulty?

With national Common Core State Standards and standardized assessments driving the agenda, PLCs run the risk of narrowing their focus to efforts to measure a few standards. Too often time is consumed trying to find a focus or engaging in long debates about content, and not enough time is devoted to reflecting about the learning of students who do not succeed. Leaders can lift the process by moving the focus to address thinking processes now emphasized in the Common Core by unpacking deeply held assumptions. When leaders focus on the thinking processes of the group, they scaffold for conceptual development and deep understanding and open the space for quality conversations. The value of communities of practice is in how educators learn to work together and how they learn to work smarter. Thus groups would be better served by focusing on the benchmarks of quality conversations.

Etienne Wenger (1998) popularized the term *communities of practice* (CPs). As with those working with PLCs, the emphasis in CPs is on doing;

however, the focus of CPs shifts from tasks to knowledge systems. In Wenger's view, a smart community designs itself as a social learning system that draws from both internal and external sources. Wenger's emphasis on group learning is twofold, focused both internally (the teacher's learning needs) and externally (the organizational learning needs). By marrying external sources of knowledge, such as standards, to internal sources of knowledge, such as experience with students, teachers work collectively to create complex maps for teaching and learning. We like to think of it as "working smarter, not harder."

IMPROVING THE QUALITY OF OUR CONVERSATIONS

As a principal, I gradually perfected an interactive design that began with mutual agenda setting and included space for what was called "think time." Think time was organized around questions that had no single answer. Staff had come to expect meetings to be well-run, efficient, and provocative. They learned that they were expected to think and to work together to delve into teaching and learning. Without realizing it, we grew together into an efficient learning organization that not only expected quality conversations, but also was skilled at conducting them without an appointed leader. Today, if those who moved into leadership were asked, "What most impacted your thinking?" they likely would say our insistence on asking questions that had no easy answers and our focus on outcomes. In addition, they learned powerful process tools—paraphrasing and questioning—that built their capacity to work interdependently, and this carried over into their classrooms. (See Chapter 9 by Robert Garmston in this book for a description of verbal questioning skills that enhance communication.)

To gain clarity and provide a practical measure for the success of quality conversations, I frame a hierarchy for assessing our conversations around what Costa and Garmston (1998) have defined as "maturing outcomes." They describe how teachers talk about and set outcomes for learners and how these outcomes mature with experience. This hierarchy also serves as a useful rubric for reflecting on the quality of group conversations. For those striving to create interdependent communities, being able to quantify the complexity of a conversation is a profound shift that improves collaborative work. When schools and groups learn to interact in a way that moves them between the different levels of conversation, their conversations have an exponential impact on practice, in that what we practice in our own lives gets replicated in the lives of our children.

By reframing Costa and Garmston's levels of maturing outcomes into five different levels of conversation, leaders can use a middle-out approach, beginning with outcome thinking to guide decisions beginning at level 3, then using the outcome thinking to shape content at level 2, and build activities at level 1. When groups start at level 1, they often create activities without strong links to learning. As communities advance to levels 4 and 5, they generate interdependent norms or habits of mind that reinforce reflective processes and create an interdependent community with an identity as a reflective, thinking-centered community. Levels 4 and 5 push groups to deep, meaningful work that improves their own personal repertoire as well as that of the group. In Figure 10.1 these levels are explicated in greater detail.

THE FOUNDATION: ACTIVITIES, CONTENT, AND PROCESS

Level 1: Activity-Based Conversations—Show and Tell

This type of conversation assumes that if teachers rub shoulders by telling about what they do in their own classrooms, they will learn from one another. In these types of conversations, individual teachers tell about something that they are doing in their classrooms, often by showing materials, and that usually is perceived by the other teachers as an activity they could try in their classrooms. In the rubbing of shoulders, some ideas stick, but most do not.

While activity-based conversations are not wrong, they have limited power to change practices. Teachers listen for "what works for them," sometimes finding something to apply immediately. This type of sharing rarely introduces the nuances and complexities of teaching, but rather stays at the surface, at the level of activities. At their worst, activities are gimmicks; at their best, they are carefully thought out sequences of instruction.

Activity-based conversations must become more than "show and tell," and interdependent facilitators need to work to take conversations to the level of deep, interdependent practices by moving the conversation through the levels of content to thinking processes and then back again to practice. When working with groups, skilled facilitators look for evidence of a collective impact on practice. It may or may not be there, as groups can arrive surreptitiously at new levels of conversation that deepen practice. However, unless the members of a community become purposeful in navigating through the various levels of conversation, it is likely to stagnate and not have a collective impact on practice. Groups that learn to purposefully navigate through the continuum move from happenstance to purposeful action that applies complex schemas of practice—a journey from novice to expert.

Figure 10.1. Costa and Garmston's Levels of Maturing

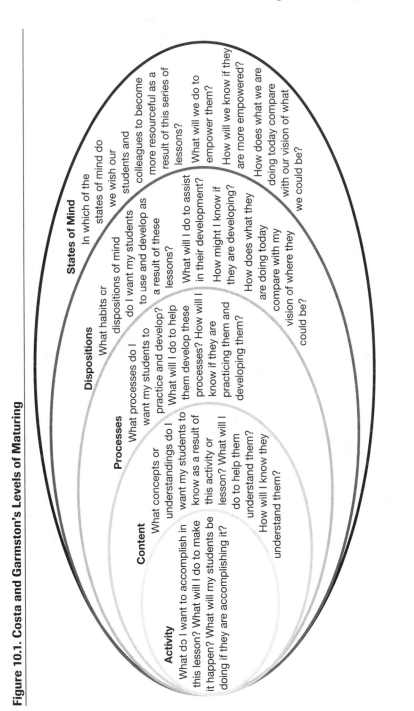

States of Mind

In which of the states of mind do we wish our students and colleagues to become more resourceful as a result of this series of lessons? What will we do to empower them? How will we know if they are more empowered? How does what we are doing today compare with our vision of what we could be?

Dispositions

What habits or dispositions of mind do I want my students to use and develop as a result of these lessons? What will I do to assist in their development? How might I know if they are developing? How does what they are doing today compare with my vision of where they could be?

Processes

What processes do I want my students to practice and develop? What will I do to help them develop these processes? How will I know if they are practicing them and developing them?

Content

What concepts or understandings do I want my students to know as a result of this activity or lesson? What will I do to help them understand them? How will I know they understand them?

Activity

What do I want to accomplish in this lesson? What will I do to make it happen? What will my students be doing if they are accomplishing it?

Level 2: Content-Based Conversations—The Debates

This type of conversation assumes that if teachers focus on content, developed either by others or by themselves, they will be better teachers. Often these types of conversations turn into debates about what the nature of the content should be, and more often than not they polarize groups.

In one school district, the community galvanized around two approaches for the teaching of algebra, so much so that the school board mandated that junior high students be allowed to choose which text they wanted to learn from, creating a nightmare for scheduling. Instead of trying to find a common understanding and coming to recognize that both avenues offer appropriate pathways for learning algebra, this community split into two camps. A leader could have asked the teachers to delve deeper into their practices to find common and divergent points of understanding instead of arguing about their own "right choice." This experience reminds us that as leaders we have a moral imperative to help groups transcend their conflicts and grow smarter together. Groups must learn how to work smarter and interdependently, not harder.

Content-based conversations have a place in communities of practice when participants learn to embrace conflict and work through it. Together, there is true value in seeking deeper understandings, nuances, and contrasting ideas that do not match one's own philosophical stance. However, content discussions often turn into autobiographical teaching conversations, where educators debate and advocate "what worked for them." The more stuck they become, the less they listen and the more they work to justify their own beliefs. This often becomes a nonproductive vicious cycle in which some fight and others retreat. One teacher once said, "In my first year of teaching I tried to tell the other teachers what I thought, but they didn't listen so I stopped talking."

Scott Peck (1987), in his work with church communities and belief systems, came to understand the emergent quality of conversations and noted that no community became a "true community" until its members were able to work through their conflicts, in contrast to groups that retreat (flee) or argue (fight). He describes the successful path as being through emptiness—the setting aside of the need to judge, or control, or fix, or convert. Likewise, moving beyond content wars requires groups to learn to work through differences of opinion and to embrace conflict as a healthy element in interdependent communities of practice. Avoiding conflict is the flip side of creating conflict.

Often when groups avoid conflict, they seek the first solution, pushing their true feelings and beliefs underground—a behavior best described by the economic term *satisficing*. This term is the clever combination of two words, "satisfy" and "suffice," and describes a decision-making phenomenon—choosing the first option that gives satisfactory results and, although it may not be optimal, suffices for the current need. Satisficing is a strategy of expediency, which works well for nonessential decisions, but creates blind spots for more complex decisions. Indeed, the satisficing phenomenon is more common than most of us would like to think. Since time is a teacher's most valuable commodity, many will adopt the first solution suggested by a group member just to get the job done. While this may be efficient in some circumstances, it is deadly for groups that are seeking shared meanings and a common language. Satisficing short-circuits the conversation and assumes that all agree, only to discover later that the only agreement was complicity of "rushing to solution."

Interdependent leaders would be well served to learn how to observe for satisficing and to use process skills (e.g., the facilitator's tool box; see Garmston & Zimmerman, 2013) to surface presuppositions that block thinking, and to invite groups to persist and think deeply about the issues at hand.

Level 3: Process-Focused Conversations—Reflective Dialogue

For process to work, it must be meaning-centered and linked to content or activities, which is why these three types of conversations—activity, content, and process—must be married to create a seamless flow that supports interdependent learning. Of course, the ultimate process is "thinking" and so communities that have learned to use meaningful processes have a reflective quality to their conversations. They talk about what they are thinking and how they are shifting viewpoints or changing their minds. When groups begin to truly listen and embrace the diversity of thought in the group, they have become interdependent. This type of conversation is called a dialogue, the necessary ingredient of all true communities. This is why working from the middle out (starting with level 3) produces more coherent, high-powered learning.

In an earlier article (Williamson & Zimmerman, 2009), we suggested that understanding and paying attention to process was the tipping point for groups as they move from good to great. It is the glue that holds all three levels of the above-mentioned conversations together, creating a structure through which the participants can navigate and create shared understandings and meanings.

Consider the contrast between empty process and meaning-centered process. A favorite meaning-centered way to get groups engaged is to find a few well-chosen quotes related to the group's work and have pairs of members talk about what a quote means, looking for nuances. Not only does this meaningful focus prime the members' attention toward the work at hand, but it moves them into a micro-community, as each person has to negotiate meaning with at least one other person.

Contrast this with an empty process icebreaker in which group members are given a paper plate with the name of an animal on the back and go around getting clues from others about the animal. While such an activity helps group members get to know one another, it does not efficiently move groups into the work at hand. The reader readily should note that this is the dilemma of the "activity trap" in which the facilitator does not pay attention to content or process. The facilitator would be well advised to begin planning by asking, "How does this opening activity provoke deeper understanding and thoughtful consideration of ideas?"

MOVING TO ADVANCED LEVELS

So far, a foundation has been established for how communities of practice might engage and measure their level of engagement by the quality of their conversations as moving from process thinking, to content, to activity, and back again. Let us now explore the next two levels—dispositions and states of mind.

Level 4: Disposition-Focused Conversations—Habits of Mind

Over time it becomes important for communities to adopt habits of mind, or dispositions, for how the group will grow and learn together. As utilized here the word *disposition* is defined as "lasting, acquired schemes of perception, thought and action" (http://en.wikipedia.org/wiki/Bourdieu#Habitus).

Any set of thinking habits, when used as a regular part of the way a group does business, becomes a set of dispositions. The essential element of dispositions, staying true to our values and beliefs, is that they become what Costa (2001) would call *Habits of Mind*. We have observed exemplary learning situations when a teacher or leader facilitates dialogue so children or adults listen with empathy, paraphrase to hear the correct message or feeling, and ask questions to probe deeper. When groups know and use Habits of Mind (Costa & Kallick, 2008), they grow in their appreciation of diverse opinions and experiences, and know how to work through disagreements and ask honest questions. People learn through active participation, not head nodding. These highly performing, collaborative groups who think together are our goal for children and adults.

Level 5: States of Mind—Virtuous Thinking Outcomes

Early in my work with Costa and Garmston around *Cognitive Coaching* (2002), we began to frame our intentions and our outcomes around a set of dispositions that we called *States of Mind*, described in more detail in Figure 10.2.

We found that by framing questions that touched on the States of Mind, we could cause a *cognitive shift*, in which a person might move from being stuck to having multiple options (flexibility), or from feeling help-less to feeling resourceful (efficacy), or from being unaware to being aware (consciousness), or from having an ill-defined plan to having a clear, precise plan (craftsmanship), or from being egocentric to being allocentric (interde-pendent). We later came to appreciate that the vocabulary of state-of-mind frames was also powerful when embedded in paraphrases as positive presup-positions for action, such as, "So you are looking for ways to be successful in this situation?" (see Costa & Garmston, 2002).

THE ULTIMATE REWARD—CREATING THE VIRTUOUS CYCLE

It is not a leader, but rather the way a leader frees a group to be open to the possibilities of creating something larger than the group, that creates a reciprocal, interdependent process for success. In systems theory, they call it the *virtuous cycle*—where positive outcomes stack together to create heightened levels of success.

Creating interdependent communities of practice is challenging and requires specific practice that focuses on refining and continuously improv-ing our facilitation skills. The missing piece of the collaborative puzzle is

Figure 10.2 Five Human Drives—States of Mind

1. The drive for *efficacy*: Humans quest for capabilities; continuous, lifelong learning; self-empowerment; and mastery and control.
2. The drive for *consciousness*: Humans uniquely strive to monitor and reflect on their own and others' thoughts and actions.
3. The drive for *flexibility*: Humans survive by developing repertoires of response patterns that allow them to create, adapt, and change.
4. The drive for *craftsmanship*: Humans yearn to become clearer, more elegant, precise, congruent, and integrated.
5. The drive for *interdependence*: Humans grow in relationship to others and are social beings in need of reciprocity and community.

Source: Costa & Garmston, 2002.

"interdependent facilitation." When all take responsibility at the five levels described here, we can work smarter, not harder.

NOTE

1. Like all emergent concepts, these ideas are the group's. I owe gratitude to all who have taught me so much about how to build interdependent communities of practitioners committed to excellence—how to create *congia la maraderie*.

REFERENCES

Costa, A. L. (2001). Habits of mind. In A. L. Costa (Ed.), *Developing minds: A resource book for teaching thinking* (3rd ed., pp. 80–86). Alexandria, VA: Association for Supervision and Curriculum Development.

Costa, A. L., & Garmston, R. J. (1998). *Maturing outcomes*. Retrieved from http://education.jhu.edu/newhorizons/Transforming%20Education/Articles/Maturing%20Outcomes/

Costa, A. L., & Garmston, R. J. (2002). *Cognitive coaching: A foundation for renaissance schools* (2nd ed.). Norwood, MA: Christopher-Gordon.

Costa, A. L., & Kallick, B. (2008). *Learning and leading with habits of mind: 16 essential characteristics for success.* Alexandria, VA: Association for Supervision and Curriculum Development.

DuFour, R., DuFour, R., Eaker, R., & Many, T. (2006). *Learning by doing: A handbook for professional learning communities at work.* Bloomington, IN: Solution Tree Press.

DuFour, R., & Eaker, R. (1998). *Professional learning communities at work: Best practices for enhancing student achievement.* Alexandria, VA: Association for Supervision and Curriculum Development.

Garmston, R., & Zimmerman, D. (2013). *Lemons to lemonade: Resolving problems in meetings, workshops, and PLCs.* Thousand Oaks, CA: Corwin Press.

Hord, S. (1997). *Professional learning communities: Communities of continuous inquiry and improvement.* Austin, TX: SEDL. Retrieved from http://www.sedl.org/pubs/change34/

Peck, M. S. (1987). *The different drum: Community making and peace.* New York: Simon & Schuster.

Senge, P. (1990). *The fifth discipline: Art and practice of the learning organization.* New York: Doubleday.

Wenger, E. (1998). *Communities of practice: Learning, meaning, and identity.* New York: Cambridge University Press.

Williamson, J., & Zimmerman, D. (2009). Collaboration takes center stage. *The Journal of the National Staff Development Council*, pp. 38–42.

CHAPTER 11

In the Company of School Leaders

Patricia Reeves

If you spend much time in the company of school administrators, you know that they are often people who wear an air of social ease and competence. While both are usually authentic, they mask other increasingly common characteristics:

- frustration about the complexity of issues associated with serving students well
- uncertainty in the face of competing and, often, ambiguous agendas
- a growing sense of urgency for effecting change
- a persistent sense of isolation and vulnerability

Effective school leaders come in both genders and all demographics and personal styles, but there are some habits and practices that set apart the leaders who navigate the complexity, uncertainty, urgency, isolation, and vulnerability from the leaders who are overwhelmed by them.

LEADING, LEARNING, AND ENGAGING

The most effective leaders focus on the work instead of themselves. These leaders are not afraid to learn from others and readily share both the grit and the glory of working to make schools better for all children. While the cultural model for a school leader is more of a Lone Ranger (Senge et al., 2000), the leaders who make fundamental and lasting changes to better their schools and districts often seek out other people as teachers, mentors, collaborators, and coaches. Moreover, they build coalitions of passionate and committed co-creators to fulfill the mission of their schools. These leaders can articulate clearly the vision they hold for their schools, their

The Power of the Social Brain, edited by Arthur L. Costa and Pat Wilson O'Leary. Copyright © 2013 by Teachers College, Columbia University. All rights reserved. Prior to photocopying items for classroom use, please contact the Copyright Clearance Center, Customer Service, 222 Rosewood Dr., Danvers, MA 01923, USA, tel. (978) 750-8400, www.copyright.com.

students, and their communities, while at the same time enlisting others to add to and deepen that vision (Marzano & Waters, 2009; Marzano, Waters, & McNulty, 2005).

So where do school leaders go to practice the habits and strategies that build strong coalitions for meaningful and constructive change in our schools? Where do they go to relieve the sense of isolation in their work? And, where do they go to authentically examine their own leadership work and find the growth edges that will make them more effective?

JOINING COMMUNITIES OF PRACTICE

Increasingly, school leaders are realizing that preparing for and getting the job are different challenges than actually doing the job. As this realization hits, more school leaders are looking for post-degree, performance-enhancing experiences. Some are turning to coaches; others seek out cohort programs where they can work with other school leaders over a period of time. In Michigan, one option for district-level leaders is a program called Courageous Journey (CJ), sponsored by the Michigan Association of School Administrators. Superintendents, aspiring superintendents, and first-line administrators join cohorts of practicing school leaders from districts all across the state and spend 3 years working together to achieve deep systemic change and improved student outcomes in their districts.

When practicing school leaders join a CJ cohort, they commit to the following work:

- deeply exploring seven research-grounded dimensions of district leadership
- authentically documenting, examining, and assessing their own personal leadership practices, dispositions, and performances
- practicing and extending high-yield leadership habits
- planning, guiding, and documenting deep, systemic change in their district
- strategically engaging, enlisting, and empowering stakeholders as critical players in the systemic change process

FORMING COLLEGIAL COHORTS

At the beginning of each new cohort, pre-existing cultural norms and time to build trust inhibit authentic conversations, but gradually these front-line leaders begin letting down their guard, and the real conversations begin. A common theme in these conversations is the challenge of achieving critical mass in, first, the motivation to change; next, the tolerance for actually embracing and making change; and, finally, the capacity to achieve and sustain change.

As one of our CJ superintendents put it, "After 2 years of blood, sweat, and tears to achieve consensus, commitment is unraveling as people begin realizing what the change will mean to them." He is not alone in this lament.

WORKING ON THE WORK

Time and again, our CJ leaders say the hard part is not exciting people with a new vision or even getting to consensus about what strategies will achieve that vision. The hard part is getting everyone to come to terms with how they must personally change in order to actually implement the strategies that will enhance learning for all students. At a recent CJ cohort session, one superintendent paraphrased a complaint heard among his staff: "They didn't tell us we would have to . . ." This superintendent was referring to the fact that, for most people, hypothetical change can be exciting and motivating, but real change that affects thought, word, and deed is scary. When not fully prepared for the reality of how change will affect them, people will abandon commitment in a heartbeat. Not surprisingly, most CJ participants express the same set of challenges in their work: how to achieve consensus around the right strategies to achieve change goals; how to ensure deep and high-fidelity implementation; and how to deal with the fact that all this work is like swimming upstream in a very rapid current through endless jagged rocks.

OVERCOMING ISOLATION

Many of our school leaders have become so isolated in their jobs that they are not used to thinking out loud about and working on meaty problems with others. In the superintendency, the lack of peers can distance these leaders from everyone else in the organization. To break this pattern of isolation, the CJ project faculty work to create a safe place for leaders to practice the authenticity that gets below the surface, so they can have more authentic and productive conversations with staff and other important stakeholders in their districts. Watching brave school leaders put aside ego in order to share their evolving leadership journey has reinforced the importance of three leadership habits:

- reflection (routinely examining, questioning, and re-interpreting)
- thinking interdependently (seeking, co-exploring, co-discovering, and co-creating)
- thinking appreciatively (responding to challenges and issues from an abundance rather than a scarcity frame of mind)

The CJ program focuses on supporting leaders who are refining these habits and using them to increase the motivation and the ability, for themselves and the people around them, to achieve better results for students. The program also engages participants in sharing, debriefing, and interpreting their work for greater insight and discovery as they document and "tell the story" of their adaptive change work.

STAYING CONNECTED

School leaders are reluctant to be away from their districts on a frequent basis, so the CJ program augments full-cohort sessions with other ways of engaging participants. Every 2 weeks, the CJ faculty offer CJ members the opportunity to blog with one another through an online community hosted by a third party. CJ faculty consult and interact with participants as they encounter or take up specific challenges or strategies in their work. The CJ program also offers trained executive coaches to assist district leaders in going deeper into their own work, and the CJ program connects participants with an array of resources (both on- and offline) and resource people for further support in their work.

CULTIVATING LASTING RELATIONSHIPS

Over the 3 years that participants work together as members of a cohort, they form relationships that extend beyond their planned CJ sessions together. They connect with one another between CJ sessions, share resources and ideas, consult with one another, and offer mutual encouragement. Some even work together to prepare for the final exhibition and provide each other feedback as they shape their final exhibitions for certification endorsement at the end of their active CJ cohort experience. After 3 years, CJ completers are so connected to one another and the shared experiences of their work that many maintain active involvement through the CJ Guild, which offers opportunities to continue engaging one another around the work of adaptive leadership.

REFLECTING AND NAVIGATING THE MILESTONES

For CJ participants, "telling their story" happens through a final exhibition at the end of their cohort experience. During these exhibitions, the superintendents talk about milestones in the leadership journey and what those milestones have taught them. Common milestones include finding their own "true north" in the work: that beacon of purpose that makes the journey worthwhile. Another milestone involves learning how to enlist, enable, and empower others to find their own beacons in service of a larger purpose. And the biggest milestone of all: learning how to fuel and harness the collective passion that transcends barriers and transports sojourners with shared purpose into new and promising territory. As described in these leaders' stories, none of these milestones are easy, certain, or predictable. Building them into a satisfying and accomplished leadership legacy involves numerous switchbacks and frequent resets in course. At the end of 3 years in the program, most participants are quick to say they have not mastered any of these milestones, but appreciate them more. As one member put it, "What is different for me now is that I am more awake to important practices and will continue working to use them better."

DEVELOPING CRITICAL HABITS

In working with Courageous Journey leaders, we have confirmed the significance of the three critical leadership habits.

First, *the habit of reflection*—where am I; how did I get here; and where am I going? This habit can be enriched by the perspectives of others who may write or say just the right thing to open up a whole new way of seeing and understanding. By seeking out and connecting cohort members with informed voices for change and renewal, we can help them see their work in new ways. We also find that reflection, when done with others, becomes more authentic and, therefore, more useful in fostering learning and growth. At the end of their time together, participants often point out the influences of authors, presenters, facilitators, and cohort colleagues as they present the story of their work. For each, the list of these influencers may be different, but what remains constant is how working on the habit of reflection brings the insights gained into sharp relief.

Second, *thinking appreciatively*. With appreciative thinking, leaders can practice together and take back to their districts a frame of mind that sees potential where there is a tendency to see problems. They also practice identifying and breaking down self-imposed boundaries ("We can't . . .

because . . .). Cohort experiences allow evolving school leaders to share the stories of their work (some of them painful), learn from the stories of others, and discover in those stories possibilities previously hidden to them. In sharing the stories of leading school districts through adaptive change, our CJ members begin to see how people can become trapped by thinking in terms of problem instead of possibility.

Leaders rehearse together, talking about the work of change in ways that start with acknowledging and appreciating the foundation of strengths available to build a strategic path toward a desired future. They also rehearse articulating that future in terms of aspiration and opportunity rather than challenge and barrier. Thinking appreciatively encourages people to take turns being lead learners, lead questioners, and lead discoverers, while offering support and encouragement to one another throughout the process. Thinking appreciatively helps people find passion for a shared vision and capacity to pursue that vision.

The third habit can be a real challenge for school leaders who were trained in the "Lone Ranger" version of leadership. This is *the habit of thinking interdependently*. They soon discover that interdependent thinking is not the polite, "I will listen to you, if you will listen to me"; rather, it involves both contributing and accepting the contributions of others in pursuit of something you can discover and own together. To think interdependently, we must let go of keeping score on who is "more right." As one participant put it, "We are all going down this path; why not go together? That way, when we stumble, we can catch each other and help regain the footing we need to achieve our goals." What this person understood is that the work of systemic change is full of surprises and, if we are open to them, amazing discoveries. Where we might be individually blind to some of the most important discoveries, we can see from many more angles if we explore and think together.

AN EVOLVING VIEW OF LEADERSHIP

Often CJ participants recall starting out thinking that effective leaders are people who have laser vision, know all the answers, and know just how to convince others to do whatever is necessary to implement those answers. All this "knowing and certainty" takes a big commitment to learning, so early in their careers many embrace the notion of leader as learner, but certainty still eludes them. Somewhere along the way in these cohort experiences, many happily abandon the quest for certainty, as they come to trust that co-creation with others can lead to great leaps of faith that send people down new paths of opportunity and innovation.

PRACTICING TO LEAD DIFFERENTLY

The hardest habit to adopt is interdependent thinking. In working with our CJ school leaders, we find that interdependent thinking is the most difficult of the three habits to fully embrace and adopt. Again, the cultural model of leader out front and in charge gets in the way. Leaders need a safe place to practice letting go of this model and replacing it with an interdependent one. One cannot lead what one cannot practice, so we provide repeated opportunities for these school leaders to engage with one another in the same ways they need to engage with the stakeholders in their schools. In practicing this kind of thinking, we have seen even the most independent and self-sufficient leaders discover that thinking interdependently removes obstacles and reveals unseen possibilities. They get to experience integrating and synthesizing ideas to the point where no one is sure where "my idea" leaves off and "our ideas" begin—moreover, nobody cares. Thinking interdependently together increases tolerance for uncertainty and creates a safe environment to "try and see what happens."

Participants' final exhibitions are a great window into how they make meaning of their experience. Their exit stories reveal how the habit of thinking interdependently takes hold in their psyches and replaces the high-stress notion that all the answers must come from them. Many discover that when the shared ideas and perspectives of collaborators are "informed" by both experience and purposeful learning, they can "unfreeze" the rock-solid status quo and make way for true adaptation and innovation. Some of our cohort members tell us that, once they experience the power of interdependent thinking and acting, it becomes a passion to experience it again. "It makes living with rapid-fire change a fun ride rather than a siege to endure."

CREATING SAFETY FOR LEARNING, GROWTH, AND ADAPTATION

Watching school leaders pursue their own breakthrough collaborations confirms that the more diverse perspectives you can bring to the work and the more you can create a safe environment in which people build trusting relationships, the more likely it is that someone or something will provide the spark that leads to new shared understandings and, thus, new shared commitments. The stories of the school leaders we serve in the Courageous Journey program remind us that the sparks can come from anyone, anywhere, anytime; the trick is to capture those sparks and ignite a true fire of renewal. When leaders pry open their own fist-hold on certainty, wondrous leadership possibilities emerge. When we give school leaders safe places to reflect, practice, reflect again, and practice more, we send them back to their work with more intentionality and more tools. Programs like Courageous Journey can help ensure that one of those tools is the capacity to lead and think interdependently. Armed with such a powerful tool, we have seen leaders achieve transformation in schools that is truly amazing.

NOTE

For more information on the Courageous Journey Program™, visit www. courageousjourney.org.

REFERENCES

Marzano, R., & Waters, T. (2009). *District leadership that works: Striking the right balance.* Bloomington, IN: Solution Tree Press.

Marzano, R., Waters, T., & McNulty, B. (2005). *School leadership that works: From research to results.* Alexandria, VA: Association for Supervision and Curriculum Development.

Senge, P., et al. (2000). *Schools that learn: A fifth discipline fieldbook.* New York: Doubleday.

CHAPTER 12

Thinking Maps for Meetings of the Mind

David Hyerle & Larry Alper

To connect is one of our most fundamental human impulses—not just with others on a personal level, but internally within our own minds with ideas that are dynamically linking together. In this sense, internally and externally we are unconsciously thinking and tackling problems interdependently, even when we believe that we are isolated actors thinking independently. The capacity of thinking interdependently begins with our internal awareness of how we see how things connect: Empathy starts within.

THE PROBLEM OF COMMUNICATING INTERDEPENDENT THINKING

One barrier to interdependent thinking is our emotional states, which often hijack our best intentions for collective, positive outcomes. Over many years of reflective practice in schools and through research in psychology and the cognitive neurosciences, we are now more aware of how we are unconsciously self-deceiving: Our individual, ever-changing brain structures sometimes are wired tight, frozen in some instances by our past experiences and the schemas that frame our thinking. Look into Daniel Goleman's first book, *Vital Lies, Simple Truths: The Psychology of Self-Deception* (1985), for a full analysis of how our emotions and cognitive states of mind deeply influence our capacities to see ourselves and others with an open mind. "Schemas are the ghost in the machine," Goleman (1985, p. 75) writes, for these *connected patterns* (schemas) drawn from experience, substantiated and reinforced in our minds, may harden and drive our perceptions of the moment and prevent transformational, conscious interdependent thinking and actions. The cumulative power of personal, interpersonal,

The Power of the Social Brain, edited by Arthur L. Costa and Pat Wilson O'Leary. Copyright © 2013 by Teachers College, Columbia University. All rights reserved. Prior to photocopying items for classroom use, please contact the Copyright Clearance Center, Customer Service, 222 Rosewood Dr., Danvers, MA 01923, USA, tel. (978) 750-8400, www.copyright.com.

social, cultural, and global frames of reference ultimately drives our mental/ emotional states and our day-to-day thoughts.

We are, as many brain researchers have noted, pattern seekers and meaning makers. In fact, in large part, it has been through the recognition of patterns that we have survived and flourished. To be a human being is to be connected to others; to be engaged with others in pairs, groups, families, and communities toward common goals; and ultimately to engage in the balancing act of improving the well-being of ourselves and others. As Margaret Wheatley (1999) observes, "Everything comes into form because of relationships. We are constantly called to be in a relationship—to information, people, events, ideas, life" (p. 145). In another context she adds, "The instinct of community is everywhere in life" (2005, p. 47).

Schools are communities built on an assumed outcome of continuous positive growth for the betterment of students and society, much like medical institutions that constantly attend to the physical and emotional well-being of people. Yet too often when individual leaders and leadership groups engage in the process of consciously thinking through problems interdependently, making decisions, and evaluating outcomes, we find ourselves feeling mentally and emotionally *disconnected*. During many one-on-one conversations, small-group discussions, faculty meetings, and professional development sessions, the conversations may begin well, as is our natural tendency, but then fall prey to people taking positions, rolling out and steamrolling their emotional states and logical arguments, and wielding power based in raw authority rather than in mindful, thoughtful judgments. People in these situations often feel embattled and separated from others—as if the face of a colleague across the table or across the hall is that of an adversary, rather than an ally on a similar journey.

A challenge that educators and others across every field face is how to *consciously* and dynamically surface thinking and identify actions in ways that catalyze ideas to be reformulated or reconstructed in a pluralistic environment. How do we bring discovery into the context of our interactions in a way that energizes and inspires insight and innovation and draws on our natural inclinations to think interdependently? When confronted with challenging decision-making conflicts, how do we become aware of the mental and emotional patterns evolving with us and in relationship to other decision-making situations?

We believe the problem is less about setting norms for communication, or using strategies for collaborative communication, or having expert facilitators mediate communication. The problem, mirroring Marshall McLuhan, is that the medium through which we normally communicate— speaking—*severely* limits our capacities to internally think interdependently (to think in nonlinear, highly connective ways) and also to then convey our "message" in an interdependent way with others. This is a radical notion, but let us explain.

This may seem strange to say, but unfortunately the mode of communication that we most covet and cherish and that we most often use as the medium to think interdependently with others—speaking—creates a glass ceiling within all of us as we generate ideas, and between us and our capacities for understanding one another's thinking. Why? This is because "spoken" representations of our thinking and emotional states are expressed almost exclusively in *linear* form (words are spoken in linear sequences, of course!), whereas our thinking from neuro-logic (brain functioning) to associative-logic (the mind informally connecting ideas), and our more formal mental operations (cognitive processes), all embody *interdependent nonlinear* thinking. For example, how often have you felt that what you are experiencing or thinking cannot be adequately expressed in words? Additionally, how often have you said to yourself and then to others, Don't you see what I mean? This is because, as brain researchers confirm, our minds work in nonlinear patterns . . . but then the medium of speaking through which we convey our thinking is forcing us into a linear presentation of the complex interdependency of our thinking pattern and ideas.

Consider that the spoken word—and written text—represents thinking in exclusively *linear* terms, while we actually are engaged in relational, associative, nonlinear, systems thinking. A more provocative statement—and one that rattles the senses because it is counterintuitive in our "literate" society—is that speaking and writing significantly under-represent our abilities to convey the rich patterns of interdependent, nonlinear thinking within which problems are found and high-quality solutions are created. An even more radical formulation is that speaking and writing (in linear text) create *cognitive* dissonance within in our own minds and in others around a table as we attempt, in fits and starts, to think in systems and interdependently with others. Peter Senge, in his work in schools and the workplace, along with leaders across many fields, believes that engaging in systems thinking is the precursor to thinking through sustainable solutions in the interdependent ecosystem we call planet earth.

If these assumptions and challenges to our normal medium of communication are by and large correct, then what is the alternative given that "speaking" is quite literally "the air we breathe"? Research from the cognitive-neurosciences and from our work in schools over the past 25 years offers a pathway that integrates speaking and writing with visual representations, based on fundamental cognitive patterns. Below we offer a new language for thinking and communicating interdependently: Thinking Maps®.[1]

THINKING MAPS AS A COMMON
VISUAL-VERBAL-SPATIAL LANGUAGE

Two insights by David Bohm (1999) in his transformational book *On Dialogue*, with an engaging Foreword by Peter Senge, capture the problem of how to richly represent one's thinking in conversation and how Thinking Maps offer an additional way of *seeing* thinking in alignment with conventional spoken and written communication:

> If we could learn to *see thought* actually producing presentations from representations, we would no longer be fooled by it. . . . A map is a kind of representation. The map is obviously much less than the territory it represents. This abstraction is advantageous because it focuses on what may be important for our purposes, with all the unnecessary detail left out. . . . It is structured and organized in a way which may be helpful and relevant. Therefore, a representation is not just "a" concept—it's really a number of concepts together. (p. 63)

The common visual language of Thinking Maps (Hyerle & Yeager, 2007) (see Figure 12.1) offers pathways for "seeing thinking" so that all individuals may visually represent *what* they are thinking simultaneously with *how* they are thinking in patterns. As we show below, in a grade-level meeting or a faculty meeting wherein every participant is fluent with Thinking Maps, interdependent thinking becomes transformative as people share and synthesize their ideas in a variety of different types of thinking patterns—in both linear and nonlinear form. Of course, as Bohm recognizes, the map is not the territory. The language of Thinking Maps works in an integrated way with the conversation at hand, offering a range of interdependent visual pathways for thinking through ideas. Like *all* representations, Thinking Maps are imperfect windows into perception, and not exacting mirror images of our minds.

Below we investigate research we have conducted over the past 10 years in the field of leadership and learning, for thinking interdependently

- within our own mind;
- in the conscious development of ideas; and
- with others.

After defining Thinking Maps, we will take one example from our research (Alper & Hyerle, 2011).

By definition, Thinking Maps are not a program or a model or simply a loose collection of useful graphics. Thinking Maps, taken as a whole, comprise

Figure 12.1. Common Visual Language of Thinking Maps

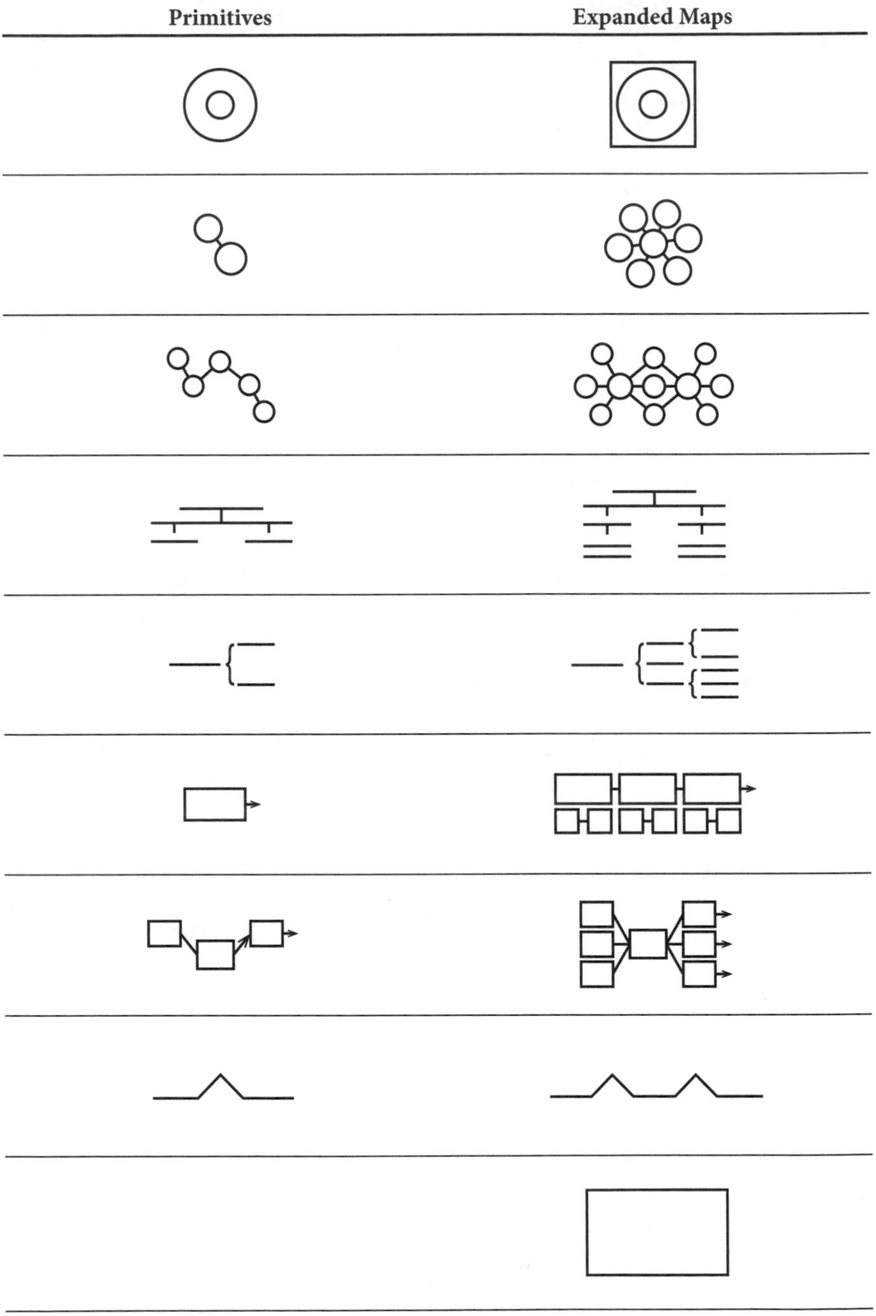

Primitives	Expanded Maps

Definitions

The Circle Map is used for seeking context. This tool enables students to generate relevant information about a topic as represented in the center of the circle. This map is often used for brainstorming.

The Bubble Map is designed for the process of describing attributes. This map is used to identify character traits (language arts), cultural traits (social studies), properties (sciences), or attributes (mathematics).

The Double Bubble Map is used for comparing and contrasting two things, such as characters in a story, two historical figures, or two social systems. It is also used for prioritizing which information is most important within a comparison.

The Tree Map enables students to do both inductive and deductive classification. Students learn to create general concepts, (main) ideas, or category headings at the top of the tree and supporting ideas and specific details in the branches below.

The Brace Map is used for identifying the part-whole, physical relationships of an object. By representing whole-part and part-subpart relationships, this map supports students' spatial reasoning and their understanding of how to determine physical boundaries.

The Flow Map is based on the use of flowcharts. It is used by students for showing sequences, order, timelines, cycles, actions, steps, and directions. This map also focuses students on seeing the relationships between stages and substages of events.

The Multi-Flow Map is a tool for seeking causes of events and the effects. The map expands when showing historical causes and predicting future events and outcomes. In its most complex form, it expands to show the interrelationships of feedback effects in a dynamic system.

The Bridge Map provides a visual pathway for creating and interpreting analogies. Beyond the use of this map for solving analogies on standardized tests, this map is used for developing analogical reasoning and metaphorical concepts for deeper content learning.

The Frame

The "metacognitive" Frame is not one of the eight Thinking Maps. It may be drawn around any of the maps at any time as a "meta-tool" for identifying and sharing one's frame of reference for the information found within one of the Thinking Maps.

Source: Thinking Maps, Inc.

a language. Consider that languages are symbolic systems composed of agreed-upon graphic marks that, combined together, enable humans to communicate simple to ever-more-complex thoughts with elegance: effectively and efficiently. Human beings traffic in symbols: They are the way we think, learn, and communicate. Every symbolic system or language has a purpose: the exchange of information and knowledge, whether it is literary, musical, mathematical, scientific, or artistic. Think of alphabets, the numbers 0 to 9 in mathematics, musical and scientific notations, Braille, and even computer code. These languages have a refined set of graphic primitives that are used interdependently to convey and make meaning. From the "Xs and Os" of a football coach diagramming the next play, to the binary "on-off" form of computer code, languages are at the heart of human communication and the conduit through which we think interdependently.

Thinking Maps, as seen in Figure 12.1, are together, in essence, a *cognitive code* that helps us to visually represent patterns of thinking as mental models: to combine and synthesize the internal thinking patterns of participants in a classroom, leadership group, or boardroom. The common visual language of Thinking Maps can be used in any learning community from classroom to faculty meeting to board meeting, to explicitly, visually represent *publicly* the connections we make as individuals internally, in our own private mental formulations. This common language may be used across any field; within the field of education, students, teachers, and administrators draw these dynamic graphics on blank pages or whiteboards, or on computers, so that they individually and collaboratively may draw out their creative and analytical thinking, whether in the teaching, learning, and assessment cycle, or for communicating and problem solving. Thinking Maps can be used in a coaching or supervisory context, in small groups such as grade-level teams, in large faculty gatherings, and across the whole school over time.

The language of Thinking Maps is used to symbolically represent, define, and activate eight specific, interdependent cognitive processes as visual-verbal-spatial patterns. These eight processes have been identified repeatedly through 70 years of cognitive science research as being fundamental operations of the human mind and brain. Bloom's taxonomy of educational objectives identified macro processes, such as the analysis and synthesis required for developing high-quality learning structures. The underlying cognitive processes, such as describing, comparing, categorizing, and seeing causes and effects, are the fundamental, interdependent operations necessary for reaching the macro objectives Bloom and others have identified:

1. Defining in context (labeling, definition)
2. Describing qualities (properties, characteristics, attributes)

3. Comparing and contrasting (similarities, differences)
4. Classification (classification, categorization, grouping)
5. Part–whole (spatial reasoning, physical structures)
6. Sequencing (ordering, seriation, cycles)
7. Cause–effect (causality, prediction, systems feedback)
8. Analogies (analogy, simile, metaphor, allegory)

Understanding these eight processes has been instrumental in identifying strengths and weaknesses in logical reasoning; they are also foundational in the areas of curriculum design and development, teaching, and standards-based testing. These are not simple, isolated logical operations. They are *interdependent* mental operations that require creative, interpretive, and reflective thinking. Our capacity for complexity in each individual cognitive process grows through adulthood; more important, however, through combination and interdependency of the eight thinking processes, our capacity for complex thinking and reflectiveness also grows. These *are not* lower order thinking skills that we somehow discard or abandon for higher order skills: Learners continue to use each of the eight processes at ever higher levels of complexity and combine them all to create, with content, the richness of ideas and concepts.

MEETINGS OF THE MIND

With this overview of Thinking Maps in mind, let's shift to consider the idea of how to facilitate interdependent thinking in the context of a common place for the meeting of minds: the often-dreaded and very necessary "meeting". During meetings it is often very difficult to remain open to our own perceptions—which means to consciously hold lightly our own point of view—while deeply listening to and reflecting on what our colleagues are saying and doing. Just try listening closely to another person without your internal dialogue interrupting the other person's words even before you verbally interrupt the person speaking! We may want to connect to what other people are saying in the moment, but often our own stories, frames of references, schemas—the ghosts in the machine as Goleman (1985) suggests—partially constrain as well as inform a constructive openness to future possibilities. We have a tendency to listen for affirmation of our own ideas. With some humor and a great deal of angst, a college professor friend of ours once stated that she would rather bite off her arm than go to a meeting! This may be because the rich, cumulative, dynamic thought processes required for highly interdependent thinking is often deflated in most meetings due to a full range of restraints, mostly the reality that the richness of each individual mind is being squeezed and pinched like toothpaste through the narrow linear opening at the end of the tube. It is bottled up in conversations, often meandering, rarely engaging the high-quality thinking of every participant.

The capacity for each of us as individuals and then collectively to identify the existing complex, nonlinear, associative mental models and frames that ground our perceptions and actions—and to consciously reflect upon, reframe, and repattern our ways of thinking—is key to creating participatory, connective leadership in one-on-one conversations, grade-level meetings, and large-group sessions such as faculty meetings. Let's look at an example of how Thinking Maps support participants in schools.

THINKING MAPS IN MEETINGS

We have all been in meetings—countless, endless, and unproductive meetings—in which we feel disengaged or powerless to influence the process or the outcomes. Often these meetings lack a clear focus and any tangible outcomes. If there is a process, it is often just that—a process that goes on without resulting in coherent ideas or actions informed by the information generated. In addition, the minutes of such a meeting frequently represent one person's interpretation of the meeting's contents and outcomes, and often *look* nothing like what various participants actually experienced.

Thinking Maps provide a clear focus and direction and naturally create the context for meaningful engagement and collaboration. The maps themselves form the "visual minutes" of the meeting and provide an accurate historical record of both the content and the thinking patterns and processes of the ideas discussed. The maps make it easy to reconstruct the conversation and re-enter the process at a later time. Sustainable schools require people to participate as leaders and contributors in highly effective ways. To sustain the level of engagement needed to address the complex issues that schools face, everyone involved must contribute skillfully and constructively.

Thinking Maps became the glue that connects people to one another and to the mission of the system through meaningful, purposeful interactions. As one teacher-leader noted:

> What's cool about the visual piece to this is that you can see your
> thinking together—it's so objective and nonjudgmental—put it on a
> visual display. . . . You can solve problems and make plans without
> it being contentious. When you're in these processes and folks
> have their own biases and assumptions, you assume certain things.

But when you plan with the maps, all this is displayed—reframes the whole way you plan with some people. The maps provide us ways to be productive with people that you might not normally be productive with.

Use of the maps makes the purpose and direction of meetings clear to participants. The group can clearly articulate guiding questions to direct its inquiry on each topic. The thinking process evident in each question guides participants in selecting the appropriate Thinking Maps to facilitate their inquiry. The use of Thinking Maps requires participants to suspend judgment and to consider how best to think about an issue. People are challenged to identify the right questions before moving too quickly to finding the right answers. Using questions and the appropriate maps opens participants to possibilities that cut across preconceived ideas and presumptions that they might have had about the topic before the collective inquiry began.

Without sacrificing the relational aspect of group process key to creating community, the use of Thinking Maps allows a group to work efficiently and in a highly attuned manner. People report the satisfaction of completing tasks not only in less time than normally expected but in a way that produces actions for which there was a high degree of commitment and enthusiasm.

The process of using Thinking Maps produces meaningful information that the group can use to inform future actions. Decision steps are embedded in a coherent process without the risk of becoming disconnected. One of the principals in our research described her use of the maps with her school's response to intervention steering committee. Together they decided which Thinking Maps to use to facilitate the conversation. Looking back on the experience, the principal remarked:

> I couldn't believe how smoothly it went—I was thinking I didn't have enough time to get through everything but it just went smoothly. . . . It was very easy for everyone to be engaged in the process.

Another principal described an end-of-the-year meeting with a team of veteran teachers to plan for the school's orientation process for teachers new to the district.

> We had a lot of people around the table for that planning process—there is a computer and a SMART Board and Thinking Maps software. We did a Circle Map, then a Flow Map with the steps,

Figure 12.2. Sample Tree Map

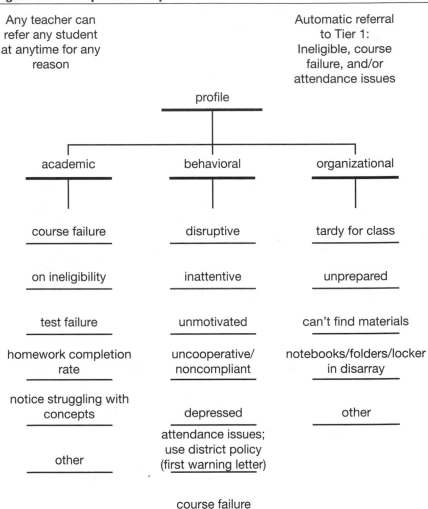

Any teacher can refer any student at anytime for any reason

Automatic referral to Tier 1: Ineligible, course failure, and/or attendance issues

profile

academic	behavioral	organizational
course failure	disruptive	tardy for class
on ineligibility	inattentive	unprepared
test failure	unmotivated	can't find materials
homework completion rate	uncooperative/ noncompliant	notebooks/folders/locker in disarray
notice struggling with concepts	depressed	other
other	attendance issues; use district policy (first warning letter)	
	course failure	

Source: Developing Connective Leadership: Successes with Thinking Maps (Alper & Hyerle, 2011)

and then a Tree Map [see Figure 12.2] for the different parts of the training. . . . The next-to-the-last day of school, sometimes folks are checking out, but when you have the maps as part of the planning document—the discussions are more focused; they can see it and stay focused. It seems like everyone's needs are met. . . . When you see this and everyone's ideas are put up on a map, everyone feels listened to and their ideas heard—facilitates more thought—no dead time, but people are visualizing what's on the maps and then processing and the light switch goes on and more ideas come out. So we come out with ten to twenty good ideas versus four to five.

When working with visually accessible information that includes the ideas of all stakeholders, people are more interested in finding a solution. Experiences such as these build momentum and organizational confidence. One senior administrator offered the following observation: "I feel a lot better where we're headed. . . . Now we can see there is a direction and a purpose. We know what we're doing, we can see the path, and we're ready to go—and how we're going to get there." Another administrator added: "The focus has always been on surviving fiscally and dealing with those issues—this feels like the first year that we've had a direction and focus on education and learning. Now we know the path and process and everyone is behind that and ready to go."

Interdependent leadership is about fostering the connections between and among people, between and among ideas within patterns of thinking, and across visual and virtual planes, which the diversity of those present and represented informs and enriches. This concept of being connected surfaces in the field of cognitive neurosciences. Networks exist in the brain, in the mind, between people, and virtually around the globe. We know that the brain constantly and unconsciously is making neural connections between the nodes: constructing, deconstructing, and reinforcing neural networks, and making patterns from sensory information drawn in from outside the body. The human mind also is making cognitive connections and consciously (or unconsciously) seeking and creating cognitive patterns based on a synthesis of what the brain already has imprinted within its neural circuitry from a lifetime of experiences.

If we can learn anything from this new synthesis of the networking brain, the mind, and the new global networks, it is that communication now depends on our capacity to seek, create, and make connections. Leaders and groups must trust that the collective wisdom of the community of learners will emerge, and that, from this, effective and meaningful solutions will be determined.

NOTE

1. Before utilizing Thinking Maps® as discussed herein, the educators high-lighted in this chapter participated in required Thinking Maps training. Resources and training are provided by Thinking Maps, Inc. (www.thinkingmaps.com). Thinking Maps® is a registered trademark of Thinking Maps, Inc.

REFERENCE

Alper, L., & Hyerle, D. (2011). *Developing connective leadership: Successes with thinking maps*. Bloomington, IN: Solution Tree Press.

Bohm, D. (1999). *On dialogue*. London: Routledge.

Goleman, D. (1985). *Vital lies, simple truths: The psychology of self-deception*. New York: Simon & Schuster.

Hyerle, D., & Yeager, C. (2007). *Thinking Maps: A language for learning*. Cary, NC: Thinking Maps, Inc.

Wheatley, M. (1999). *Leadership and the new sciences: Discovering order in a chaotic world*. San Francisco: Berrett-Koehler.

Wheatley, M. (2005). *Finding our way: Leadership for an uncertain time*. San Francisco: Berrett-Koehler.

Reflecting on Part II

Part II of this book focuses on the facilitation strategies that promote the growth of groups that work and think together. Groups that think together do not just happen. Examine the groups to which you belong and that you facilitate in your school, church, work, or community. Use the suggestions from this part of the book to monitor, analyze, and enhance the conditions that you have and that you want to create. Start this dialogue with your colleagues and co-facilitators. Think together to continue your useful practices and gain others.

GUIDING QUESTIONS

1. Assume the role of the facilitator was distributed rather than assigned. What would it look like, sound like, and feel like if everyone consciously used the skills of interdependent thinking at every meeting? What are the advantages of everyone being responsible for facilitation at each meeting?
2. We know that it is helpful to debrief the process of a meeting as well as the decisions and products of a meeting. We are used to debriefing questions like, "What results of this meeting are you most pleased with?" or "What results of this meeting will most benefit students?" What would happen at your meetings if you asked questions about interdependent thinking, such as: "What did you change your mind about today at this meeting? What information or facilitation skills encouraged you to examine your opinion or plan and replace it with another opinion or plan?"
3. In your head, list the various groups to which you belong. Select a group that you believe could be called a *smart group* using Robert Garmston's definition. Think of one of your groups that has not yet become a smart group according to Garmston's definition. Without naming names, analyze how that group might get smarter.
4. If you were facilitating a group, what one skill would you invite your group to consciously employ to experience immediate interdependent thought? How would you know it was successful?

PART III

Fostering Dispositons of Interdependent Thought

> All higher mental functions . . . are initially created through collaborative
> activity.
>
> —Berk & Winsler, *Scaffolding Children's Learning:*
> *Vygotsky and Early Childhood Education*

Individuals' different skills make collaboration possible. One reads
instructions; another interprets them. One deftly manipulates
complicated devices. Another's strong memory keeps track of turns. One
notices small effects that others miss. Another has the interpersonal skill
to forestall or solve disputes. Children expand their skills by observing
others and exercise their strengths by working with others.

Collaboration stimulates children to explain, share observations,
engage in dialogue, combine strategies, exercise patience, and complete
tasks. Explaining something to another builds one's own understanding.
Ultimately it is through talk focused on problem solving—particularly
among children who approach tasks differently—that learning occurs.

Teachers can make collaborative behaviors explicit by talking to
children about their different individual strengths. Teachers can pose
metacognitive questions to cause students to become aware of their
own thought processes and thereby build reciprocity—helping children
understand both the process and benefit of consciously sharing what
they know with another.

This part of the book contains both research information and
instructional strategies intended to build interdependent classrooms
as well as to help students take charge of their mental processes when
interdependent thinking is necessary for group productivity.

REFERENCE

Berk, L. E., & Winsler, A. (1995). *Scaffolding children's learning: Vygotsky and early childhood education*. Washington, DC: National Association for the Education of Young Children.

CHAPTER 13

Cooperative Learning: Accessing Our Highest Human Potential

Judy Willis

The brain has neural networks that, with guidance, can prepare students with *executive functions, emotional self-awareness and control*, and *social interactive skills* to become thoughtful participants, problem solvers, and innovators in the 21st century. As educators, we can and must provide opportunities to prepare all students for the new challenges and opportunities that await them.

Correlations between neuroscience research and cooperative learning offer insights about the conditions that promote optimal development of the neural networks in the prefrontal cortex. Successfully planned rich learning tasks in which students must think and act together provide the cognitive stimuli needed to activate and enrich executive functions, such as judgment, critical analysis, flexible perspective taking, inductive reasoning, prioritizing, risk assessment, creative problem solving, innovation, metacognition, and goal-directed behavior. The interactive and interdependent components of cooperative learning offer the emotional and interpersonal experiences needed to stimulate development of the prefrontal cortex networks that direct emotional awareness, successful communication, collaboration, adaptation, and resilience.

NEUROSCIENCE LIGHTS UP PATHWAYS TO THE HIGHEST BRAIN

Humans' brains have the largest *prefrontal cortex* (PFC) by volume of all animals. This 20% of high-value cortical real estate contains the networks that direct the advanced systems of executive functions, long-term

The Power of the Social Brain, edited by Arthur L. Costa and Pat Wilson O'Leary. Copyright © 2013 by Teachers College, Columbia University. All rights reserved. Prior to photocopying items for classroom use, please contact the Copyright Clearance Center, Customer Service, 222 Rosewood Dr., Danvers, MA 01923, USA, tel. (978) 750-8400, www.copyright.com.

conceptual memory, and emotional self-awareness that most characterize our humanity.

Through neuroimaging techniques, first with positron-emission tomography scans and later with functional MRI (fMRI) scans, we have seen patterns of varying metabolic activity in the awake, thinking human brain that correlate physical and mental actions and responses. We also can see the age ranges when different areas of the brain undergo the most rapid phases of physical maturation.

Maturation in the prefrontal cortex involves both the pruning away of networks with relatively low electrical activity and the strengthening of the networks that are most frequently activated by use. The PFC is the last part of the brain to mature, going through its most active changes between ages 8 and 18. As children spend a large percentage of their time in school during these years, educators are vital caretakers of the development of the PFC circuitry—the tools that children need most for their future social, emotional, and cognitive success and fulfillment.

GET INFORMATION IN AND RESPONSES OUT
OF THE HIGHEST BRAIN

To recognize the challenge of even getting the sensory data that make up learning into the PFC, consider the complexity of the brain's physical construction. A neural circuit holding even a small memory, such as an address, requires communication among thousands of neurons and about 100 feet of connections (axons and dendrites).

All learning starts as input from the senses, but not all sensory information available is accepted for intake. The admission criteria for passage through this filter, called the *reticular activating system*, are more exclusive than they are for the best universities in the world. Each second there are millions of bits of sensory data seeking entry, and less than 1% of these are selected.

Emotions exert powerful influences on all aspects of the learning process, including attention, memory construction and retrieval, and higher order thinking. The *amygdala* is a switching station deep in the brain's primitive, emotionally reactive limbic system (LeDoux, 1994). When stress is high, the increased metabolic activity in the amygdala directs incoming information down to the lower automatic brain (Pawlak, Magarinos, Melchor, McEwen, & Strickland, 2003). In fMRI scans of children in states of high stress or anxiety, the increased metabolic activity is accompanied by decreased activity in the PFC as new information/learning is blocked from entering memory construction (Toga & Thompson, 2003).

Without the reflective input from the PFC, when the amygdala diverts intake to the lower brain, behavior output is driven by survival instincts. Under these stress conditions, emotion is dominant over cognition and rational thinking. Responses are narrowed to fight, fright, or freeze (Thorsten et al., 2008).

Sustained boredom can put the amygdala into the stress state, so that in the absence of input to the PFC, the brain creates its own stimulation. When students don't have frequent opportunities to engage with learning in meaningful, successful, and enjoyable ways, the stress of sustained boredom or frustration that diverts control to the lower brain's fight/flight/freeze responses also results in the behaviors interpreted as *acting out* or *zoning out*.

Common threats to students' perceptions of safety, such as making embarrassing mistakes in front of the whole class, being called on when they don't know the answer, concerns about their mastery of English as a Second Language, and, for older children, fear of appearing too smart or not smart enough and risking ostracism by peers, are reduced by the interdependence of group collaboration.

A positive emotional state promotes the flow of input through the amygdala to the PFC (Subramanian, Kounios, Bowden, Parrish, & Jung-Beeman, 2009). Students' expectations of pleasure increase attention and memory, and reduce the impact of stressors that otherwise might present as behavior management problems (Talmi, Anderson, Riggs, Caplan, & Moscovitch, 2008).

Well-planned cooperative group learning experiences reduce stress, decrease boredom and frustration, and increase expectations and experiences of pleasure. With goals designed to connect with students' interests and authentic performance tasks that they consider relevant, students want the knowledge tools they need to succeed. Students are then in the ideal state for motivated, attentive learning because they *want* to know what they *have* to learn.

NEURO-*LOGICAL* SUCCESS CYCLE

Because the executive functions of judgment, analysis, and the ability to delay immediate gratification for long-term goals are still maturing well into one's 20s, many students do not have the insight that effort toward a goal promotes progress. Many students equate their potentials with grades received based only on summative assessments. These students often develop fixed mindsets that limit their efforts when they do not believe they have the capacity to succeed (Dweck, 2000).

A neuro-*logical* success cycle, promoted by cooperative group learning, can reduce pre-existing negativity and increase PFC activity supported by the emotionally positive impact of group cohesiveness, choice, and opportunities for students to participate through their strengths. In contrast to whole-class instruction, successful cooperative groupwork includes opportunities for more frequent and specific feedback and revision.

When students begin to experience successful cooperative groupwork and the feedback illuminates the association between their effort and their incremental goal progress, the resulting intrinsic gratification activates the release of *dopamine*. Dopamine is a neurotransmitter that, when increased sufficiently, promotes feelings of pleasure, deep satisfaction, and motivation to repeat or continue the action that is associated with its release (Willis, 2011).

As students continue to have positive learning experiences in cooperative groups, they develop more-positive attitudes about school and more characteristics associated with growth mindsets (Dweck, 2000). With the addition of the dopamine-pleasure influence of intrinsic motivation, students develop greater confidence and resistance to amygdala-blocking stressors, such as participation and mistake fear.

The cycle continues as students have more positive experiences in their small groups and become more comfortable with participation and academic risk taking (willingness to risk being wrong, offer suggestions, defend their opinions). As students transition toward a growth mindset, they dedicate more effort to academic work, especially when they know that it will increase their successful participation in a group (e.g., homework that practices a math skill that they want to use to gather data for a project).

Increased confidence, positive connections to learning-group goals, and opportunities to participate through their strengths all build students' resilience to previous stressors as their amygdala to support and promote passage of input to the PFC.

HOW THE BRAIN GROWS SMARTER

Unlike the physical maturation going on in students' bodies, their networks of executive functions and emotional controls will not develop passively. Their brains have the framework of rudimentary executive-function neural circuits that are undergoing pruning and myelination at their fastest rate during the school years. Students need experiences during these years to promote the development of their executive functions and emotional resources if they are to be prepared with these skill sets. Experiences in which students must think interdependently can provide the guided network activation necessary if students are to achieve their highest potentials during this "use it or lose it" stage of PFC development. The analysis of many neuroimaging studies supports correlations between frequency and duration of practice (the use of the networks to direct the mental or physical tasks they control), the amount and extent of neural activity seen in the associated region of cortex, and the density of myelin that improves the speed, accuracy, or proficiency with which a task is performed. For example, specific regions of visual cortex demonstrated notable increases in activity and density of connections (dendrites and synapses) and myelin within networks when subjects learned to juggle. These regions continued to increase in metabolic activity and density of interneural connections with practice as juggling skills improved (Draganski et al., 2004).

Studies, such as these, cannot be considered *proof* of the effectiveness of any classroom strategy. Valid laboratory research in the medical model requires limiting the difference between the control and experimental groups to a single variable. Because classrooms can never be matched in such a controlled way, the most we can do is make correlations and predictions relating the neuroscience research to educational interventions.

It is only an extrapolation from neuroscience research, such as those mentioned, to offer theories about how the practices in cooperative learning promote improved executive function and emotional awareness/self-control. The interpretations of the research that follow offer a bridge between information from research and the impact of an instructional intervention. The bridge is not ready for motor vehicles, but reasonable for foot traffic.

ONLY THE PERSON WHO THINKS, LEARNS

There are two components of the brain's neuroplasticity. Pruning is the brain's self-destruction of unused circuits to increase the efficiency of those that are most used. Neuroplastic growth refers to the increase in connections (dendrites, synapses) between neurons and more layers of insulating myelin constructed around axons in circuits that are frequently activated. The increased myelin insulation increases network durability (resistance to pruning) and the speed at which it conducts the electrical impulses that carry information from neuron to neuron (e.g., faster memory retrieval, cue identification, and pattern recognition).

Neuronal circuits of PFC functions are most effectively activated when students do the active thinking—evaluate, opine, predict, and so on. Passive listening and reading for isolated facts in order to answer questions, do little to activate the higher cognitive executive functions. During whole-group instruction, active thinking is not as prominent in students as it is when they are learning in one-to-one mentoring or through cooperative group experiences.

Jeanne Gibbs (1995), in her book *Tribes,* reported that in traditionally structured classes each student has about 5 to 10 minutes a day of individual time to engage in classroom academic discourse. In groupwork, that amount of time increases dramatically. She found that students experienced a greater level of understanding of concepts and ideas when they talked, explained, and argued about them with their group, compared with listening to a lecture or reading a text.

Cooperative group activities, unlike whole-class discussions or independent work, provide the most opportunities for students to think together—finding their voices, sharing their ideas, posing questions, drawing conclusions, and making associations verbally and through other formats. The small size and interdependent support of cooperative groups lowers the perceived risk of making a mistake or being wrong in front of the whole class. This is especially critical during adolescence when "fitting in" is such a strong need that individuality can become stifled (Jernigan, Hesselink, Sowell, & Tallal, 1990).

PRACTICE MAKES PERMANENT

Long-term memory networks are developed and reinforced through neuroplasticity by a number of cooperative group interactions and activities. The greater participation of each student in small groups and the variety of links to more circuits of memory further increase understanding and memory when group activities include processing the new learning in multiple sensory systems.

Information ultimately is stored in the part of the brain that holds sensory information related to each sensory response system (e.g., visual memories stored in the occipital lobes and auditory memories stored in the temporal lobe). This multihemispheric memory storage improves students' abilities to retrieve the information through a variety of cues. As the related neural networks are repeatedly co-activated and develop more and more dendrites, synapses, and myelin layers, the extended circuits of relational patterns promote concept network construction, making the learning more readily available to transfer to new applications (Geake & Hansen, 2005).

The interactive meaning making inherent in thinking interdependently promotes long-term memory construction. Opportunities to teach others are excellent ways for students to clarify and cement their own understanding of a concept. Activities in which students use symbolic thinking to transform information into other modalities, such as narratives or novel representations (posters, PowerPoints, videos, skits), provide powerful ways for students to commit learning to long-term, pruning-resistant memory.

Like long-term memory networks, executive-function networks also are strengthened when students practice the skills that contribute to the function. For example, estimating skill improves when children estimate quantities in a weekly estimation jar, receive feedback about the correct answers, and apply those experiences to make better and better estimations. Those estimation skill-building experiences can promote the executive functions of judgment and analysis-based prediction.

Opportunities to learn and use higher level thinking skills are one of the recommendations from the PISA assessment analysis of attributes of top-performing students (OECD, 2009). Cooperative group learning gives students a small, safer place to try out the higher thinking skills of executive function that they might not express to the entire class. They can experiment with critical thinking in a structured small-group setting, with scaffolding provided as needed via teacher prompts about what to discuss and how to run the discussion. This process empowers students to become more active not only in whole-class discussions, but in their homework, and in expressing their opinions outside of the classroom.

EMOTIONAL, SOCIAL, AND COMMUNICATION SKILLS

Communication success is related to emotional awareness and control. Active engagement in cooperative learning experiences builds cognition and emotional control circuits. Students do not have enough one-on-one teacher experiences throughout the day to provide this feedback, but as cooperative groups build their cohesiveness, trust, and collaborative skill sets, students become less dependent on their teachers for this feedback.

The nature of cooperative group interdependence also increases emotional sensitivity and communication skills. The planning of cooperative learning transfers the responsibility of decision making and conflict resolution to the students. Inevitably, unpredictable social and emotional challenges arise, such as different opinions about the choices regarding their investigation or about group member roles and responsibilities. These occur in safe settings and provide opportunities for students to build self-awareness and learning skills as they participate in discussions, ask questions, make predictions, disagree or agree with interpretations of others, and collaborate on common goals.

PICKING UP CUES

With less interpersonal contact, as children spend more time in the digital world, cooperative groups become increasingly important for the brain's construction of emotional cue awareness. In preparation for the higher demands on communication that accompany globalization, students need to build the PFC networks to identify emotional cues, and employ conscious strategies to maintain the reflective behavioral self-control to take actions to sustain collaboration.

When students engage in group projects and tasks, there are frequent unpredictable situations that arouse emotions, such as differences of opinion, sudden insights with the desire to interrupt, or disappointment when the consensus directs group decisions contrary to a student's desire. The brain makes predictions regarding social and emotional decisions or choices the same way it makes cognitive predictions of answers to questions—based on prior experiences.

Cooperative groups are powerful and authentic playing fields for these experiences, so students develop skills of recognizing nonlinguistic emotional cues. This will become increasingly critical when global interactions and interdependencies require communicating with others with whom they do not share a language or cultural norms. In these situations, accurate interpretations of cues will serve to prevent misunderstandings and conflicts that otherwise could disrupt collaboration.

With experiences in which they must think together and receive feedback, students develop increased ability to interpret the emotions and cues of others and respond with interventions that sustain successful communication. They may even be gaining emotional network development that increases group intelligence.

THE FUTURE

The qualities sought for the top jobs in emerging industries go beyond strong foundational knowledge to focus on applicants' abilities as innovators and creative problem solvers who can interpret and utilize new information, communicate clearly, collaborate successfully, and solve problems creatively. As globalization progresses, with more advances in information and technology, there will be more-complex, multifaceted problems, often beyond the domains of experts in single specialties.

Solving these problems will require interdependence, open-mindedness, flexibility, and strong communication skills for successful collaboration. The most capable applicants will be those who have developed their highest executive and social/emotional assets. The neurological classification of executive functions includes judgment, planning, estimation, analysis-based prediction, prioritization, pattern recognition and extension, metacognition, risk assessment, flexibility, clarity of communication, and goal-directed behaviors.

Through trial and error, instruction in specific strategies, observation of other groups' successful strategies, metacognition, and the other components of successful cooperative group learning, students build their executive functions, communication skills, and awareness of and appropriate response to emotional cues.

When students have more opportunities to activate and strengthen their circuits of long-term conceptual memory, executive function, and emotional awareness/control, they develop the prerequisites for success and personal satisfaction in the world in which they will live and work—to understand new information as it continues to increase in availability, analyze this information for accuracy, evaluate opinion versus fact, and identify bias. They will deduce novel uses for new information and technology, communicate and collaborate with others to solve new problems, and contribute innovations and ideas to expand the benefits of the global information pool to all people throughout the globe. Consider now the components of the required skill sets for 21st-century success, the thinking and behaviors defined as executive functions, and the cognitive, social, and emotional behaviors necessary for successful cooperative groupwork. You'll recognize these as essentially one and the same. Students who participate in successful cooperative group learning throughout their education, and develop PFC networks with the full array of executive functions and emotional control networks, will have the 21st-century skill sets. These students will be equipped with the *Habits of Mind* that will be their passports to personal fulfillment and achievement of their brains' highest capabilities.

REFERENCES

Draganski, B., Gaser, C., Busch, V., Schuierer, G., Bogdahn, U., & May, A. (2004). Neuroplasticity: Changes in grey matter induced by training. *Nature, 427,* 311–312.

Dweck, C. (2000). Self-theories: Their role in motivation, personality, and development. In *Essays in social psychology* (pp. 142–145). New York: Psychology Press.

Geake, J. G., & Hansen, P. C. (2005). Neural correlates of intelligence as revealed by fMRI of fluid analogies. *Neuroimage, 26,* 555–564.

Gibbs, J. (1995). *Tribes.* Sausalito, CA: CenterSource Systems.

Jernigan, T. L., Hesselink, J. R., Sowell, E., & Tallal, P. (1990). Cerebral morphology on MRI in language/learning-impaired children. *Archives of Neurology, 48*, 539–545.

LeDoux, J. E. (1994, June). Emotion, memory and the brain. *Scientific American,* pp. 50–57.

Organisation for Economic Co-operation and Development (OECD). (2009). *Programme for international student assessment (PISA) framework: Key competencies in reading, mathematics and science.* Paris: Author.

Pawlak, R., Magarinos, A. M., Melchor, J., McEwen, B., & Strickland, S. (2003, February). Amygdala is critical for stress-induced anxiety-like behavior. *Nature Neuroscience, 6*(2) 168–174.

Subramanian, K., Kounios, J., Bowden, E., Parrish, T., & Jung-Beeman, M. (2009). Positive mood and anxiety modulate anterior cingulate activity and cognitive preparation for insight. *Journal of Cognitive Neuroscience, 21*, 415–432.

Talmi, D., Anderson, A. K., Riggs, L., Caplan, J. B., & Moscovitch, M. (2008). Immediate memory consequences of the effect of emotion on attention to pictures. *Learning Memory 15*, 172–182.

Thorsten, T., Hariri, A., Schlagenhauf, F., Wrase, J., Sterzer, P., Buchholz, H., . . . Heinz, A. (2008). Dopamine in amygdala gates limbic processing of aversive stimuli in humans. *Nature Neuroscience, 11*(12), 1381–1382.

Toga, A., & Thompson, P. (2003). Temporal dynamics of brain anatomy. *Annual Review of Biomedical Engineering, 5*, 119–145.

Willis, J. (2011). A neurologist makes the case for the video game model as a learning tool. *Edutopia.* Retrieved from http://www.edutopia.org/blog/video-games-learning-student-engagement-judy-willis

CHAPTER 14

We Instead of Me

The Teacher's Role in Engendering Interdependent Student Thinking

Patricia A. Roy

Imagine two groups working on a solution to a problem-based learning project. One group has divided the work into component parts, sending each member off to complete work alone. Later, the members compile the segments and plan their presentation. Their conversations focus on logistics, format, transitions, organization, and graphic displays. Each member has done a competent job on his or her component, and the product looks polished, colorful, and well designed.

The second group has organized itself differently. While each member has been given a component to learn about in order to compose a first draft, the group's time together looks and sounds distinctly different. When one member presents his or her work, the others make comments, ask questions, propose refinements, express their concerns, argue for alternatives, recommend revisions, and praise strengths. The presenter listens intently, counters with rationales and explanations, proposes new refinements, and offers alternatives. By the time this segment of the work is completed, the original has become an amalgamation of the entire group's thinking—forged through a combination of thoughtful debate, positive support, and interdependent thinking. Members feel confident in their product and secure in their presentation. Each member's contribution to the joint effort is acknowledged, yet the group knows that the product is greater than the sum of its parts.

The first group was efficient in completing the task—dividing and conquering the content. The second group amplified the work by jointly transforming the efforts into something no single member could have

The Power of the Social Brain, edited by Arthur L. Costa and Pat Wilson O'Leary. Copyright © 2013 by Teachers College, Columbia University. All rights reserved. Prior to photocopying items for classroom use, please contact the Copyright Clearance Center, Customer Service, 222 Rosewood Dr., Danvers, MA 01923, USA, tel. (978) 750-8400, www.copyright.com.

completed on his or her own. These differences did not happen by chance but because of a knowledgeable teacher. The educator plays a critical role in creating conditions, reward structures, complex thinking tasks, and interactional skills so that group members engage in interdependent work and complex thinking.

What is the teacher's role in building the skills necessary for groups to work effectively, think interdependently, and develop and build on one another's expertise? First, the teacher implements research-identified critical attributes of cooperative learning. These attributes describe the fundamental conditions required for effective cooperative learning and increased interdependent thinking. Not all groups are cooperative groups, and these attributes explain why. Second, research on maximizing achievement within cooperative groups informs the teacher's work. Third, the teacher engineers a culture that supports interdependent thinking, develops appropriate group tasks, and interacts as a facilitator.

COOPERATIVE GROUPS ARE MORE THAN A SEATING ARRANGEMENT: CRITICAL ATTRIBUTES OF COOPERATIVE LEARNING

Many teachers comment that they are not getting the results they expected from the use of cooperative learning groups. Frequently this occurs because groups are not structured well or students have not been taught skills to ensure cooperative interaction. According to a meta-analysis of research, there are five critical attributes essential to high-functioning cooperative learning groups (Dean, Hubbell, Pitler, & Stone, 2012; Johnson & Johnson, 2009; Marzano, Pickering, & Pollock, 2001). A sixth is also critical for students to learn to work within learning groups of heterogeneous membership. A comparison of the critical attributes in cooperative learning groups versus simple groupwork can be seen in Figure 14.1.

CRITICAL THINKING IN COOPERATIVE SETTINGS

Research into critical thinking and cooperative learning has yielded significant results for students who have worked within collaborative settings. Generally, students are more likely to use higher thinking levels when they participate in structured group settings opposed to working individually. Members' diversity of knowledge and experience enhances the learning process for all. Further, improved problem-solving skills in cooperative settings result when students are "confronted with different interpretations" of

Figure 14.1. A Comparison of the Critical Attributes in Cooperative Learning Groups Versus Simple Groupwork

Cooperative Learning Groups	Common Groupwork
Positive Interdependence	*No Interdependence*
Each member benefits from the learning of others; reward system is based on how the group works and learns together	One student can complete the work alone; other members do nothing; one member can dominate the group
Individual Accountability	*Group Accountability*
Each member is responsible for demonstrating his or her learning; group incentives are based on how well individuals perform	A single group grade is given for the group product; individual learning is not examined or assessed
Face to Face—Interdependent Thinking	*Individual Thinking*
Group members are taught how to give help and provide explanations, exchange information and resources, challenge one another's thinking and assumptions, and develop new ideas	Students think and act on their own, coming together at the end of work time to combine individual efforts for the group product
Interpersonal and Small-Group Skill Development	*Assignment of Roles*
Teacher deliberately develops interpersonal behaviors for working in a group; focuses on communication, trust, leadership, thinking better together, and conflict resolution skills and behaviors	Roles are assigned to complete the task: leader, recorder, materials manager, checker, etc.; interpersonal skills are not addressed or developed
Group Processing of Interaction	*No Processing*
The group reflects on the strengths of group interaction for thinking, task accomplishment, and social relationship maintenance, while setting goals that improve group functioning	The group does not reflect on how effectively or ineffectively members worked or thought together; individual members may complain to the teacher about the lack of cooperation or involvement
Heterogeneous Group Composition	*Pseudo Teamwork*
Students who have different talents, skills, and learning styles are configured into groups by methods involving teacher selection, random selection, or student selection with criteria. Social skills that are taught allow for collaborative results	There is an assumption that students know how to collaborate, and that good teamwork results from the right "mix" of students in a group

the problem and peers assist them to "internalize both external knowledge and critical thinking skills and to convert them into tools for intellectual functioning" (Gokhale, 1995, p. 5).

When Gokhale compared group and individual work, group members scored significantly higher on critical-thinking items. A meta-analysis of cooperative learning studies found that quality of reasoning was significantly higher within cooperative settings compared with competitive or individualistic settings (Johnson & Johnson, 2009). Another review of studies found cooperative learning to be more effective on higher level tasks compared with other instructional methods (Jacobs, Lee, & Ng, 1997). Further, cooperative learning was superior for solving word problems, non-linguistic problems, and both well-defined and ill-defined problems (Qin, Johnson, & Johnson, 1995).

Teachers recognize that merely placing students in physical proximity and directing them to learn together does not ensure quality group inter-action or learning. Webb's (1985) research investigated and identified the mediating variables of cooperative interaction that are critical to successful learning and skilled problem solving, that are fundamental to interdependent thinking, and that influence achievement:

- Giving help to others increases achievement when it involves giving rationales or explanations—not merely repeating answers.
- Engaging actively in the thinking and learning process is essential—merely observing or listening to others is not sufficient.
- Receiving help improves achievement when that help is accompanied by an explanation and support.
- Using a reward system that rewards the group (*positive interdependence*) results in more helping behavior.
- Establishing heterogeneous group membership leads to higher frequency of elaborative behaviors (*information processing*).

This work reinforces the need to structure positive interdependence, teach interpersonal and interactional skills, and design curriculum tasks to maximize learning and increase the occurrence of interdependent thinking among group members.

THE TEACHER'S ROLE IN STIMULATING INTERDEPENDENT THINKING

The teacher needs to create a collaborative culture, foster co-cognition, develop thinking skills, create learning tasks that require interdependent thinking, and use facilitative interventions when groups need to refocus. Let's look at each of these in turn.

Creating a Collaborative Culture

The teacher can establish and clearly define for students how effective groups interact. It is not just a matter of developing individual social or interpersonal skills but of defining and coaching group norms of interaction, which include the following cooperative learning norms:

- Clarify the group goal and task.
- Talk, discuss, and decide before starting the task.
- The goal is to reach consensus, not "win."
- Use active listening.
- Everyone participates equally.
- Encourage others to participate.
- Rotate roles during groupwork.
- Check understanding of all group members.
- Everyone is responsible for the success of the group.

These norms are more than slogans. They are taught and improved over time through group training activities, teacher reinforcement, feedback, and monitoring. Effective group interaction is a product of interpersonal skill development—not luck.

Practicing Co-Cognition

Many students, and even adults, are unaware of how they think and feel during group interaction (i.e., metacognition). The beauty of well-executed cooperative learning is that we can develop and polish co-cognition—thinking about the group's thinking—while using metacognition—thinking about one's own thinking. This, too, is not just luck. Prompts for metacognitive thinking can be given along with directions for the group task; they are monitored by the students and the teacher and included in group debriefing at the end of the task. Figure 14.2 presents a sample list of metacognitive prompts and questions.

The teacher reinforces positive interdependence by providing a group reward, not a group grade, when *all* members are successful. This reward system emphasizes the concept that everyone benefits when each person learns and that students have a responsibility to help one another learn. While there are many strategies for structuring interdependence (Dishon & O'Leary, 1998; Roy, 1990), it remains the teacher's responsibility to

Figure 14.2. Metacognitive Prompts and Questions

Critical Attributes	Examples of Metacognitive Prompts and Questions
Positive interdependence	• How did you feel when Jessie paraphrased your idea? • How did Lisa's sharing of her research expand your thoughts? • As you reflect on your group's finished product, how did each member's contribution get woven together?
Individual accountability	• How will you monitor your own participation in the group task? • How well do you think you practiced your good listening skills? What is some evidence? • What did you tell yourself when you were tempted to interrupt?
Face to face—interdependent thinking	• What were you aware of in your own reaction when Maryann challenged your idea? • How did you decide to respond to Maryann? • What might be some alternative ways to respond?
Interpersonal and small-group skill training	• When your group reached an impasse, what were you aware of in how you reacted? • By what criteria did your group decide to allocate roles? • What were you aware of in your group members' reaction when you agreed (disagreed) about your plan?
Group processing of interaction	• As you reflect on your group's progress, what were you aware of in group members' contributions to its success? • What suggestions might you make for improving your group's working together? How might you and others in your group monitor that performance?
Heterogeneous group composition	• How did Paul's demonstration help the group envision your presentation strategy? • How did representing your ideas on a concept map help clarify your understanding of the task? • What effect did Marco's insistence on having a logical plan have on the group's actions?

structure and use reward systems that create positive interdependence within the group.

Processing time allows team members to reflect on how well they functioned as a group (words, actions, and thinking) by identifying strengths, recognizing ineffective behaviors, and setting goals for future improvement. Research into processing found that groups that took time to process achieved more and retained the information longer than groups that did not process (Yager, Johnson, Johnson, & Snider, 1986).

The teacher can foster processing with questions or by providing sentence stems for students to complete until students incorporate these steps by themselves. The focus is on "how" the group worked together rather than whether it completed the task. Processing strategies include:

1. *Teacher conducted:* The teacher meets with each group one at a time. The teacher can model processing by asking each member to name an effective skill he or she saw occur during the group's work time.

2. *Buzz session:* The teacher brings the whole class together and asks a processing question; each small group buzzes for a minute; and the groups share their responses with the teacher and the whole class. The teacher might ask the team to give themselves a grade on how well they helped other members without doing the work for them.

3. *Independent processing:* Each member can be provided a processing form that might contain statements and a continuum. The members mark the form individually and compare their responses with others in the group. For example, answers might range on a continuum from Always to Sometimes to Not Yet.

4. *Strength bombardment:* Every member monitors one person and gives that person feedback on a strength or behavior that contributes to group success.

5. *Goal setting:* Teams identify an area of improvement and set a goal. They might complete the stem, "To be an even better group, we can. . . ." The next time, the group reviews the statement and sets a goal for each person to make a commitment to practice that skill.

Develop Thinking Skills

Whether developing interpersonal or thinking skills, the steps are similar: Name the skill, define it, help students monitor and practice it, and provide time for them to reflect on the use of the skill.

Teachers may want to develop students' ability to engage in dialogue. Dialogue has been defined as the "free and creative exploration of complex issues, a deep 'listening' to one another, and suspending of one's own views" (Senge, 1990, p. 237). The purpose of dialogue is to understand other people's thoughts rather than to win others over to one's position. It is not about debate but exploration and openness.

One way to unpack this concept for students is to provide prompts or sentence starters, which give them a strategy to practice. Dialogue starters might include, "Help me understand why; What is the difference between _____ and _____?; Tell me more about . . . ; or, Your perspective is. . . . What else are you thinking?" The practice at first will be mechanical, but once students understand the purpose, they will create their own ways to engage in dialogue.

The teacher might prepare a poster, possibly a "T" chart of behaviors that look and sound like dialogue. This chart remains posted to remind students of the purpose and definition of dialogue, along with the sentence starters. Groups might be asked to add new sentence starters to the poster. The teacher will continue to remind students of appropriate time to use dialogue while in their groups until dialogue becomes common practice.

Develop Group Tasks Requiring Interdependent Complex Thinking

The learning tasks must require the use of complex thinking. If group members are asked merely to complete worksheets or drill one another on spelling, complex interdependent thinking is not required. The following are some group learning activities that involve higher-level group thinking:

- *Socratic seminar:* A Socratic seminar is a discussion of an essential question emerging from a common text. Students' opinions are shared, proven, refuted, and refined through dialogue with other students. Typically, it is conducted in a fishbowl setting—with an inner and outer group. Students mine the text for deeper understanding and meaning while inviting other members to also explore, challenge, offer alternatives, and disagree. In some versions of the Socratic seminar, students develop the essential questions, and the seminar is conducted completely by students. The seminar format provides opportunities to practice critical thinking, encourage divergent thinking, promote respect for diverse opinions and points of view, and gain deeper understanding of concepts, principles, and values.
- *Content-based controversy:* Students spend time researching the pro or con side of a topic such as whether there is global climate change or whether the American financial system requires more

government regulation. They research, study, and organize their arguments. Next, they present their information to the other side and later switch their positions, arguing the opposing perspective. Finally, both sides come together to meld information into a single solution that uses the best information from both positions (Johnson & Johnson, 1979).

- *Problem-based learning:* Students are presented with a complex problem such as addressing pollution in their town or inventing a new sport for astronauts to play on the moon for exercise. Teams work for 3 to 8 weeks, research background information, use critical thinking to create viable solutions with evidence, prepare presentations, and learn to collaborate as a team. Problem-based learning topics cover a wide variety of content areas and require team members to be critical thinkers and to synthesize a wide range of content. Problem-based learning addresses 21st-century content and skills and opportunities for interdependent thinking (Pearlman, 2006).

Teacher Interventions

When groups are working, the teacher's responsibility is to monitor group task, group interaction, and group thinking. An observation tool helps the teacher determine whether students are focusing on critical concepts and interacting collaboratively. The teacher uses observation data, not opinions, to give feedback to groups to help them improve their work and their interactions.

Teachers need to remember that they are *not* members of the group. As much as they would like to jump in and rescue the group's intellectual or interpersonal challenges, they should *not*. This admonition does not mean that teachers should ignore groups but rather should empower groups to solve their own issues—learning how to solve their own dilemmas, whether they have to do with content or group interaction. A teacher needs to interact with the group to help it solve its own problem, not intervene and solve the problem for the group. One of the indicators of interdependent thinking is that students are able to figure out what to do when they don't know what to do (Costa & O'Leary, 1992). Rescuing groups robs them of the opportunity to figure out their next steps and resolve their dilemmas.

During groupwork, the teacher facilitates groups by using a number of behaviors (Cohen & Lotan, 1991). The teacher:

- monitors groups to clarify tasks or remind them of expectations or time limits;

- reinforces group norms by labeling and acknowledging the use of the norms or reminding members of the norms;
- assists "stuck" groups—if a group has tried to resolve issues but seems to be at an impasse, the teacher can step in and ask questions or use a problem-solving protocol to help members determine how to keep their work moving;
- provides specific positive or negative feedback on how the group is functioning or completing the task; and
- asks questions to push the group to think more deeply about an issue or a statement.

CONCLUSION

Structuring cooperative learning groups differs significantly from grouping students and demanding that they cooperate. The teacher's role is to engineer the conditions that will facilitate high levels of learning and complex thinking. Mere physical proximity and teacher expectation of joint work will not produce the results described in the cooperative learning research. Groups must be structured with clear positive interdependence and individual accountability; team members need to have opportunities to learn effective interactional and thinking skills; tasks must require the use of higher level and interdependent thinking; and the teacher needs to delegate authority to the groups so that members can tackle challenges and learn how to resolve them. Using cooperative learning to engender interdependent thinking is not easy, but research and experience have shown it is well worth the effort.

REFERENCES

Cohen, E., & Lotan, R. (1991). *Program for complex instruction*. Palo Alto, CA: Stanford University, School of Education.

Costa, A. L., & O'Leary, P. W. (1992). Co-cognition: The cooperative development of the intellect. In. N. Davidson & T. Worsham (Eds.), *Enhancing thinking through cooperative learning* (pp. 41–65). New York: Teachers College Press.

Dean, C., Hubbell, E., Pitler, H., & Stone, B. (2012). *Classroom instruction that works: Research-based strategies for increasing student achievement*. Alexandria, VA: Association for Supervision and Curriculum Development & Denver: Mid-continent Research for Education and Learning.

Dishon, D., & O'Leary, P. W. (1998). *A guidebook for cooperative learning: Techniques for creating more effective schools*. Holmes Beach, FL: Learning Publications.

Gokhale, A. (1995, Fall). Collaborative learning enhances critical thinking. *Journal of Technology Education, 7*(1), 5. Retrieved from http://scholar.lib. vt.edu/ejournals/JTE/v7n1/gokhale.jte-v7n1.html

Jacobs, G. M., Lee, C., & Ng, M. (1997, June). *Co-operative learning in the thinking classroom*. Paper presented at the International Conference on Thinking, Singapore.

Johnson, D. W., & Johnson, R. T. (1979). Conflict in the classroom: Controversy and learning. *Review of Educational Research, 49*, 51–70.

Johnson, D. W., & Johnson, R. T. (2009). An educational psychology success story: Social interdependence theory and cooperative learning. *Educational Researcher*, 38(5), 365–379. Retrieved from http://edr.sagepub.com/cgi/content/abstract/38/5/365

Marzano, R., Pickering, D., & Pollock, J. (2001). *Classroom instruction that works: Research-based strategies for increasing student achievement*. Alexandria, VA: Association for Supervision and Curriculum Development.

Pearlman, B. (2006). Students thrive on cooperation and problem solving. *Edutopia*. Retrieved from www.edutopia.org/new-skills-new-century

Qin, Z., Johnson, D. W., & Johnson, R. T. (1995). Cooperative versus competitive efforts and problem solving. *Review of Educational Research*, 65(2), 129–143.

Roy, P. (1990). *Students learning together*. Richfield, MN: Patricia Roy Company.

Senge, P. (1990). *The fifth discipline*. New York: Doubleday.

Webb, N. (1985). Interaction and learning in small groups. *Review of Educational Research, 52*, 421–445.

Yager, S., Johnson, R. T., Johnson, D. W., & Snider, B. (1986). The impact of group processing on achievement in cooperative learning groups. *Journal of Social Psychology, 126*(30), 389–397.

CHAPTER 15

We Think Better Together

Classroom Strategies for Interdependent Learning

Jill Barton, Mary Burke, & Sabrina French

Great minds don't always think alike, as the old adage goes, but we can improve how minds think together. This chapter helps set the stage for applying interdependent thinking in the classroom, and addresses how to solve problems when they arise.

While cooperative learning is always groupwork, groupwork is not always cooperative learning. A model of conscious cooperative learning, not loosely structured classroom groups, needs to be employed to create interdependent thinking.

For many children and teens, the school years are hard to navigate. Students are struggling to define themselves as individuals while also striving to identify with their peers. Not all students arrive at school with the skills necessary to work cooperatively. Students don't always know how to interact socially with one another, because, in many instances, these skills are not learned at home or in communities. It is critical that healthy, respectful relationships are nurtured in the classroom.

SETTING THE STAGE FOR THINKING

Effective group thought occurs in an atmosphere where each learner feels supported, protected, and accountable to the other members of the group. When group collaboration is at its best, each member of the group feels a personal responsibility for meeting group goals. This type of learning situation will pay high dividends for all group members as they develop positive interdependence and individual accountability.

The Power of the Social Brain, edited by Arthur L. Costa and Pat Wilson O'Leary. Copyright © 2013 by Teachers College, Columbia University. All rights reserved. Prior to photocopying items for classroom use, please contact the Copyright Clearance Center, Customer Service, 222 Rosewood Dr., Danvers, MA 01923, USA, tel. (978) 750-8400, www.copyright.com.

Cooperative learning activities do not automatically yield cooperative thinking. The risk is that students can appear to be sharing and considering others' thoughts and ideas simply because they are sitting together. In reality, these students might still be thinking in isolation. The challenge is to create cooperative groups of learners that actually compose thoughts together. In order to create an environment that fosters this kind of cooperative thinking, it is imperative to carefully and thoughtfully set the tone in the classroom.

An important first step in setting up a collaborative environment is to establish group norms. These norms are the foundation by which groups will work and interact together. Having norms in place goes a long way toward establishing interdependent thinking that is sustainable over time. In order to do this, the attributes of positive group interaction should be explicitly defined. This is accomplished by reaching group consensus about what positive daily behaviors are expected in the instructional setting.

Examples of elementary classroom norms
- We will be good listeners and one person will talk at a time.
- We will all take turns sharing ideas equally.
- We will keep our hands and feet to ourselves.

Examples of secondary classroom norms
- We will be respectful to everyone in words and actions.
- We will be active listeners.
- We will agree to disagree politely.
- Everyone will contribute ideas to the group equally.
- We will participate equally by rotating roles.

In the intervention setting, where groups of students are pulled out from their regular classroom to a small group in order to meet specialized academic needs, it is also important to acknowledge and establish common norms. Regardless of the members or duration of a group, norms should be established to ensure cohesiveness among all participants.

After the class has established norms, it is critical that students practice and monitor their use of the norms so good habits are started and maintained throughout the year. New norms may be added as the need arises. The norms become a classroom contract by which all abide. It is beneficial for students to take part in individual and group reflection on the norms. Periodic and intentional assessment of the norms builds positive interdependence and individual accountability. One way to accomplish this is to create rubrics for individual and group behavior. A rubric should include reference to the established norms. Students and groups benefit by maintaining a record of where they fall on the rubric. An example of a rubric for individual behavior is provided in Figure 15.1.

Figure 15.1. Contributor Rubric

Criterion	Elegantly Cooperative	Cooperative	Beginner	Novice
Respecting others	The group member listens to, acknowledges, builds upon, and responds to the opinions and ideas of others by clarifying, paraphrasing, and empathizing. Consciously monitors the participation of each group member and invites contributions from all. Advocates the use of skillful listening to show respect to all group members.	The group member listens to, acknowledges, and builds upon the opinions and ideas of others with paraphrasing and respectful comments. Voluntarily contributes ideas to the group conversation.	The group member attempts to listen to and acknowledge the opinions and ideas of others with respectful comments. When invited, contributes ideas to the group conversation.	The group member over-talks or interrupts, argues from his or her own point of view, and maintains personal opinions even in light of conflicting data or group consensus. Dominates the conversation or withdraws/remains silent.

The value of a classroom where thinking together is the expectation, not the exception, is priceless and must be deliberately crafted by the teacher. When a teacher encourages cooperative groups to think and reflect, not just complete a task, students will have the support of the group to think for analysis, creativity, and problem solving. Communicating their thinking with peers allows students access to multiple viewpoints which can be discussed and defended. Even when there are disagreements, students can develop and practice valuable problem solving strategies. For additional information about cooperative learning and its effects on the brain and thinking, see Chapter 13 in this text.

BUILDING A FOUNDATION

Listening and Responding to One Another

Before expecting students to do any kind of thinking together to problem solve, they need to be given the language and skills to do so. Students don't inherently know how to listen and respond to one another, so a great deal of time may be spent at the beginning of the school year building these social skills. It is far easier to introduce how to be a good listener than to immediately expect students to have the skills necessary to work cooperatively. These skills can be applied to learning tasks or team-building topics.

A strategy to help students develop communication and listening skills is to have them summarize or paraphrase the words of their partner or clearly express their opinions. Sometimes it is necessary to provide students with prompts like, "My partner said, '_____,'" or, "I believe _____," in order for them to articulate their listening or thinking. Later these prompts for paraphrasing can be posted prominently in the room so students can reference them continually when speaking in groups. This is an activity where students learn to listen as they think. It is a first step in teaching them to recognize patterns in thinking. Students need to be given ample opportunities to practice communication with peers using review topics or skills before expecting them to dive into complex scenarios. The ultimate goal of any activity is to help students be responsible for their own thoughts and expression, while also assisting them to recognize the importance of what others have to offer.

There are additional considerations when planning for instruction in a "thinking classroom." One of the considerations is to provide learning opportunities where there are multiple entry points and more than one solution. There is no faster way to stifle collaborative thinking than to present a question where there is one right/correct answer and one defined path to the solution. A hierarchy is swiftly established with closed questions or tasks because the high-achieving students usually arrive at the correct solution first. Students around them quickly begin to feel that their ideas and opinions are not valuable to the group and will be hesitant to share in the future.

Delivering Instructional Content

When introducing a new social skill, instructional activities may include the review of content and concepts. A social skill is named, discussed, and a "sounds like, looks like" chart is developed by the class and hung in the room for reference. This allows students to focus on the new social expectation while working with familiar concepts. After the social skill is firmly embedded, the instructor can scaffold the activities to target higher order thinking skills. As the year or unit progresses, these carefully designed social skill lessons will have students thinking critically and cooperatively together. Figure 15.2 offers cooperative strategies (Dishon & O'Leary, 1998) and conversation starters.

Moving forward, a question to consider is, "What do students need to know for the cooperative activity?" It is important to know what prior knowledge a student brings to the activity. A pre-assessment is a valuable tool because it can help to form groups. Students may need some kind of common experience that can prompt their prior knowledge. This allows them to connect with the event and move to higher levels of discussion that go beyond simply guessing or defining. These experiences can level the playing field for students who have had very little exposure to the content and

Figure 15.2. Cooperative Conversation Starters

Cooperative Strategies	Conversation Starters for Elementary	Conversation Starters for Secondary
Turn to your neighbor	"Based on your knowledge of the elements of poetry, turn to your neighbor and generate a list of ways the author used figurative language. Which is most imaginative? Which is most humorous?"	"Using the maps, turn to your neighbor and compare the weather fronts. Then predict the kind of weather each might bring." In which prediction do each of you have the greatest confidence? Why?"
Think-pair-share	"Based on your knowledge of the elements of poetry, generate a list of ways the author used figurative language. Now pair with another person and tell each other your ideas. Be prepared to paraphrase what your partner said or what consensus you reached."	"Use the maps to compare the weather fronts. Then predict the kind of weather each might bring. Now join your partner and explain your ideas. Be prepared to describe what your neighbor said or what consensus you reached."
Pairs of pairs	"Based on your knowledge of the elements of poetry, in pairs, generate a list of ways the author used figurative language. Record your ideas on a sticky note. Join another pair to create a combined list of ways the author used figurative language."	"In pairs, use the maps to compare weather fronts. Predict the kind of weather each might bring. Record your ideas on a sticky note. Join another pair to create a combined list of weather fronts and your predictions of the weather each might bring. Work together to identify the predictions you think are most likely to be correct."

can provide the group with a common language. Teacher-selected groups provide a method for pulling students with varied strengths and skill sets together. Heterogeneous groups provide opportunities for rich debate and discussion. At the elementary level, this might mean grouping advanced, grade-level, and struggling readers to discuss the elements of a story. At the secondary level, it could mean pairing a student with knowledge of mechanical skills with a student who lacks that information in order to discuss the benefits of simple machines in our lives.

When introducing students to new and sometimes more abstract ideas, providing common background knowledge is critical. Structuring the activity with clear outcomes and tasks will allow students to move to the higher level of thinking. It is advantageous for teachers to have several questions planned in advance that will assist students in their thinking. Possible content cues are, "What do you know about this topic already?" "What data or information do you have to support your ideas?" and "How does this information relate to . . . ?" Coaching questions may include, "What patterns do you notice?" "What do you need to know and do to move forward?" and "What might happen if . . . ?" Questions must encourage thinking, not just doing.

Student groups occasionally will come to roadblocks they can't work through on their own. An effective teacher has already anticipated where the students might struggle and has a plan in place to guide them through the thinking process.

PROBLEMS TEACHERS/INSTRUCTORS MIGHT RUN INTO AND POSSIBLE SOLUTIONS

The following examples address potential problems teachers/instructors may encounter while implementing a classroom culture where students are expected to think interdependently.

Problem 1: Conflicts hinder students' willingness to work together.

> *Possible solution 1:* Review norms and rubrics with individuals and groups.
> *Possible solution 2:* Add to or revise the norms to address specific behavior expectations.
> *Possible solution 3:* Have students identify social skills that will help them overcome the problem.
> *Possible solution 4:* Have a frank and open discussion with students about the possibility of working cooperatively within a group without having to be best friends. The staff of the school can be used to illustrate this concept. Students are often surprised to

learn that all of the educators in their school are not necessarily best friends, even though students often observe them working together in a collegial manner.

Problem 2: The high-achieving students are reluctant to hear or accept the ideas of others.

Possible solution 1: Given a prompt, each person writes his or her idea down on a sticky note at the same time. Then the teacher utilizes a random selection strategy (e.g., the student whose birthday is closest to the date) to determine the order in which students will state their ideas within each group.

Possible solution 2: Revisit the norm, "We will all take turns sharing ideas and opinions." This also will assist in refocusing the group on positive interdependent thinking.

Problem 3: Students who struggle academically are afraid to voice their thoughts.

Possible solution 1: Provide students with questions where there is no one right answer and where problems can be approached in multiple ways. This is key to building confidence.

Possible solution 2: Play to a student's strengths, by drawing upon his or her background knowledge, interests, and learning profile. Not only does this boost the self-confidence of the student, but it also shows peers that every person has something to contribute to the group.

Possible solution 3: As another strategy, build in "speaking time," using a timer or talking chips. This strategy allows the students to have the opportunity to talk uninterrupted for a specific amount time or until he or she runs out of talking chips.

Problem 4: There is a student who is not able to function at the level of the rest of the group.

Possible solution 1: Utilize "thinking partners" where a student is paired with a more capable peer. Together, these partners share their ideas with the rest of the group. For example, suppose the group has been asked to draw comparisons between two cultures and create a poster to present to the class. Prior to the whole-group discussion, the teacher has paired individuals and given them talk time to create lists about the cultures. Then the group comes together to share ideas and accomplish the task.

The struggling student, who might have a tendency to fade into the background or be unable to share ideas, is now able to participate with support. This practice builds accountability for both students, while fostering a beneficial relationship. The more capable student is forced to practice explaining things in more than one way, and the struggling student benefits from the positive modeling of thought.

Possible solution 2: Provide learning supports prior to the lesson. These supports will aid the student during the group lesson or discussion. Examples of supports might include graphic organizers, a pre-reading of the information, or scaffolding of concepts by the instructor. A preview of information or expected skills activates prior knowledge. This experience can take place in an intervention setting or in the regular classroom, depending on the needs of the students. When students meet as partners or groups in class, the struggling student will have received tools that help him or her share his or her thoughts and ideas.

Problem 5: Students latch onto the thinking of one student and claim it as their own.

Possible solution 1: Periodically have students think, write, and share. Before sharing ideas, students take time to organize their thoughts and then write down what they are thinking. Students must record their ideas even if that means they write, "I'm very confused about this topic, and need to hear some other ideas to help me with my own thoughts." Knowing that they are going to be held accountable for their thinking raises their level of concern.

Possible solution 2: Revisit the norm, "Everyone will contribute ideas to the group equally."

Problem 6: The group hits a roadblock and cannot move forward.

Possible solution 1: Have all students write their ideas down on paper, and then read all ideas to the group and look for patterns. Trends in the responses should direct the group in ways to move forward with the task.

Possible solution 2: Gently guide the group with questions intended to prompt the students. For example, a group is using multiple resources to make a claim about how humans can influence weathering on structures. The students have done some research as well as some in-class testing. However, they are not sure how to process their data. At this juncture, it would be critical to ask, "What research data do you have?" "What does each piece of research data tell you?" "What do your investigation data tell you?" "Is there a relationship between the research and your investigation data?" "What further information do you need?" and "What do you need to do to make a claim?" Anticipation by the teacher is key in dealing with situations such as these. It is necessary to have the group reach its own conclusion, not for the teacher to give the answer to the group.

CONCLUDING THOUGHTS

Relying on cooperative thinking as a means of delivering high-quality learning experiences moves students to a deeper understanding, both socially and academically. It is key for developing positive interdependence and individual accountability.

In rigorous learning settings, there will be times when all students will falter and need help. What a gift it is for students to be provided cooperative thinking opportunities and a learning environment where they are assured that when they fall, the group will lift them up, and when they fly, they will fly together.

REFERENCES

Dishon, D., & O'Leary, P. W. (1998). *A guidebook for cooperative learning: Techniques for creating more effective schools*. Holmes Beach, FL: Learning Publications.

CHAPTER 16

Theater

Celebrating Interdependent Thinking

Sandra Brace

The theater is a celebration of interdependent thinking. It is an ancient cultural form that has functioned for centuries to bring people together in both thought and feeling. Theater can be both an example of and a template for highly effective group thought. Theatrical conventions, traditions, and practices are invaluable tools for education and the professional disciplines. As social beings, people seek a connection that is met singularly by the theater on both sides of the stage. When we view group thought through the lens of theater, we are provided with the ancient Greek standard of effective group thought at its highest level: *that all minds in attendance are brought into a shared experience of beauty and/or understanding and/or catharsis.* In live performance, matrixes of unspoken agreements exist as disbelief is suspended and a world is co-created that both audience and performers bring to life together. The essence and point of theater is interdependence, and it remains something we can experience only as a group—perhaps the most important piece of all. Drama, dance, music, and performance come together in the theater in countless combinations but with singular intent: to express. These ancient arts remain as timeless as this basic human need, and are living celebrations of interdependence.

Theater has a vital place in classrooms for children and adult learners because it is so rich in practices and strategies that develop a group's capacity for thinking and performing together. Staging theatrical productions requires authentic use of systems and processes, provides opportunities for students to become more aware of both independent and interdependent thinking, and is structured around good practices for effective group thought across disciplines. Theater comes with clear assessment tools, feedback structures, and lists of responsibilities so wide that the strengths of every individual in the classroom and learning community are valued.

The Power of the Social Brain, edited by Arthur L. Costa and Pat Wilson O'Leary. Copyright © 2013 by Teachers College, Columbia University. All rights reserved. Prior to photocopying items for classroom use, please contact the Copyright Clearance Center, Customer Service, 222 Rosewood Dr., Danvers, MA 01923, USA, tel. (978) 750-8400, www.copyright.com.

The purpose of this chapter is twofold: to describe the attributes of effective group thought in theatrical settings, and to present some strategies from theater that apply in many other settings, particularly in classrooms, to develop and enhance those capacities. If indeed, as William Shakespeare proposed, "all the world's a stage," we want all of our players to be in top form.

EFFECTIVE GROUP THOUGHT IN THEATER

The attributes of effective group thought are very similar in dance, drama, and theater. The cast is united by a clear common goal and/or vision: the work. There is an acknowledged leader and an agreed-upon protocol. There is trust and willingness, and the cast and director are in partnership in creating the work. Each individual strives to his or her highest potential to serve the work. The group values the work foremost; defers to the director, who in turn respects the interpretations and contributions of cast and production company; and works through roadblocks with humor and enthusiasm. During the rehearsal process, effective group thought in drama and dance presents itself as the ease with which the cast makes errors and corrections, and the respect cast members show to one another throughout the process. Individuals are comfortable in extending themselves and take risks when group thought is effective, and there is comfort with proximity, as well as a heightened awareness of one another's physical space. The effective ensemble is caught up in the "flow" of the work, there is more "yes" than "no" heard on stage, and there exists a willingness to consider every angle and try the same thing in a variety of ways. In performance, the effective cast of actors and/or dancers demonstrate continual and focused awareness of one another, and, in the case of dance, move and breathe as one. In every situation, the most effective cast demonstrates a willingness to make sacrifices for the greater cause, hear the ideas of others, and celebrate both individual and group achievement.

DEVELOPING EFFECTIVE GROUP THOUGHT IN THEATER

Trust

Building and maintaining trust are similar across disciplines and are the core of effective thought in theater. The director and production team model honesty, clarity, transparency, and respect, and make these viable requirements for the cast. Establishing a shared and common vision is key, as is a focus on building and valuing complementary skills and celebrating individual growth alongside group achievement. Theater honors the tradition of "circle" from the first read-through to opening night. In circle, the cast of actors or dancers become "one" in a chain that is only as strong as its weakest link. There is clear focus and purpose; and the performers use circle to share and balance energy and connect their thoughts and intentions. Trust in the theater is based on consistency, respect, and decorum. An excellent director will build trust exercises into the rehearsal process and consistently stretch the cast members to their full potential—individually and as a group.

Team Building

There is no better way to build group awareness and interdependence than play. Theatrical tradition maintains a rich repertoire of games, improvisation, and physical challenges, which, when valued and practiced throughout the rehearsal process, prove to be excellent team-building activities. Catch phrases and slogans are useful to redirect focus, and consistent reinforcement and ongoing assessment of the group's progress by the director and cast is key. For example, a director working with a group of first-time actors might have the ensemble place their right hands in the center of the circle at the close of each rehearsal with the call, "Doing it!" As their hands all come together and in one voice the group would respond, "And doing it well!!" Team handshakes, theme songs, and bits of choreography are playful ways to enhance effective interdependence in theater and in the classroom. Many theater warm-ups are playful—from physical capering and childhood games to vocal warm-ups, tongue twisters, and limericks. Laughter can be critical in successful team building on stage and in the classroom. In both settings, movement and vocal warm-ups that are consistently done together are powerful tools to unify a group.

Notes

Built into the theatrical tradition is the convention of "notes" after rehearsals and some performances. An effective director will call attention to the details, successes, and needs of the scenes, and comment on group achievement during rehearsal—theater's ongoing assessment piece. Similarly, the effective teacher also keeps ongoing student assessments that motivate and inform students of their progress. The most effective directors and teachers provide continuing opportunities for individual independent growth, while inspiring interdependence as the means to the end of serving the work, or learning.

Rewards and Recognitions

Within theatrical traditions, there are practices in which the group supports individual growth. The dancer who falls as a result of effort in the ballet class receives applause for her risk taking, just as the actor may get a round of applause in "notes." On stage and in the classroom, rewards and recognition present an opportunity to celebrate and support group effort, identify individual achievement, and inspire further achievement.

ENGAGING IN TOTAL GROUP THOUGHT

For minds to come together, they must have something to wrap around. In the professional theatrical model, the intention is always clear: There is a show to do and a director in charge. In education, leadership is also clear, and the "show" is learning. Finding a common goal and vision will unite a group, and the best place to start is from a shared value for what will be achieved together, whether it is realizing the director's vision of an existing work or creating a new work. Setting a learning goal together as a group when embarking on a project likewise can be very powerful in the classroom. Posters, charts, and "success-o-meters" draw focus and give value to the process, in the same way sketches of the set and costumes help create a unified vision in both drama and dance. Unit studies with themes that can be developed creatively, and provide opportunities for role play, music, dance, costumes, and videography, bring learning to life in the classroom. In both settings, leadership functions to bring together the cast/class in purpose, vision, and enthusiasm.

DELIBERATE INTERDEPENDENCE

Interdependent thought flourishes where it is valued. The director/teacher will set the tone throughout the theatrical process by modeling the behaviors desired of the group. Directors and teachers use "circle" as a symbol of partnership and understanding, as well as responsibility to one another. The group seeks to strengthen its bond throughout the process at hand and, with good leadership, becomes solid and even (as is often the case in theater) "family." Providing opportunities to be constantly showcasing the growth of individuals as well as the group is key in sustaining group effort. Group outcome in education traditionally was framed by competition and individualization, but educators are rethinking structures constantly to include cooperation and team thinking.

The theatrical process of blocking, choreographing, and rehearsing scenes or dances requires effective interdependence. Within this process is also the heart of best practice: play, improvisation, moving together as a group, trying the same thing in a variety of ways, and making discoveries.

Successful interdependence depends on the accountability of the group's members. The director is aware when the group's focus waxes and wanes, and alerts the cast when there is a shift, something an effective teacher does as well.

In the theater, cue lines are crucial. Actors very often learn one another's parts and the cue lines of other characters in the scenes they are in; in case a line is dropped, this helps the scene to move forward. The theater has practices to develop accuracy, such as "speed-throughs"—running the lines at lightning speed so that everyone *has* to know their lines.

THE DREAM AS EVIDENCE

I have choreographed Shakespeare's *A Midsummer Night's Dream* three times in my career: as a student in Los Angeles, at a boarding school in Hawaii, and most recently in a rural area school in the Far North of New Zealand. The three productions were in vastly different venues: a black box theater in LA's downtown Skid Row area, a state-of-the-art stage at a Hawaii boarding school, and a dilapidated stage in the school hall of a New Zealand rural area school. The three casts were widely different as well: up and coming LA professionals and hopefuls, privileged and high-achieving international boarding school students with backgrounds and training in the arts, and students in rural New Zealand with very limited experience of dramatic production outside the cultural arts. But in all three productions, similar tried-and-true practices drove the process and built interdependence. They were: a shared reverence for the work, a common purpose and a shared vision, clear expectations and consequences, "circle," consistent physical and vocal warm-ups (similar to skill and knowledge building in classrooms), opportunities to build trust among the cast members in rehearsal, opportunities for the cast members to interact with one another in a variety of settings, feedback, and celebrations of individual and group success. In every case, the quality of the production was a product of talent, leadership, and the cast's ability to come together interdependently as an ensemble.

In all productions, there was attention to input and systems of assessing and refining practice. To varying degrees, the productions developed a shared language and vernacular that grew from knowledge and repetition of the lines, and all casts found great delight in the plot twists and character buffoonery of the comedy. In all productions, Shakespeare's beautiful and complex language presented an ongoing challenge and ready assessment for progress in fluency and retention skills. All groups valued individual and group development, demonstrated responsibility, and were able to achieve individual satisfaction when the group was functioning at a high level. To serve Shakespeare's complex comedy well, students and players across settings also had to develop additional attributes well applied to real-life settings. On stage and in rehearsal, they developed their awareness of what was going on at all times in their environment, while adapting communication skills to successfully navigate audience reaction.

OVERCOMING ROADBLOCKS AND OBSTACLES

The New Zealand "Dream" production was an endless succession of road-blocks and obstacles. The students' prior teacher was relaxed and "free-form" in her constructivist approach. Turning to Shakespeare, the students' biggest challenges were focus and discipline. Most of the students were unfamiliar with Shakespeare's play, and the school culture as a whole was not entirely supportive and had mixed feelings about drama. Student expectation had been fairly low in the past, and the quality of the performances had reflected this in prior years. The students' work ethics and ability to focus were unknown to me, and they seemed an unlikely group to succeed the rigors of Shakespeare. Yet, they were a perfect fit for the play, and when I mentioned it as an idea in our planning session they were unanimously enthusiastic. We discussed levels of interest and what was required for full-scale production versus an informal workshop treatment. We agreed on a full-scale, top-notch production worthy of a $10 ticket—which they later delivered with aplomb.

Using a co-constructive model that was comfortable to them, we established clearly stated rules, practices, and intentions for the production. To satisfy a variety of achievement standards, the students also choreographed, composed, performed, and satisfied technical roles and responsibilities. We were in agreement that the project was daunting and we took time to anticipate roadblocks and obstacles and set systems in place in advance to deal with them as they came up. We established protocol to deal with challenges and were in agreement that positivity and flexibility best drove our efforts. Theatrical conventions, practice, and etiquette were new to the students, but the tried-and-true traditions prevailed throughout the process. The students performed to sold-out audiences, setting both attendance and revenue records for the school.

INDEPENDENT THINKING IN INTERDEPENDENT SETTINGS

The success of the New Zealand production was based in its interdependence as well as the individual strengths of the students. With few exceptions, the students were utterly committed to their personal best while willingly focusing on the needs of the group as a whole. The skills needed to navigate the abridged script were learned as a group, and we used choral reading and recitations to become familiar with the language. As director, I tried to offer a variety of settings for them to examine their thinking as a group and as individuals, and provided consistent encouragement of the group intention. Reinforcement for hesitant performers ("Faeries rock!"), credos ("Shakespeare rules!"), hand gestures, and unspoken reminders like a snap by the forehead were used to get students used to the idea of "checking in" with their thinking, "tuning in" to group thought, and keeping the focus on the work.

A RELEVANT ASSESSMENT

In theater, the assessment is the performance. In education, the assessment is more; it involves the students' understanding of and ability to reproduce the skills they have learned to achieve successful performance in their lives. An effective classroom produces students working at peak level both individually and cooperatively—much in the same way as a cast works together to serve a work. In both settings, effective interdependence produces success worthy of celebration.

There is a singular event in theater that happens only after the finest of performances. It happens after the last line, note, or movement: the final "lights-out." The audience knows the performance is over and that applause is the expected convention—but the silence stretches. For a moment the audience will not let the performance be over. Each audience member must unhook his or her mind from the performance and re-enter reality—a shift that is held by the group in this silent, suspended, and reluctant moment. It is in this moment that every part of the theatrical process comes to a still point, every mind in attendance is together, and interdependence is experienced as both means *and* end to something transcendent. Then the audience explodes in simultaneous applause.

CHAPTER 17

Thinking Interdependently
The Family as a Team

Lauren A. Carner & Angela Iadavaia-Cox

Consider this common scenario of family life: Douglas and Bethany Grant have just realized that Doug's recently widowed mother is not doing well and that some kind of intervention probably will be necessary. They are considering asking her to come live with them, and their minds are racing with all the implications. How will they find space for her? How will they manage their already complex and stressful schedules? How will their two children accommodate to the needs of their elderly and ailing—yet beloved—grandmother?

Situations like this offer an opportunity for family members to think interdependently—engaging with the "outside world." Such situations challenge a person's sense of identity, not just as an individual but also as a member of the family and of the larger community. Thinking interdependently is *collaborating with a sense of purpose and mission*. It is a way of thinking, communicating, and working in which each person's strengths are valued and encouraged, while the talents of the group compensate for relative weaknesses. It is the ability to speak up, contribute to the discussion, and advocate for a particular position or plan. It is also knowing when it is time to take your own plan off the table if it doesn't seem to fit where the group is going.

When a family thinks interdependently, the abilities and efforts of its members are magnified synergistically. As members of the family collaborate and cooperate—not just on finding a solution, but on discovering many different ways to approach problems—the power of their thinking is multiplied by the dynamic interchanges that happen between them. They become more than the sum of each individual member's contributions and talents. A family (indeed, *any* group) learns from every experience with interdependent

The Power of the Social Brain, edited by Arthur L. Costa and Pat Wilson O'Leary. Copyright © 2013 by Teachers College, Columbia University. All rights reserved. Prior to photocopying items for classroom use, please contact the Copyright Clearance Center, Customer Service, 222 Rosewood Dr., Danvers, MA 01923, USA, tel. (978) 750-8400, www.copyright.com.

thinking how to do it better next time. The family members become increasingly adept at reading one another's cues, listening, knowing when to advocate for an idea and when to throw their support behind another's idea, and how to put each person's abilities to the most effective use.

Family life benefits in many ways from intentionally activating thinking *together*. Creating interdependence within the family builds a positive structure that gives family members a firm foundation and a strong identity from which to venture out into the world. For children, it provides the security of feeling good about where they come from and what their family stands for. It creates positive expectations and confidence that each one in the family is valued for exactly who he or she is and that each one has important contributions to make. When a family develops the habit of thinking and working interdependently, children are listened to, and they in turn learn how to listen and communicate well. Interdependent thinking teaches them how to manage differences of opinion and how to get their own needs met, while still respecting the needs of others. Children who are part of a family that deliberately thinks, works, and plays together interdependently are going to bring those skills of relating and working with others into the world with them, where those skills will be very much needed.

Thinking interdependently can improve one's ability to navigate within and contribute to any size group—from friendship to marriage to family, school, work, and beyond. In this chapter we present some of the principles we have learned from research that can inform ways we work together as a family team. We also will describe ways of encouraging interdependent thinking in the home–school connection.

BUILDING FAMILY IDENTITY

It is important for a group, organization, or team to have a clearly articulated vision or sense of identity—a vision that its members think about, understand, verbalize, agree with, and try to live up to. Many schools and corporations create "vision statements" for their organizations. They set out on paper the aspirations and values they hope to live up to. When treated as a living, working document, the vision statement can serve as a guide to behavior. According to Larson and LaFasto (1989), a key element of effective leadership is to establish a vision of how things can and should be. If we assume that parents provide the leadership within a family, then, together, a couple can begin this process. They might start by clarifying and making explicit what their values, goals, hopes, and dreams are—first as individuals, then together as partners, and finally as a family. Having a vision in mind of the kind of person one aspires to be, and the kind of life one wants to live, can help keep the focus on what is truly important.

An individual might start with questions for him- or herself, such as, When are you happiest and most at peace? In what settings do you feel healthy and safe? What kinds of social situations make you shine? What kind of work do you love doing? Where do you picture yourself in 5, 10, or 20 years, and what do you hope to be doing then? What hopes and dreams did you have when you were younger? What dreams do you have now? What are the most important values you hold? What do you need to do in order to actually live by those values? The answers to these questions can be pondered, tinkered with, and crafted into a personal vision statement of the life one hopes and plans to have.

The most profound adjustment for couples is the transition from "I" to "we." If there is no common, agreed-upon vision for the marriage, conflict is bound to arise, often repeatedly over the same issues. Even if couples did spend time before marriage in deep conversations, chances are the realities of life have intruded with challenges and obstacles and opportunities they may never have imagined. In addition, long-buried scripts from the couple's *parents'* marriages find their way into the present. These ghosts of marriages past can intrude on a couple's best intentions and can create difficulty unless they are brought to the light of day, discussed, and understood jointly.

Gottman and Silver (1999) emphasize the importance of each partner affirming and honoring the hopes and dreams of the other. They propose guided questions for couples to consider together—not all at once, but one or two at a time in recurring conversations. The questions cover broad topics such as how each partner views his or her role in the relationship; how they want their home to be; what importance they place on extended family, religion, education, money; how they believe children should be disciplined; how they would prioritize spending leisure time, and so on. For each question, partners are encouraged to think about what the situation is *currently*, what the situation *was* as they were growing up, and finally what they hope the situation could be in the *future*. These conversations can be powerful tools for creating increased understanding, intimacy, and shared goals. With greater clarity of goals and expectations between partners, one would expect to see more cohesiveness and increased ability and willingness to pull together on behalf of each other.

Steven Covey (1997) takes this process one step further by encouraging in-depth conversations to include the children in developing a family mission statement. Making the time and effort for partners and the family as a whole to have these conversations can be a profound contribution to developing a clear, strong, and protective sense of family identity. Below are some additional suggestions for enhancing a sense of family identity.

TALK, TALK, TALK!

There are so many toxic influences competing for children's time and attention, we cannot assume that children will absorb parental values unless time is given to make it so. We recommend taking the time to have conversations about "how we want our family to be." As you talk together about what a happy family looks like, sounds like, and feels like, take notes so you can build on what is said. Questions such as, What feels best about being in our family? What makes you feel glad to come home? What are some things that maybe don't feel so good, or that you wish you could change? can stimulate unexpected perceptions and insights. It is important for these conversations to be carried out in a respectful and affirmative way. This is a time for everyone in the family to think and speak freely. If older siblings are used to interrupting or crowding out younger ones, parents will want to make sure that everyone's contribution is encouraged and valued. This is a perfect time to listen with empathy and understanding and to teach listening skills to the children (Carner & Iadavaia-Cox, 2012). If anyone in the family uses this time to bring up a complaint or concern, parents can use their empathic listening skills to paraphrase, come to a good understanding of what the concern is, and use the moment for everyone to figure out some ways to make it better. These conversations do not have to be heavy or somber. They can be woven into the conversation at dinner, while playing board games, or on family car trips. They invite everyone in the family to think about ways they can actively create the family they want to be.

TAKE THE TIME TO BE TOGETHER

Taking the time to be together conveys more emphatically than words that parents want and *choose* to be with their children. While children are still young, parents should establish that doing things together is their best idea of a good time. This message is conveyed by attending children's practices and games, going to school events, seeking children out for company when doing everyday chores, or taking a few minutes to throw a ball or to play with the dog together. Not all the time, of course—everyone needs some alone time as well as time with friends—but enough to leave no doubt that you value and enjoy their company.

The ways in which parents and children interact obviously will change over time. Parents will need to frequently recalibrate their responses to their children in order to keep in tune with kids' ever-growing maturity level. One way to do this is to look for ways of tapping into children's increasing competencies. Many adults who are not "digital natives" rely on their offspring to help them navigate the mysteries of newer technology. Another way is to learn something new together. One family decided to start a garden, and each person chose an aspect of gardening that was most interesting to him or her. One did some research on what the hardiest plants for the climate would be. Another took on the project of composting kitchen scraps to make good soil. One of the children loved to draw and sketched out possible designs for the garden. The youngest just loved digging in the dirt, but along the way became quite adept at distinguishing between beneficial insects and garden pests. Each family member had a slightly different relationship and commitment to the garden, but it clearly became an *interdependent* family project.

DEVELOP FAMILY RITUALS

Most families have their own rituals around holiday celebrations, but other opportunities to create loving rituals abound: how family members greet one another in the morning and upon reuniting after a day of school and work; the way they say goodnight; how they celebrate the first day of school or the first day of summer vacation. Some families have a pasta and movie night on Friday to unwind from the week. Others take the whole family to their favorite local restaurant, and others share the tradition of Shabbat dinner or a church service. There can be rituals for going places and for staying in on a rainy day. Whatever they are, family rituals can impart a sense of delicious anticipation in their familiarity and comfort. They are like secret handshakes that contribute to a sense of secure belonging.

PROMOTE POSITIVE FAMILY TRAITS

When thinking about your own family history, what stories of courage, overcoming adversity, persistence against the odds, resilience, strength, and ingenuity can be summoned? When children hear such tales from parents' earlier days or from long ago, they develop the conviction that "that is the stuff I am made of. I can do this too." By making family values and dispositions explicit—traits such as optimism, kindness, persistence, generosity, ingenuity, courage, or the willingness to work hard—they become sources of pride and reasons to celebrate. When parents talk about and promote these traits as part of a family identity, children are enabled to see them as something they can aspire to and eventually achieve.

The family identity, which comes through time spent together, conversation, shared rituals, and a clear sense of one's positive family traits, is the first step toward thinking interdependently as a family. In the case of the Grant family, described at the beginning of the chapter, Douglas recalled telling his children of the time their grandmother took in a high school classmate of his whose own mother had passed away. Douglas had been moved by her compassion and generosity, and wanted to convey to his own children the value he had absorbed of the importance of doing the right thing. That value would figure prominently in whatever decision they ultimately would come to.

DECISION MAKING TOGETHER IS CRITICAL

A second element of interdependent thinking is making decisions together as a family. A generation or two back, it was the norm for parents to not share information or decision making with their children. Big issues such as money or sexual responsibility were rarely talked about. It was considered impolite to talk about politics and religion because it was assumed that an argument would ensue. Children rarely had the opportunity to witness, let alone participate in, a problem-solving kind of discussion. When conflicts arose, a typical response would be to shut down thinking and discussion, either by leaving the room or by having loud arguments. With so few models and opportunities to practice, it is no wonder that the ability to listen carefully, to find common ground, and to come up with good, mutually agreed-upon solutions seems so daunting now. Good communication can improve not only understanding but also our connectedness to one another. When we paraphrase what a family member has said, we not only are making sure we are getting it right, we are showing we *care* enough to get it right. When we monitor our own tone of voice and body language when dealing with a problem situation, we make sure that we are in sync with one another. As we question and pose potential problems, we encourage children to think more deeply and to come up with possibilities on their own. The positive presuppositions with which parents enter into a conversation convey confidence that, together, any problem can be worked through to a good resolution. The family is the perfect place within which to nurture these important attitudes and skills. (For a detailed explanation of these communication skills, see Garmston, Chapter 9, this volume.)

MANAGING CONFLICT

Another key element of high-functioning families is their ability to resolve conflicts peacefully. When a family thinks interdependently, its members let go of the idea of prevailing or winning. Instead, they work toward solutions that support all. When working through a conflict on a family level, it is important for all members to feel they have been heard and understood. Someone in the family, most likely an adult, but perhaps an older child, may have to assume the role of mediator, to ensure that each person gets to speak without being interrupted. At some point a group paraphrase such as, "Sounds like none of us are happy with the messy way the house is looking, but we have different ideas about what to do about it. Can we begin to find agreement on some of those ideas?" might get the discussion moving in a positive direction. Successful conflict resolution requires that there be no "losers."

THINKING INTERDEPENDENTLY:
THE HOME–SCHOOL CONNECTION

When parents chat with their children about the school day, we suggest that they begin to frame some comments and questions in a way that supports interdependent thinking. The older, more competitive model would emphasize how a child performed in comparison with other students and would be reflected in questions such as, "How did the other kids do? Was yours the highest grade?" It is natural and understandable that parents want to know how their child compares with others. Parents need some kind of frame of reference in order to determine whether their child is learning at an appropriate rate and level. Questions and comments that evoke comparisons with others, however, do not help children build on their intrinsic interest and motivation for learning. Rather, conversations that focus on what is inherently interesting in the material they are learning, on the challenges and triumphs experienced in mastering those skills and content, and on the problems and satisfactions of working with others are more conducive to encouraging interdependent thinking.

If parents keep in mind the ideas of *vision/identity, good communication and decision-making skills*, and *conflict resolution*, questions and comments should come more easily. Parents might ask what groupwork their child is engaged in and how the child likes working that way. They might ask the child to explain how the children in the group make sure everyone gets a chance to participate and what happens if there are disagreements. A child might be asked to reflect on what he or she has learned from others in the group and what, in turn, they may have learned from him or her. Parents may discover that their child is so accustomed to working this way that it is almost second nature. Or, they may find that there are indeed some problems that crop up and the child would appreciate some support or suggestions. Let us look more closely at the three factors that contribute to successful group functioning, and how parents can support their child's development of those skills at school.

Vision/Identity

Parents can encourage and motivate their child in her group experiences. Questions such as, "How would you describe the group you are in now?" "What are some of the things you like about your group?" or "Are there things you can think of that would make it work even better?" can stimulate thinking about the "we-ness" of the cooperative learning group. A sense of belonging and identity with the group enhance motivation. Questions such as, "How do you and your friends celebrate your successes?" or, "How do you encourage one another when the going gets tough?" remind children that celebrations and support for one another through tough times are normal functions of groups.

Parents are encouraged to respond to their child's comments in ways that foster appreciation for others. Comments such as the following can reinforce understanding of the qualities that contribute to good collaboration:

- It sounds like everyone is really motivated and working hard.
- From what you describe, each person is carrying his own weight. That must be such a good feeling—that together you can get your job done.
- Isn't it interesting how each person has something valuable to offer? James brings a lot of energy to the group, and Keisha had a really creative idea.

If a child reports that she has done something that promoted interdependent thinking, for example, that she encouraged a quiet child to contribute, or that she asked questions in a way that helped the group to clarify its thinking, parents should point out appreciatively that those behaviors are exactly what makes for great teamwork.

Communication—Decision Making

Parents can refer to times when using good communication skills helped resolve a family conflict, and then encourage their child to think about how those same skills might be used at school. Similarly, they can extend their child's thinking about those skills by telling "stories" about how they used pausing or paraphrasing or empathic listening to defuse a situation at work. *Pausing* or providing *wait-time* is a particularly salient communication skill. Parents might point out the advantages of waiting and thinking about what the other person has said, before jumping in with a comment. If this is something that is actively worked on at home, one can imagine the benefits when the child brings that skill to school.

Paraphrasing can be explicitly taught. Parents can explain how much better it feels when someone is actively trying to understand someone else instead of arguing with the person. Then parents and children can take turns practicing paraphrasing. One can talk for a minute or two while the other tries to paraphrase for content and feeling. They can review how it felt to be so carefully listened to. They can explain how useful paraphrasing is in a group situation by encouraging everyone to fully express their thoughts and feelings.

Similarly, *probing and clarifying* can be an extremely useful tool for dealing with the common experience of misunderstanding or misinterpreting the motives and intentions of others (or for when the other person seems to have misunderstood). Children and adults can be taught the metacognitive strategy of monitoring their own reactions and not jumping to conclusions. Parents can teach their child to "check it out" by asking a clarifying question or by paraphrasing. If the child reports that someone got angry with him for no apparent reason, parents can suggest that he ask the other child whether there might have been a misunderstanding and offer to work it out.

Conflict Resolution

Parents can use examples from their own family's experiences with successful conflict resolution to encourage thinking about managing conflict with peers. Children need to understand that conflict is a normal part of life, but it is how we handle it that makes all the difference. Children may need help in developing a few strategies to deal with some of the strong emotions that come with conflict so they can stay calm and clearheaded. Doing deep breathing, counting to ten, taking a little break, or having some little "mantra" or slogan to mentally rehearse such as, "I'm good at staying calm," are useful strategies that most children can master. Parents can reflect on how difficult it sometimes can be for people to let go of their own need to "win." Children can be encouraged to ask the group, "How can we figure this out so that everyone is happy?"

Imagine the possibilities if the next generation learns from an early age the satisfactions of thinking and working interdependently, of creating and sustaining a vision for a better world, and has the skills to actually put it into practice.

REFERENCES

Carner, L., & Iadavaia-Cox, A. (2012). *Raising caring capable kids with habits of mind*. Westport, CT: Institute for Habits of Mind.

Covey, S. (1997). *The 7 habits of highly effective families*. New York: Golden Books.

Gottman, J., & Silver, N. (1999). *Seven principles for making marriage work*. New York: Crown.

Larson, C. E., & LaFasto, F. (1989). *Teamwork: What must go right/what can go wrong*. Newbury Park, CA: Sage.

CHAPTER 18

The Seven Habits of Highly Interdependent Teachers

Jeremy Little

I am the proud dad of a 4-year-old boy and a 2-year-old girl. On long car rides, the Disney/Pixar hit *Finding Nemo* is a staple in our family minivan. There is a particular section of the movie that hits home with the educator in me every time I listen to it.

To set the scene, Marlin has been searching for his son Nemo. Along the way, Marlin meets Dory, who agrees to help him, in spite of her "short-term memory loss" problem. As the pair search for Nemo, Marlin becomes increasingly frustrated with Dory and her inability to focus on getting his son back. After a run-in with hungry sharks and a mime-happy school of fish, my favorite part arrives:

> Dory: Oh dear. Hey, hey come back! Hey, what's the matter?
> Marlin: What's the matter? While they're doing their silly little impressions, I am miles from home, with a fish that can't even remember her own name.
> Dory: Boy, bet that's frustrating.
> Marlin: Yeah. Meanwhile my son is out there.
> Dory: Your son Chico?
> Marlin: Nemo.
> Dory: Right. Got it.
> Marlin: But it doesn't matter, 'cause no fish in this entire ocean is gonna help me.
> Dory: Well, I'm helping you.

I particularly enjoy that section because I tend to behave like Marlin: focused, wanting to do things my way, sometimes not interested in others'

The Power of the Social Brain, edited by Arthur L. Costa and Pat Wilson O'Leary. Copyright © 2013 by Teachers College, Columbia University. All rights reserved. Prior to photocopying items for classroom use, please contact the Copyright Clearance Center, Customer Service, 222 Rosewood Dr., Danvers, MA 01923, USA, tel (978) 750-8400, www.copyright.com.

help or opinions, and usually tending to think that by doing something alone, I will get it done more efficiently. However, one of the unifying themes of *Finding Nemo* is how interdependent we really are on one another. When Dory says, "Well, I'm helping you," not only is she correct, but, as it turns out, her ability to read the diver's mask (to find out Nemo is in Sydney, Australia) and her questions to other fish (to find out how to get to Sydney) prove to be exactly what Marlin needs in order to find his son.

As a high school choir teacher, the more I teach, the more I realize how interdependent I am:

- on my colleagues, for new ideas and for modeling wonderful teaching strategies or assessments;
- on my students, for bringing their creative and insightful points of view to class and for displaying an attitude of wanting to learn from and with others; and
- on my administration and school community for providing a positive atmosphere in which to teach and learn and work as a team.

As I reflect on the journey from thinking, "I can do it all, leave me alone," toward, "Let's see how I can team with others to create a better product than any one of us could have dreamed of," there were seven essential habits that I was fortunate enough to develop that led toward this mindset.

HABIT 1: HOLD THE MIRROR UP TO YOURSELF

My favorite book on teaching is *The Courage to Teach* by Parker Palmer (2007). I read it every summer, and think I could read it for 30 more summers without fully mining all of its depths. This book forces me to continually examine myself as a teacher, my fears and anxieties when working with my students, and how I can use these feelings to become a better teacher and human being. In order to fully connect with others, we as teachers must be comfortable in our own skin. We must make a continual effort to examine our own intentions, methods, lessons, strategies, units, and assessments, simply to remind ourselves why we use what we use, or do what we do. As Palmer states, "As we learn more about who we are, we can learn techniques that reveal rather than conceal the personhood from which good teaching comes" (p. 24).

Jhumpa Lahiri, the Pulitzer Prize–winning Indian American author, wrote:

For much of my life, I wanted to be other people; here was the central dilemma, the reason, I believe, for my creative stasis. I was always falling short of other people's expectations: my immigrant parents', my Indian relatives', my American peers', and above all my own. The writer in me wanted to edit myself. . . . How could I want to be a writer, to articulate what was within me, when I did not wish to be myself? (2011, p. 80)

We need to know our own strengths, our own resources and points of view, the very things that we can bring to a group. For interdependent thinking to happen, we must see one another as having different resources (information, thinking style, points of view, strength within a group, etc.). Below are some strategies for knowing oneself as a teacher.

- Keep a classroom journal, with daily reflections of your own teaching, what you did well, what you can improve on, and how this is making a difference to your students. Force yourself to adhere to this every day, and then read through it at the end of the semester and school year.
- Read Palmer's *The Courage to Teach* every summer, highlight passages, write down quotes, and put them in your office as daily reminders of your focus.
- Search for different ways to evaluate your own teaching: Randomly video record a lesson and watch it; ask a colleague or administrator to observe your teaching.
- Invite feedback from your students. At the end of the year that our first child was born, I gave my students an end-of-the-year evaluation of my teaching. One student commented, "This year was great, although Mr. Little seemed much more tired and cranky at times. He was also much more relaxed and understanding when we had problems than before Elliot was born." After I read this, I reflected on my demeanor and thankfully realized this insightful student had provided me with powerful feedback that I could use to improve my teaching.
- Allow the students to see the "mirror-holding" habit in you: Ask them individually or as a class about specific aspects of your lesson that could be improved, give them time to evaluate your teaching (formally or informally), and let them see that you are working at becoming a better teacher for them.

In her environmental classic, *The Sense of Wonder,* Rachel Carson states:

If I had influence with the good fairy who is supposed to preside over the christening of all children, I should ask that her gift to each child in the world would be a sense of wonder so indestructible that it would last throughout life, as an unfailing antidote to the boredom and disenchantment of later years, the sterile preoccupation with things that are artificial, the alienation from the sources of our strength. (1965, pp. 42–43)

I have this quote directly above my computer in my office, and every time I read it, I am reinvigorated to step into my classroom and teach. I believe that this "sense of wonder" has allowed me to view my own teaching as being highly interdependent on others, and thus has allowed me the freedom to use my own experiences, thoughts, and feelings to connect with those around me as I learn and grow.

HABIT 2: CREATE AN ENVIRONMENT OF MIRROR HOLDING IN YOUR CLASSROOM

When my students see my willingness to improve and be introspective, they do likewise (with my intentional assistance). When students are presented with regular opportunities to ask questions of themselves, to generate and refine their own thoughts, and to share these thoughts with friends and with me, we begin to foster interdependence. In *Letters to a Young Poet*, Rainer Maria Rilke encourages this process:

> Therefore, my dear friend, I know of no other advice than this: Go within and scale the depths of your being from which your very life springs forth. At its source you will find the answer to the question, whether you *must* write. . . . For the creative artist must be a world of his own and must find everything within himself and in nature, to which he has betrothed himself. (2002, p. 13)

If we want students to learn to recognize the strengths of others, to see the value in working as a team, they must be given opportunities to search within themselves for their own value, to realize their own strengths and ideas, and to develop the habit of refining their own thinking about working in a group.

We need to help students know themselves. In my class, almost all instruction is tied to a specific learning outcome, which each student knows in advance. As we work toward these outcomes, students complete weekly self-assessments that they first share with peers and then turn in for my assessment. In one specific column, I ask the students to rate their own understanding of the outcome, to pose any questions about it, and to detail their progress toward the outcome that week. This activity requires students to think about their progress toward our class outcomes, while giving me a chance to interact with their own thinking and make comments that spark further thought.

HABIT 3: PUT YOUR SUBJECT UNDER THE MICROSCOPE

One of the best aspects of my job as a choir teacher is also one of the most daunting. Every year we have new music, and thus the lesson plans I designed for all of the previous year's pieces need to be retooled and written anew for the pieces we will study and perform this year. Because I have most students for 4 years, I have to write lesson plans for literally hundreds of pieces before I can begin to reuse them. This has forced me to distill the skills, ideas, and attitudes that I teach through these pieces into a series of course outcomes. However, because each piece of music is relatively unique, I have the opportunity to look for ways to help students become interdependent while studying the specific subject matter.

For example, this past year, we were investigating a piece by J.S. Bach entitled "Sicut Locutus Est." The text, taken from Luke 1:55, is, "As he spoke to our fathers, to Abraham, and to his offspring forever." As we dove into the text further, I asked my students to describe traditions in their families, to journal about their thoughts on eternity, to interview an older family member about what it was like for that person to go through high school, and to speculate on what popular songs or ideas of today will be talked about 100 years from now. Each activity or journal prompt allowed students to think on their own, interact with and listen to their peers, and deepen our sense of community as a class. Furthermore, because it was tied to our subject matter (Bach's *Magnificat* is an historically significant work), we did all of this in the context of our subject.

When examining your subject matter for potential lessons, scour it for places to develop interdependent thinking and create outcomes (taken from your curriculum) that foster interdependent thinking. A few of my course outcomes, developed using principles from Costa and Kallick's *Learning and Leading with Habits of Mind* (2008), can be seen in Figure 18.1.

HABIT 4: INTENTIONALLY PLAN ACTIVITIES AND EXPERIENCES THAT DIRECTLY CONNECT YOUR CLASSROOM LIFE TO REAL LIFE

Students in my class study many works of great art. This art was not created in a vacuum; each piece of music was written by a living, breathing person, in an historical context. We study these pieces as if each contains a mystery to be solved.

- Why do you think the composer wrote this work? Who or what occasion did he or she write it for?

Figure 18.1. Affective and Habit Goals

How am I making our performance better (when I'm singing and during down time)?

Habits of Mind Used: finding problems to solve, striving for accuracy, persisting, applying past knowledge, listening with understanding/empathy, remaining open to more learning

- My vocal line: What spots are difficult for me? How is each difficult?
- My section's "take": tuning, rhythms, participation/energy, memorized?
- Another section's "take": same as above (Key Points: Where did they start? What goal/concept was Mr. Little working on with them? How can I use their performance to make mine better?)

How am I making our class better?

Habits of Mind Used: managing impulsivity, thinking interdependently, finding humor

- In daily rehearsal: Am I focused on the goals, thinking about my own thinking/performance? Am I listening when I should and talking when I should?
- Week-to-week: tardiness, sectional attendance, assignments, music theory/vocal progress over time

How am I making my life better?

Habits of Mind Used: responding with wonderment and awe

- Personal reflection: Am I connecting with the songs and rehearsal experiences? Is expressing myself in this way satisfying? Do I enjoy the process as well as the product?

Our Ultimate Goal

Affective response[1]—a meaningful connection (spiritual, intellectual, emotional, physical) between us and

- the music (aesthetic awareness)
- themselves (self-awareness)
- other students or people (relational awareness)
- the bigger world around them
- a life-changing idea or insight

Summary: Our goal is that through these affective responses, we will grow in personal knowledge (our opinions, values, dreams, wishes, habits, etc.), have a heightened awareness and sensitivity to all of humanity (current or historical), and grow in our awareness of the transcendent (whether spiritual, religious, or other).

1. This definition of affective response is adapted from a definition put forth by Randall Swiggum of the Wisconsin Music Educators Association's Comprehensive Musicianship through Performance project (CMP). For more information about CMP, visit www.wmea.com/CMP.

- How might the local and world societal events at that time have influenced the composer and the composition?
- How is the piece constructed? What makes this either unique or similar to other pieces by the same composer?
- If there is a text: Why did the poet write this? What is the message of the poem?
- As you compare these pieces of music, why do you think one speaks to us in such a powerful way and others do not?

Through studying, performing, asking questions of, and generating responses to these great works of art, students discover connections between themselves and other cultures, both past and present. They learn how great art is created and how they too can create. They use this art to help make sense of their lives and the world around them.

It is through these intentional, affective-domain-focused experiences that students learn

- how to listen with empathy and care for not just what is being said (content) but who is saying it;
- how to function each day as a group and delay instant gratification;
- that ambiguity is often a part of art (and in life) and how to search for more than one answer to a problem;
- that asking questions (of a piece, of a situation, of ourselves) is valuable and makes our lives richer and more meaningful than merely skimming the surface of things that don't instantly reveal themselves; and
- that remaining open to different art, situations, people, or problems, and learning how to relate to and make connections with the "new and different," can be very beneficial.

When students begin to understand how their thinking, their being, their life fits into the world around them and into history, they perform the music better, they treat one another better, and they become better human beings. This to me is the essence of thinking interdependently.

Following is an example of how subject matter can connect to real life: Last year, we studied and performed a series of pieces that were written by children at Terezin concentration camp during World War II. Of the many survivor testimonies, videos, and discussions we had, one of the most powerful interdependent learning experiences took place when our class went to the Illinois Holocaust Museum. As we were looking through the exhibit, one student noticed a ticket on display. It was a boarding ticket for a ship that fled Europe in 1939 toward the United States. One of my students began to cry. She remembered her grandmother telling her stories about the voyage on that ship, about how she came to America. After this student shared her story with our class, our struggle to make sense of the context of this work, our interactions with one another, and our daily commitment to honoring the memory of those killed and those who survived World War II was enhanced greatly.

HABIT 5: RESTRUCTURE YOUR PHYSICAL ENVIRONMENTS (LESSON PLANNING MATERIALS AND CLASSROOM SET-UP)

Over the years, I have noticed that I fall into certain "ruts" as a teacher. As I planned lessons, I would keep the same format. I knew I should vary things up more, but the craziness of the school year came, and by the time a particular lesson arrived again, I would resort to what I did in past years. Because of this, I felt my students were stuck in a "rut" as well. Many times they could predict what was going to come next in my lesson, and hence became disinterested. Furthermore, I noticed the physical classroom environment varied little as well. Students sat in the same chairs, talked to the same people, and fell into the same "holding pattern" that I had.

Following are some strategies for adding variety to your teaching:

- Create lesson plan templates that require interdependent thinking activities or habits each week. When I see that the part of my lesson plan sheet reserved for "Interdependent Thinking Activity" is blank, I sit down and devise one method to allow students to do this.
- Every so often, re-arrange the chairs or tables, and so on, in your classroom to force students to work in small groups. Students often appreciate this departure from their regular routine and usually will be more inclined to share their opinions and learn from one another in a new setting.
- Place quotes or reminders around your office. As I'm typing this, I'm looking at two fortune cookie sayings I have taped to my bulletin board:
  » "Laughing brains are more absorbent."
  » "We learn from everyone we meet."
  To me, these sayings act as "anchors" and remind me to create space for students to think, learn, and interact with one another in a meaningful and interdependent way.

HABIT 6: TEACH FROM A POSITION OF WEAKNESS

A master teacher I know, who had just retired after more than 35 years of teaching, once described the essence of his teaching philosophy like this: "I always want to remain like a 2nd-year teacher. Competent enough to handle my subject, but always looking to try new things, to branch out, to get better." I enjoy hearing him talk because he reminds me to never stay complacent. Even after all of his accomplishments, accolades, and student successes, he was always looking to try something he'd never done before!

I want to model this attitude to my students; to show them I'm growing, that we create knowledge together, and that we find understanding through our relationships with one another and with the subject matter.

Most musicians have a great sense of reading and performing rhythms. I, however, have always struggled with it. Early in my career, I shied away from performing pieces that were rhythmically complicated because I didn't want my students to think I was an incompetent teacher. I had to know everything, be able to do everything right; I was the pitcher and they were the glasses. As I began to realize I was shortchanging their music education by deliberately withholding rhythmically challenging pieces, I had to confront a reality: If we were to study and perform these kinds of pieces, I would have to be "okay" with them seeing my vulnerability and "incompetence." As I began to teach more rhythmically complex pieces, a funny thing started to happen: I became more interdependent on my students (I want you to pair up and take turns demonstrating this rhythm to each other. Did your partner perform it correctly? How do you know? Now you perform it and have your neighbor evaluate it). My students in turn became more interdependent on one another, and we all began to grow.

Here are some strategies for teaching from weakness:

- Find at least one new project, unit, primary source, or idea in each of your courses per year. Take the time to develop new plans, plan new assessments, and create new outcomes.
- Utilize the resources around you (friends, students, community, etc.) and bring outside professionals into your classroom to speak about relevant topics or to give students the opportunity to ask questions of someone practicing in their field.
- Put students in cooperative groups to research together and provide feedback to one another.

HABIT 7: FIND A COLLEAGUE—ACTUALLY BE INTERDEPENDENT

Ironically, interacting with hundreds of students every day can be a very lonely venture. I often feel isolated from other adults, cut off from adult discourse and interaction. Furthermore, because I am the only choir teacher at my school, I can't bounce ideas off anyone else or receive content-specific feedback. When I feel cut off from other professionals, I tend to teach "the subject" and not "the students."

When I seek out other professionals in my building who are fostering interdependent thinking in their classrooms, however, I begin to feel, well, interdependent! I observe them, talk with them, and bounce ideas off them. We begin to create a better teaching and learning environment through our shared experiences. When I attend workshops and presentations by other professionals in my content field, I am revived and encouraged to come back to my classroom to create more-significant experiences for my students.

In our school district, professional learning communities are used to bring teachers with common goals together to create meaningful professional development that ultimately will benefit students. I regularly witness the power of teams of teachers learning, researching, brainstorming, experimenting, and analyzing data together. It is through these regular and sustained interactions with other professionals that we as teachers grow and in turn create better experiences for our students.

CONCLUSION

In reading this chapter in a book about interdependent thinking, you may have found irony in the fact that each habit focused on one primary person: you, the teacher. However, isn't the idea that self-knowledge leads to betterment, what we want to promote to our students?

In 2006, *Time* magazine named "You" the person of the year. John Steinbeck once wrote, "For the most part people are not curious except about themselves." By taking our human inclination for self-interest and intentionally examining our fears and frustrations, our shortcomings, our subject matter, and our classrooms, we find that, indeed, "no man is an island," as John Donne figured out long ago. As we become more interdependent on the professionals working in our building, other colleagues in our field, and, most important, on the wonderful students sitting in front of us every day, we realize how wonderfully connected and invigorating this profession called "teaching" truly is.

REFERENCES

Carson, R. (1965). *The sense of wonder.* New York: Harper Row.

Costa, A. L., & Kallick, B. (2008). *Learning and leading with habits of mind: 16 essential characteristics for success.* Alexandria, VA: Association for Supervision and Curriculum Development.

Lahiri, J. (2011, June 13). Trading stories: Notes from an apprenticeship. *New Yorker,* p. 80.

Palmer, P. (2007). *The courage to teach. Exploring the inner landscape of a teacher's life.* San Francisco: Jossey-Bass.

Rilke, M. R. (2002). *Letter to a young poet.* London: Dover.

CHAPTER 19

Teaching the Dispositions of Interdependent Thought

Arthur L. Costa & Pat Wilson O'Leary

Throughout this book, certain patterns of behavior have emerged among people and groups that think interdependently. We refer to them as "dispositions." Dispositions, according to Ron Ritchart, are:

> acquired patterns of behavior that are under one's control and will as opposed to being automatically activated. Dispositions are overarching sets of behaviors, not just single specific behaviors. They are dynamic and idiosyncratic in their contextualized deployment rather than prescribed actions to be rigidly carried out. More than desire and will, dispositions must be coupled with the requisite ability. Dispositions motivate, activate, and direct our abilities. (2002, p. 31)

We found at least eight dispositions of interdependent thinking that seem to recur throughout the chapters in this book. Readers may find more to add to this list. The important point here is that we begin early in a child's education to develop these dispositions so that children will be successful in their interdependent interactions in the future. We will present some teaching strategies that are intended to enhance these dispositions:

1. Persisting through group tasks
2. Positivity
3. Listening with understanding and empathy
4. Flexibility
5. Metacognition—monitoring and executing one's own thinking
6. Precision of language and thought
7. Questioning and posing problems
8. Creating, imagining, and innovating

The Power of the Social Brain, edited by Arthur L. Costa and Pat Wilson O'Leary. Copyright © 2013 by Teachers College, Columbia University. All rights reserved. Prior to photocopying items for classroom use, please contact the Copyright Clearance Center, Customer Service, 222 Rosewood Dr., Danvers, MA 01923, USA, tel. (978) 750-8400, www.copyright.com.

These dispositions can best be experienced, practiced, analyzed, and applied in collaborative settings. For each of the dispositions discussed in this chapter, a learner activity is suggested to engage students in working cooperatively to develop the disposition. Suggestions are offered for teacher behaviors to mediate students' learning from these experiences and help them to apply or transfer these dispositions beyond the classroom setting. The teacher is critical as a mediator of this process, as can be seen in seven major roles:

1. *Structuring* the group (including giving directions) to maximize positive interdependence; presenting the group with some dilemma, problem, decision to make, or discrepancy to resolve; organizing/assigning tasks within the group; and communicating multiple and simultaneous goals.

2. *Mediating* the group's work by asking questions, building vocabulary, keeping clearly in mind the multiple nested objectives of the activity, responding nonjudgmentally, inviting the group's metacognition, reflecting on the processes of interdependent thinking by debriefing after groupwork, making the disposition explicit by labeling actions; and inviting transfer or bridging beyond this setting to other life situations.

3. *Teaching* students specific cooperative skills as needed, including generating criteria, listening, empathizing, communicating, helping by not giving answers, observing, role playing, consensus seeking, and evaluating (Dishon & O'Leary, 1998).

4. *Monitoring* by observing students getting better at these dispositions, assisting them to become aware of their own and others' growth in these behaviors, providing specific feedback, and finding other examples of the use of the behaviors beyond the context in which they were learned.

5. *Modeling* all the dispositions in one's own conduct.

6. *Collaborating* as a member of a school-based team. Thinking interdependently is not just for classrooms. To work well, schools, too, must become interdependent. Teachers can reinforce these skills throughout the grade levels and across the subject areas. Parents can become involved in reinforcing these behaviors at home (see Chapter 17 this volume). Teachers should coach one another, plan together, construct collaborative visions, trust one another, and problem solve together. Finally, they should assess themselves throughout the cooperative thinking process.

7. *Reflecting* on these dispositions has to be taught. It is common to debrief a product. However, teachers can provide students

with the activities and discussions to debrief their cooperative behaviors and cooperative thinking skills. Students can develop habits to improve their interdependent thinking.

Students and teachers may cooperatively assess their growth in the performance of the dispositions of interdependent thinking in group and individual settings by using a "How are we doing?" checklist (see Figure 19.1). For each disposition, the teacher would fill in appropriate attributes and observable indicators. The columns for rating and performance are labeled "Often," Sometimes," and "Not Yet."

The examples can serve as a model. The intent is to have students develop and keep a checklist of indicators of what they would see a person doing or hear a person saying if he or she was employing the disposition. It is not intended for the student to use the checklist to evaluate other students. Rather, students should use the list to observe themselves and their own performance in groups. In several of the activities, a member of the group can be designated as a process observer and invited to record indicators of performance on this checklist, and to share his or her observations with the group after the activity. The desire is that students will become better able to develop, retain, and apply a set of internal criteria for monitoring and evaluating their own performance.

PERSISTING

When people work interdependently, it is more likely that they will persist than when they work alone. They stick to a task and see it through to completion.

Individual students may lack the ability to analyze a problem, to develop a system, structure, or strategy of attack. Although students are reluctant to go it alone, they devote much energy and time to a difficult task when

Figure 19.1. "How Are We Doing?" Checklist

ATTRIBUTE: _____

Observable Indicators	Often	Sometimes	Not Yet

they do it with others, probably because of their feelings of responsibility to and camaraderie with others.

Suggestions for Teachers

Talk with your students about persisting and build their vocabulary related to it: perseverance; stick-to-it; hang in there; if at first you don't succeed, try, try again; tenacity; focused. Discuss with them why it is necessary to persevere. Read them the story *The Little Engine That Could* or something similar. Perhaps some of them have seen the movie *Stand and Deliver*, the story of Jaime Escalante, a teacher who coached Hispanic inner-city students to become math experts. Discuss how persistence by both the teacher and the students paid off. Another example is Nelson Mandela, who spent 27 years in prison but never gave up his beliefs.

Have students recall times when they persevered or persisted. In groups, have them describe what they would see a person doing or hear a person saying that would indicate that he or she was persisting. Enter the following indicators on the "How are we doing?" checklist: "Seeks alternative sources of data or other resources to support the group's work"; "May take a break, but returns to the task"; "Says, 'Wait, I want to finish.'" A student can serve as a group process observer by tallying observations of a group's performance during and after the following activity.

Activity: Spatial Reasoning

Place your students in groups of three. The task is easy enough for a small group, which helps keep more people involved more of the time. Give each group one piece of paper with a "maze" of geometric shapes, such as a checkerboard as in Figure 19.2, or many triangles or squares within a larger triangle or square. See Johnson and Johnson (2012) for other team activities. Ask the groups to agree upon a system to use to count the number of squares. Every person is responsible for knowing the final number and how to find all of the squares recognized by the group, and for being able to explain the system. While working, one person serves as recorder.

After 15 minutes, time is called. Students sign the group paper, the signature meaning, "I understand and I helped." Several or all of the groups are checked for accuracy and understanding. The teacher picks one person from each checked group to show all of the shapes without help from group mates. Students are asked to recall specific behaviors they used to encourage one another.

Figure 19.2. Checkerboard

Follow-up Discussion

During the processing, ask students: "How long would you have worked on this task had I assigned it as homework for you to do at home alone?" Some students state they would have given up. Many would have found one immediate solution that satisfied them and their job would have been finished.

Ask them to compare that response with what they actually did. They often will say they worked longer, found it more interesting, explored a variety of solutions, and checked for more accuracy.

Ask students to discuss and explain why people often persist longer in groups than when alone. Ask them when else it is necessary to persist and persevere. Have them describe their thinking—what goes on inside their heads—when they need to continue to work to solve a problem but don't know what else to do. Ask whether there was ever a time when they wished they had persisted, but didn't. What were the consequences?

Evidence of Growth/Improvement

Students may demonstrate growth in their interdependent thinking by realizing that a group is more productive and efficient than individual effort. As two students said:

It's not about what you want or somebody else does. It's about working as a team to get the job done.

At first I was not a good group worker because I felt controlling and perfectionist. I had to step back and examine my thinking and adjust to be cooperative and open. I've changed the way I thought about my role in the group process.

POSITIVITY

Interdependent thinking is encouraged by positivity. Students are more likely to offer ideas and opinions to their group when they know that their contributions will be received positively, even if their information is not included in the final group decision. To develop well, interdependent thinking also requires the positivity of accepting that our combined and synergistic efforts are worth the time and effort it takes.

It is our role to help students become aware of the positive results of thinking, the joys of inquiry, and the thrill of discovery. We must teach and model taking the time to think. We value and practice collaborative learning because several brains can help our brain think better. It is positive when students have classmates who share the effort as well as enhance everyone's deep thinking. Working in cooperative groups may take more time. However, when students are positive, they are more apt to explore new ideas, ask one another for help, and take advantage of added knowledge and experiences from group mates. Cooperative groups provide an optimal opportunity for students to learn more together. A "we can do it" attitude benefits everyone's learning.

Suggestions for Teachers

Build the vocabulary of positivity: "helpful, constructive, encouraging, affirmative, appreciative, open-minded, inquiring, optimistic, synergistic," and so forth. Read stories of fables, such as *Swimmy* by Leo Lionni (1991). Ask students why and when it is important to use positivity. Ask why is it easier to be engaged and learn in a positive environment than in a negative one. Ask them to interview their parents to determine when in their jobs they have to be positive about people, situations, and ideas, and what effect it has working conditions. Ask them to recall times when they wish they had been positive but weren't. What were the consequences?

Activity: Below the Surface

After reading a story, poem, newspaper article, or a chapter, give your students five or six questions to answer. The questions need to be open-ended—for example, "What if . . . ?" "How do you think the character/ politician/scientist feels when . . . ?" "What would you have done if . . . ?" "Why do you suppose . . . ?"

Place your students in groups of four or five. This fun and challenging activity benefits from the added resources of a group larger than a pair or trio. Each group gets one response sheet with the questions and spaces for three possible answers. The students take turns writing the three answers on which the group agrees. Then the group discusses and agrees on which of the three is the "best" choice. Every group member must be able to define the group's definition of "best."

An appropriate social skill for this activity is "responding positively to ideas." Students may need to brainstorm and write a chart about what this social skill "looks like" and "sounds like" before this activity takes place. This conversation and number of group members needs 20 to 25 minutes work time. When time is called, group members are asked to sign the worksheet, which means, "I participated and I agree." If someone cannot agree, they sign, briefly stating why they can't agree or writing a different answer. Everyone in the group should be able to explain the dissenting, as well as the majority, responses: "It is not a tug of war." "Time ran out before further resources could be checked." "Further consensus could not be reached." A randomly selected reporter then reads to the class the group's "best" responses plus the rationale for each selection, while the teacher facilitates perspective taking and continued thinking by noting similarities and differences in the answers from all groups. The teacher asks groups to state how often their third or fourth alternative was their best (a common result), why students think that happened, and how it felt to develop a thoughtful, in-depth response, rather than just a quick one.

Students are asked to recall the ways in which they "responded positively" and how those positive behaviors kept them willing to contribute alternatives and rationale for their answers. For example, each group mate tells his or her group, "I felt _____ when some responded positively to my idea because _____." Or, "One way I responded positively to an idea I didn't agree with was _____." Or, "Something we decided that was a new thought was _____."

Follow-up Discussion

Invite the group process observer, a role that rotates with each activity, to share observations from the "How are we doing?" checklist. The teacher also can facilitate thinking by asking such questions as, "What happened in your group when you still had to come up with the third alternative?" or, "Did you find your group coming up with four or more alternatives to each question?" "Why?" "What did that do to your group's thinking?"

Ask when were times during this activity in which students were aware of their temptation to respond negatively and how they managed their thoughts. What went on in their head when they did so? What effect did their positivity have on their group's functioning? When else in life or in other school settings is it important to manage their positivity?

Evidence of Growth/Improvement

Students will increase their positivity as we preview and process their positive behaviors. Before a cooperative learning activity, we might discuss the consequences of their negative actions, the taking of time to consider a response before giving it, and how to listen to, acknowledge, and consider alternative points of view without making premature value judgments. After the group activity, we always discuss, "How did we do?" "What went well? What was your role in making it successful?" "How can we do better next time?" (See Aguilar, 2012, for more about positive processing.)

LISTENING WITH UNDERSTANDING AND EMPATHY

The ability to listen may well be one of the highest forms of interdependent thinking. Interdependent thinkers spend a lot of time trying to understand another person's point of view. People who lack this disposition spend most of their energy trying to persuade others to accept their point of view.

One of the most complex forms of listening is empathic listening. Carl Rogers, one of the most influential psychologists of the 20th century, said,

> The way of being with another person which is termed empathic . . . means temporarily living in his/her life, moving about in it delicately, without making judgments. . . . [T]o be with another in this way means that for the time being you lay aside the views and values you hold for yourself in order to enter the other's world without prejudice . . . a complex, demanding, strong yet subtle and gentle way of being. (1975, p. 4)

Suggestions for Teachers

Discuss the need for listening. Why is it important? Ask students to ask their parents whether they need to listen in their jobs. What does it mean for them? Build the vocabulary of listening: attending, not interrupting, paraphrasing, discussing, discourse, dialectical, empathy, rapport, eye contact, and so on.

Have students describe the feelings they experienced while being listened to. Ask what went on inside their heads when they served as listeners. Invite them to share experiences in which they wish they had been listened to and, further, experiences in which they wish they had been better listeners.

Activity: Digital Recorder Dyads

Partners sit facing each other without desk or table. Partner A starts by responding to a question or topic presented by the teacher. After 1 minute the teacher stops the action and asks partner B, who has been listening quietly, serving as the "digital voice recorder," to "play back" what partner A has just said. Partner A listens carefully and corrects or adds to what partner B has heard. Then the partners reverse roles. This method can be developed in stages: Start with learning to summarize and paraphrase, and then move on to reflecting feelings, and more active listening techniques (Graves & Graves, 1989).

As students practice their listening skills, they will notice themselves and others practicing such techniques as maintaining eye contact, paraphrasing others' responses, asking questions related to the subject, using body language like an appropriate nod, and so on. (See Robert Garmston's Chapter 9 for an in-depth description of skillful listening.)

Follow-up Discussion

Discuss with students what people do when they listen to one another. Ask whether they have ever been listened to. How do they know they have been listened to? What goes on in their heads when they listen? What would you see people doing or hear them saying if they really were listening? Enter their statements into the "How are we doing?" checklist and have them use the checklist with their cooperative groups.

Evidence of Growth in Students' Listening Skills

One high school student wrote in his journal:

Listening before prejudging someone's contribution makes sense. Being patient helps. I was surprised at the great ideas and how much everyone added.

Figure 19.3 presents an "I Can" rubric composed by elementary school students to guide their self-directed assessment of their ability to listen with understanding and empathy.

FLEXIBILITY IN THINKING

Interdependent thinkers show flexibility by empathizing with others and considering other points of view. They can generate alternative, creative solutions to problems and can approach problems from differing vantage points. They can find the humor in situations. Flexible thinkers are able to celebrate uncertainty; they enjoy a state of tentativeness and are often uneasy with answers or solutions arrived at prematurely.

Some students have difficulty considering alternative points of view or dealing with several sources of information simultaneously. Their way to solve a problem seems to be the only way. They may decide that their answer is the only correct answer. They are compelled to know whether their answer is correct, rather than being challenged by the process of finding the answer. They are unable to sustain a process of group problem solving over time and therefore avoid ambiguous situations. They have a need for certainty rather than an inclination to doubt or to pursue alternatives. Their minds are made up, and they resist being influenced by data or reasoning that contradicts their set beliefs. Solving problems in a cooperative setting

Figure 19.3. "I Can" Rubric

Listening with Understanding and Empathy	Evidence	Not Yet But I Will Try
1. I wait until someone is finished before I take my turn to speak.		
2. I show respect to the speaker by facing the person.		
3. I show that I am listening by making eye contact with the individual who is speaking.		
4. I show that I am listening by nodding and shaking my head.		
5. I make connections between what you say and what the person directly before you (and before them) has said.		
6. I ask relevant questions.		
7. When I disagree, I paraphrase first to show that I understand and then justify my answer with references.		

will provide students many opportunities to develop, test, reflect upon, and apply alternative and creative solutions.

Suggestions for Teachers

Have students read stories or passages written from differing perspectives (Chris van Allsberg's *Two Bad Ants*, 1988, is an example). Discuss with students the need for flexibility. Build the vocabulary of flexibility: alternatives, "shades of gray," vantage point, reorientation, paradigm shift, transformation, ambiguous. Share with them stories or incidences in which flexibility of thinking in a group produced solutions to problems. Invite them to share examples of instances in which they have had to develop alternative, creative ways of solving problems, either alone or with others.

The purpose of the following activity is to have students realize the possibility of considering alternative points of view. Students will find that there is more than one way to view a problem. They will need to exhibit and practice flexibility in considering others' solutions. Develop your "How are we doing?" checklist. Possible indicators include, "All group mates' points of view are heard."

Activity: Current Events

Every content area or grade level can address current events. Have groups of three or five pick a topic of current interest within the subject objective, grade level, or community—for instance, recycling of household waste; school policies regarding dress, parties, or field trips; issues of community government. Starting with less controversial issues will help build the use of social skills before emotion is strong around any inflammatory topics. Appropriate social skills to assign (one at a time) would be, "respond respectfully to ideas"; "paraphrase"; "disagree in an agreeable way." Each group must reach consensus and write lists of reasons plus a rationale for at least two sides of the issue, and sign the group paper to indicate participation. The reporter from each group must present the decisions to the rest of the class.

A variation would be to divide the class into small groups, with half of the groups working on a rationale for one side of an issue while the other half is working on the opposite side of the same issue. Then group members are asked to switch their position before reporting to the whole class. The analysis might result in the creation of a class continuum representing the many points of view regarding the issue and then lead into a problem-solving situation.

Follow-up Discussion

Invite the group process observer to share indicators. Discuss with students what went on inside their heads when they thought flexibly. How did they approach the problem from a different vantage point? What were the effects of their reorientation? Discuss with students when else in life they need to remain flexible. Ask them what they will take from this learning to other subject areas, to home situations, or to other life situations.

When students are learning to be flexible in their thinking, they will exhibit such behaviors as willingness to change their mind, ability to accept another point of view ("I understand . . . "; "I see and . . . "), accepting or offering more than one alternative to the problem, being able to compromise, and so forth.

METACOGNITION:
MONITORING AND EXECUTING ONE'S OWN THINKING

Interdependent thinkers are mindful of and are in control of their own mental processes. When they are confronted with a problem, they formulate a plan of action in their minds; then they monitor that plan while they are implementing it. After it is completed, they reflect on the plan to determine whether it worked as they hoped it would to produce a reasonable conclusion. Once students are coached to develop this capacity, they can bring these skills to the next level. When working with others, they are able to think metacognitively about the group process, with phrases like, "I think we have a clear understanding of this part of the problem, but I think we need to look a little more deeply at. . . ." Or, "I feel us getting stuck. What do we need to do to move forward?"

Teaching is a prime example of an individual engaged in metacognitive process. As a teacher, one develops a lesson plan, envisions the lesson and sees the action as it unfolds, hears planned questions and expected student responses, and anticipates where student misunderstandings might arise and plans for that. Then, when teaching, good teachers monitor that plan to determine whether it is working and is producing the desired results. (Teachers report that they talk to themselves inside their head: "I need to speed up"; "Go back and review"; "Remember to teach that point in tomorrow's lesson"; "This isn't working!") Then, after the lesson, they reflect to determine what worked and what didn't, where to go next, or what to do differently in future situations. This is metacognitive teaching.

Some students are unaware of their own thinking processes while they are thinking. They lack a plan of action to solve a problem before they begin.

If they do have a plan, they are often unable to determine whether that plan is working or whether it should be discarded and another plan employed. They seldom evaluate their strategy to determine its efficacy or whether there could have been a more efficient approach. When asked, "How did you solve that problem?" they may reply, "I don't know, I just did it." They are unable to describe the steps and sequences they used before, during, and after the act of problem solving. They cannot transform into words the visual images held in their mind. They seldom plan for, reflect on, or evaluate the quality of their own thinking skills and decision-making strategies.

Students can better learn metacognitive skills in cooperative groups (Webb, 1985; Weinstein et al., 1989; Yager et al., 1985, 1986). The teacher can invite students to develop group criteria or operational definitions for their own performance as interdependent thinkers: what they would be doing or saying if they were listening, being positive, thinking flexibly, and so forth. These indicators serve as criteria with which to monitor their own and others' performance. Thus, through collaboration, students develop a common set of criteria, internalize those criteria, hold them in their heads as they work together, and then evaluate their own and the group's performance. Thus, *co-cognition* is the cooperative development of the intellect: collaboratively developing concepts, visions, and operational definitions of interdependent thought, which, in turn, are used to guide, reflect upon, and evaluate one's own performance while in groups (co-cognition) or when alone (metacognition) (Costa & O'Leary, 1992).

Suggestions for Teachers

Help students to understand metacognition with several of these activities: Read to students or have them read passages from such books as Tim Gallwey's *The Inner Game of Tennis* (1974), Jack Nicklaus's *Golf My Way* (1974), and Charles Garfield's *Peak Performers* (1986). Interview athletic coaches, inviting them to describe how athletes positively envision their own performance inside their heads. Invite musicians to describe how they "audiate" or play tunes inside their heads. Ask students whether they ever talk to themselves. Have them describe that process. Build the vocabulary of metacognition: inner speech, inner dialogue, talking to oneself, audiation, mental rehearsal, envisioning, thinking about one's own thinking.

Activity: Thinking Aloud Allowed

Have students get into trios and assign the following tasks: One student will be the problem solver. The problem solver's task is to solve the problem and to verbalize what is going on inside the heads of the trio members while doing this—what strategy is being attempted, what steps they are using to reach the solution.

The second student will be the listener. The teacher will need to teach listening skills, as it requires special abilities to listen effectively to another person's thought processes.

The third student should assume the role of the coach for the listener. The coach's task is to listen to, record evidence of, and give feedback regarding the listener's performance of the "effective listener" skills. The rules of listening that the teacher will need to demonstrate, give reasons for using, have the students practice, and help the coach give feedback about are as follows:

- *Check for accuracy.* Listeners are encouraged to enable the problem solver to check for accuracy by asking such questions as, "How do you know you are right?" or, "What other ways could you solve this problem to prove that you are correct?"
- *Clarify.* Listeners are encouraged to invite the problem solver to elaborate or explain more fully the strategy of solving the problem. They might use such clarifications as, "I still don't understand; help me," or, "Run that by one more time." Listeners are cautioned not to interrupt the problem solver's thinking, but rather to wait until the problem solver comes to the end of a sentence or pauses, then ask for clarification: "When you say, 'I just did it,' how did you know where to start?"
- *Point out errors.* The listener may identify any errors the problem solver may have made such as in computing, in reading, or in listening adequately. Remind students to do this respectfully. Such statements as, "I think there may be a problem with your computation," or, "I think you have misread the information," or, "You didn't hear all the directions," would be some examples of pointing out errors.
- *Do not correct the errors.* It is very tempting for listeners to tell problem solvers how to solve the problem or to tell them when they have arrived at the right answer. This must be avoided. Explain that the purpose of metacognitive discussions is to keep the problem solver thinking rather than arriving at the conclusion. Telling the problem solver that the answer is "correct" may discourage further thinking.
- *Keep talking.* Listeners often will have to remind problem solvers to verbalize what is going on inside their heads as they are solving the problem. Particularly if the problem solvers write something on paper, they will be tempted to interact with the pencil and paper rather than verbalizing the strategy.

- *Encourage persistence.* There will be times when problem solvers might say, "I hate these kinds of problems," or, "I'm not good at solving these problems." The listener may need to encourage the problem solver to persist with phrases like, "Keep it up," "You're making headway," "You're doing fine," or, "What would you do/ say if you could solve these problems?"

Check to ensure that all members of the trio understand their roles. Present the trios with the following or similar problems suitable for their age/grade level:

1. A new student has just been transferred into your room. The teacher has asked if you will be study buddy/friend/mentor to the new kid. You agreed. When the new kid arrives you see that she has obvious learning and social disabilities. Your friends say, "You aren't going to help that girl, are you?" What do you do?
2. It is second-semester final exam time. Someone has gotten a copy of the test for chemistry from last year. Do you take a look? Tell the teacher? Something else? Why?
3. You have taken an interest in computer games. After an introduction during a 6-week enrichment class, you decide to do and learn more. Where do you go for help? What goals do you set for yourself? How do you fit this extra study into your already full schedule of school and soccer?

After the problem solver has solved the problem and the listener has facilitated the metacognition, have the coach give feedback as to which of the behaviors the listener used. Invite the problem solvers to describe what the listeners did to help or hinder the problem-solving process. Ask what they might do differently next time to be even more helpful. Change roles and repeat the process with other similar problems.

The purpose of these activities is to cause students to become more aware of and take charge of their own thought processes. Thinking and then talking about their thinking begets more thinking. Have students encounter many problems. Have them describe what's going on inside their heads when they can't figure out the meaning of an unfamiliar word, or describe their decision-making process as they generate ideas for a story or an essay. As they progress, scaffold them to the next level and invite them to practice metacognitive thinking in groups, asking questions as they problem solve about whether their computation is correct, whether they have examined all solutions, whether they have looked at some aspect superficially to which they should return their attention, what they have done well.

Follow-up Discussion

Have students describe indicators of what people do when they metacogitate—when they are mindful of their own thinking. Have them record their own experiences as they get better at their awareness of their own thinking. Some indicators are: "Can list the steps used to solve a problem," "Learns from mistakes," and so on. Have them move from this to indicators of metacognition when people think together.

Evidence of Growth/Improvement

Students are becoming more aware of their own thinking if they are able to describe what goes on in their heads when they think. When asked, they can describe what they know and what they need to know. These descriptors apply to interdependent thinking as well. Students can describe what data are lacking and their plans for producing those data. They can describe their plan of action before they begin to solve a problem. They can list the steps and tell where they are in the sequence of a problem-solving strategy; they can trace the pathways and blind alleys they took on the road to a problem solution.

They can apply cognitive vocabulary correctly as they describe their thinking and strategies. We will hear students using such terms and phrases as: "I/we have a hypothesis . . . ," "My/our theory is . . . ," "When I/we compare these points of view . . . ," "By way of summary . . . ," "What I/we need to know is . . . ," or, "The assumptions that underlie my/our work are. . . ."

THINKING AND COMMUNICATING
WITH CLARITY AND PRECISION

Language and thinking are closely entwined. Like the two sides of a coin, they are inseparable. Another disposition of interdependent thinkers is their desire to communicate clearly, both orally and in writing. They use specific terminology, refrain from overgeneralization, and support their assumptions with valid data.

Some students' language is confused, vague, and imprecise. They describe attributes of objects or events with such nonspecific words as "weird," "nice," or "okay." Objects are referred to as "stuff," "junk," and "things." Their sentences are punctuated with "ya' know," "er," and "uh." We might hear them use vague nouns and pronouns: "*They* told me to." "*Everybody* has one." "*Teachers* don't understand me." Verbs are often nonspecific: "Let's *do* it." Comparatives go unqualified: "This soda is *better*." "I like it *more*."

Suggestions for Teachers

Talking with students about the need for precise meanings and striving for clarity are essential. Describe times when communicating with precision is not important, and how one knows when it is and when it is not important. Invite them to think of times when they have had to use clear and exact terms because precision was essential to completing a task. Ask them whether they have ever experienced a time when they wish they had communicated more precisely but didn't. What were the consequences? List such experiences on the board or a chart. Add your own situations to their list. Tell them stories in which lack of clear oral or written communication caused difficulty, like missing a meeting because of forgetting to specify differences in time zones.

Build the vocabulary of clear communication: checking, accuracy, correct, error, mistake, proof, reliable, clarifying, clarity, vague, perfect, fidelity, conscientious, exact, craftsmanship, pride, and so on.

Oral language is rife with omissions, vagueness, and generalizations. It is conceptual rather than operational, value-laden, and sometimes deceptive. To encourage careful, precise, and accurate communication and thinking, teachers must teach students to define their terms to become specific about their actions, to make precise comparisons, and to use accurate descriptors. They also should be alert to vague or unspecified terms in the speech of other group members.

Ask students to describe what they would see a person doing or hear a person saying if he or she was communicating with clarity. Enter the behaviors in your "How are we doing?" checklist. Indicators could be, "Uses correct names and labels," "Uses precise analogies," and so forth. Have students keep track of their behaviors during the following activities.

Alert students to vague terms such as those in the left-hand column of Figure 19.4. Practice with them by sharing some statements that need to become more specific. Have them respond by seeking clarity and specificity. In

Figure 19.4. Fostering Clarity of Communication

When you hear such vague terms as . . .	Seek clarity by responding . . .
"He *never* listens to me."	"Never?" "Never ever?"
"*Everybody* has one."	"Everybody?" "Everybody in the whole world has one?"
"*Things* go better with . . ."	"Which things specifically?"
"Things *go* better with . . ."	"Go? Go? How, specifically?"
"Things go *better* with . . ."	"Better than what?"
"*They* made me take it."	"Who are they?" "How did they force you?"

groups, have one student make a vague statement. Group members respond using examples such as those in the right-hand column of Figure 19.4.

Activity: Communicating with Clarity and Precision

Group editing of individual writing efforts can be perfect places for students to work on clarity of communication. The goal is, of course, for students to transfer their editing efforts to their own work in future assignments. Begin students in groups of three on small tasks. Students read their sentence, paragraph, or paper to the group. Orally or in writing, each group mate responds with one positive comment and one suggestion for change or revision. The student receiving the comments hears/takes all suggestions and says, "Thank you," or says nothing. It is not helpful at this time for the receiver to defend or select options, although in some interdependent processes such dialogue would be encouraged. Students then continue around the circle until everyone has received feedback from the group. Revisions are then done at home or during individual work time and brought back to the group at a later time. The complexity of the editing increases as students increase their writing skills and build trust within the group. Appropriate group skills for this activity include "using names," "eye contact," and "responding positively to ideas." Ask students to make a quick verbal "whip" around their group after editing with one topic such as, "I felt _____ during the editing of my paper because _____," or, "It's helpful to give and receive feedback in other situations like _____."

Follow-up Discussion

Ask students what they do when they monitor their own oral language for clarity. What strategies do they employ to monitor and decide what to do when they realize they may have made an error, used vague language, or overgeneralized?

Evidence of Growth/Improvement

As students progress, they will seek clarity from others. You should hear students asking, "Would you please explain that one more time? I'm not sure I understand," or, "How do you know you are correct—what evidence do you have?" You may even hear students question your directions on assignments when they are vague. Value their alertness to imprecision!

As students' language becomes more precise, they will use more-descriptive words to distinguish attributes. They will use more names correctly. They will spontaneously provide criteria for why they think one product is better than another. They will speak in complete sentences, voluntarily provide supportive evidence for their ideas, elaborate, clarify, and operationally define their terminology. Their oral and written expressions will become more concise, descriptive, and coherent. They will voluntarily seek corrective feedback and constructive criticism from their peers and their teacher.

QUESTIONING AND PROBLEM POSING

One of the distinguishing characteristics of humans is our inclination and ability to find problems to solve. Yet students sometimes depend on others to solve problems, find answers, and ask questions for them. They sometimes are reluctant to ask questions for fear of displaying ignorance.

Interdependent thinkers know how to ask questions to produce the data they need. They know how to fill in the gaps between what they know and what they don't know.

Isadore Rabbi, a Nobel Prize–winning physicist, tells a story of when he was growing up in the Jewish ghetto of New York. When other children came home from school, their mothers would ask them, "What did you learn in school today?" But Isadore's mother would ask him, "What good questions did you ask today?" Dr. Rabbi suggests that he became a physicist and won the Nobel Prize because he was valued more for the questions he was asking than the answers he was giving (Barell, 2012).

Suggestions for Teachers

Build the vocabulary of questioning and problem posing: dilemma, controversy, resolution, paradox, interrogation, examine, data collection, and so on.

Talk with students about the nature of questions, why they are important, and what their various functions are. Some of the functions of questions might be: to gather data and verify information; to clarify meaning ("Would you explain what you mean by that?"); to form experimental hypotheses ("If we were to conduct this experiment in a darkened room, would the same results be reproduced?"); to seek opinions ("From your point of view, what do you think will be the effects of this election?"). The following activity will cause students to pose questions.

Activity: Posing Questions

Teachers might introduce a problem and simply have students generate questions about the problem: not solve the problem or generate solutions, just pose questions.

One way to build ownership of asking questions is to ask students in groups of four to determine what questions they want to answer in preparation for a test or assessment situation. The teacher first asks students to decide and write what questions they have. Then individuals join together to compare and contrast their questions and to come up with one list to pose to the rest of the class. Frequently they will have similar questions, which they find reassuring. Also, they will each have questions that others in the group don't understand. A discussion will clarify or delete the unclear questions. A master list is created by the teacher on easel paper as group readers report their lists. Individuals can then use the list for home study, or further group investigation can offer possible answers as a review activity.

Follow-up Discussion

A useful debriefing can be to ask individuals to decide and explain what happened to their original questions as discussion within the group continued. Many of the questions asked in this assignment might be of the recall nature, mostly facts, dates, and basic information. However, it is a beginning for any age group of students who are not used to posing their own questions or being precise in their questioning. Then more complex questioning strategies can be added to the students' repertoire.

Build your "How are we doing?" checklist. Possible indicators are, "Asks thoughtful, focused questions," and "Seeks clarification and verification."

Evidence of Growth/Improvement

Teachers can use the checklists over time to observe a shift from their asking questions and posing problems toward the students asking questions and finding problems for themselves. Furthermore, the types of questions students ask should change and become more specific and profound. For example, questions that reflect empathy and flexibility ("From whose point of view are you seeing this?") and requests for data to support others' conclusions and assumptions ("What evidence do you have . . . ?" or, "How do you know that is true?") increasingly will be heard. Students will pose more hypothetical problems characterized by "what if" questions: "What do you think would happen if . . . ?" "If that is true, then what might happen when . . . ?" "From whose perspective are you viewing this?" or, "What are the assumptions underlying your argument?"

We want students to be alert to phenomena in their environment and to recognize discrepancies and inquire about their causes: "Why do cats purr?" "How high can birds fly?" "Why does the hair on my head grow so fast but the hair on my arms and legs grow so slowly?" "What would happen if we put a saltwater fish in a freshwater aquarium?" "What are some alternative solutions to international conflicts other than wars?" Keep a "How are we doing?" checklist for your class indicating increases in the frequency, complexity, and purposefulness of the questions.

INGENUITY, ORIGINALITY, INSIGHTFULNESS, AND CREATIVITY

Interdependent human beings are creative. They often try to conceive problem solutions differently, examining alternative possibilities from many angles. They tend to project themselves into different roles using analogies, starting with a vision and working backward, imagining they are the objects being considered. David Perkins (1991) suggests that creative people test their limits, take risks, and live on the edge of their competence. They are more intrinsically than extrinsically motivated, working on a task because of the aesthetic challenge more than the material rewards. Creative people are open to criticism. They hold up their products for others to judge and seek feedback in an ever-increasing effort to refine their technique. They are uneasy with the status quo. They constantly strive for greater fluency, elaboration, novelty, simplicity, flexibility, insightfulness, craftsmanship, perfection, beauty, harmony, humor, and balance.

Interdependently functioning people know that working in groups can cause the "creative juices" to flow. They know how to use such strategies as brainstorming, metaphor, or mind-mapping to generate new ways of perceiving problems and their solutions.

Working in groups causes greater stimulation of ideas and thus provides a setting in which to generate creative thought. Students will want to pay attention to how their ideas flow more freely when they listen to and "bounce off" others' ideas in a freewheeling atmosphere.

Suggestions for Teachers

Build the vocabulary of creativity: insight, intuition, clever, creative, originality, fluency, inventive, divergent. Have students discuss the meaning of the old saying, "Necessity is the mother of invention." Invite them to think of times when they had to invent an original solution to a problem. What were the circumstances? Have them describe what went on in their heads when they had to think of an original idea.

Have the students interview their parents, caregivers, or community members—when do they have to draw on their originality, ingenuity, and creativity in their work with partners or teams? Have students read stories of Sir Isaac Newton, Albert Einstein, Michelangelo, Elizabeth Barrett Browning, Alexander Graham Bell, Emily and Charlotte Brontë, Thomas

Edison, Madame Curie, Leonardo da Vinci, Steve Jobs, James D. Watson and Francis Crick, and other noteworthy artists, scientists, inventors, engineers, entrepreneurs, and philosophers who are known for their inventions and creative insights. In some cases these individuals worked alone, but in many others it was the creativity of the groups they worked in that pushed toward higher accomplishment and discovery.

Activity: Cheerios as a Metaphor

The following activities are intended to have students work in groups to experience and then to describe the metacognition involved in the creative thinking proesses of fluency, and simile or metaphor.

Give each group of four to six students a handful of Cheerios. Place the pile of cereal in the center of the table on a piece of paper. (Some students will want to eat the cereal. Tell them they may after the activity.) Ask one student to be the recorder to capture as many of the group's ideas as possible.

Ask them to monitor what goes on in their heads when they are thinking fluently. Their task is to think of as many uses for a Cheerio as they can in 1 minute (e.g., life preserver for ants, wheels for a mini car, packing material, counters, to keep babies quiet, etc.).

After 1 minute call time and have the recorders share the groups' lists of uses for the Cheerios. Then ask the students what went on in their heads when they were thinking fluently. They often will describe their thinking as building on ideas of others—they listened to one another and those ideas stimulated them to generate even more ideas. Others will say something like, "I let my mind run wild to think of anything—sometimes different ideas," or, "I opened my mind to anything it could think of."

Ask students to think of and tell about situations in which they might need to think fluently. Invite them to think of jobs or careers in which people get paid to think fluently (advertising agents, artists, composers, writers). These ideas are stated, by volunteers, to the whole class.

The second activity in which they will engage is metaphorical thinking. Explain that similes are comparisons between two unlike objects or events, introduced by "like" or "as." Give some examples (e.g., "cheeks like roses," "hard as nails"). Have students find examples of similes in short stories, advertising, speeches, and so on. Explain that metaphors compare unlike objects in a way that illuminates or highlights the essence of one by comparison to the other. For example, "spaghetti junction" describes a tangle of roadway interchanges.

Now have the students complete the following: A Cheerio is like a _____ because _____. They will have 1 minute to think of as many similes as they can while the group recorder captures these.

After 1 minute, share the similes. (A Cheerio is like a doughnut, ring, or circle because it's round. A Cheerio is like a sponge because it soaks up liquid. A Cheerio is like a dull book because it's dry.)

Invite students to describe what went on in their heads when they were thinking in similes and metaphors. They may say they searched their memory for comparisons. They may say they thought of the attributes of Cheerios—round, crunchy, spongy, tan color, puffy—and then thought of other similar objects. Again, they no doubt will report that they built upon and "bounced" off others' ideas as they were stimulated to greater creativity when listening nonjudgmentally to others.

Follow-up Discussion

Debrief by having students consider the following questions: What went on in their heads as they brainstormed? How did working in groups facilitate their creative thinking? When else in life do people succeed by thinking creatively in groups? Invite them to ask their parents how they must create, what the circumstances are, and how they draw upon others to enhance their creativity.

Develop indicators of creativity/insightfulness. Have students monitor their own and their group's growth of originality, fluency, and creativity by keeping their "How are we doing?" checklist. Indicators could be: "Play with ideas and things," "Think divergently," "When talking, extend ideas," "Use prior skills and knowledge in new ways," and so forth.

SUMMARY

In this chapter we have suggested some teaching strategies that can contribute to the development of the dispositions of interdependent thinkers recurring throughout the chapters in this book. Working in collaborative ways in classrooms, schools, school districts, and communities produces intellectual growth in all parties involved. Interaction, dialogue, resolving conflicts, solving problems, making decisions, brainstorming, envisioning, and planning in groups not only enhance the quality of the solutions generated, but also contribute to the growth of the dispositions of thoughtful interdependence of every member of the group, allowing individuals to become more precise, more creative, more persistent, more flexible, more curious, more thoughtful, more self-aware, and more empathic toward others. These are behaviors of interdependence. These are the dispositions we believe to be essential for human survival, productivity, and enjoyment, now and in the future.

REFERENCES

Aguilar, E. (2012). *The secret to making it a great school year.* Retrieved from http://edutopia.org/blog

Barell, J. (2012, November 20). *Fostering curiosity here, there and everywhere.* Retrieved from http://smartblogs.com/education/2012/11/20/fostering-curiosity-here-there-everywhere-john-barell/

Costa, A. L., & O'Leary, P. W. (1992). Co-cognition: The cooperative development of the intellect. In. N. Davidson & T. Worsham (Eds.), *Enhancing thinking through cooperative learning* (pp. 41–65). New York: Teachers College Press.

Dishon, D., & O'Leary, P. W. (1998). *A guidebook for cooperative learning: Techniques for creating more effective schools.* Holmes Beach, FL: Learning Publications.

Gallwey, W. T. (1974). *The inner game of tennis.* New York: Random House.

Garfield, C. (1986). *Peak performers: The new heroes of American business.* New York: William Morrow.

Graves, N., & Graves, T. (1989). *What's cooperative learning? Tips for teachers 'n trainers.* Santa Cruz: Cooperative College of California.

Johnson, D. W., & Johnson, F. P. (2012). *Joining together: Group theory and group skills.* Princeton, NC: Merrill.

Lionni, L. (1991). *Swimmy.* New York: Dragonfly Books, Random House.

Nicklaus, J. (1974). *Golf my way.* New York: Simon & Schuster.

Perkins, D. (1991). What creative thinking is. In A. L. Costa (Ed.), *Developing minds: A resource book for teaching thinking* (pp. 85–88). Alexandria, VA: Association for Supervision and Curriculum Development.

Ritchart, R. (2002). *Intellectual character: What it is, why it matters, and how to get it.* San Francisco: Jossey-Bass.

Rogers, C. (1975). Empathic; An unappreciated way of being. *Counseling Psychologist, 5*(2), 2–10.

Van Allsberg, C. (1988). *Two bad ants.* Boston: Houghton Mifflin.

Webb, N. (1985). Interaction and learning in small groups. *Review of Educational Research, 52,* 421–445.

Weinstein, C., Ridley, D., Dahl, R., & Weber, S. (1989). Helping students develop strategies for effective learning. *Educational Leadership, 46*(4), 17–19.

Yager, S., Johnson, R. T., & Johnson, D. W. (1985). Oral discussion, group-to-individual transfer, and achievement in cooperative learning groups. *Journal of Educational Psychology, 77,* 60–66.

Yager, S., Johnson, R. T., Johnson, D. W., & Snider, B. (1986). The impact of group processing on achievement in cooperative learning groups. *The Journal of Social Psychology, 126*(30), 389–397.

Reflecting on Part III

Teaching begins at home and ends in the classroom. Part III contains chapters from practitioners in the areas of adult professional development, K–12 classrooms, and the home. Use their field-tested strategies to teach your own children and the students in your classroom the dispositions of contributing members of groups that think interdependently.

GUIDING QUESTIONS

1. Smart groups are made not born. What deliberate teaching of interdependent thinking do you presently use in your student groups, teacher groups, and/or administrator groups to grow their "smartness"?
2. As a classroom teacher, how do your cooperative learning group assignments result in interdependent thinking? How do you know? What might you do to make those group assignments even more thought-full? How might you promote interdependent thinking throughout your school's curriculum and instruction?
3. Duplicate the record-keeping rubric from Chapter 19 for one of the dispositions of interdependent thinking. Complete it for 2 to 4 weeks. What specific behaviors become more consciously used when you are keeping track?
4. As you observe children interacting in groups, what interdependent thinking skills do you see and hear them using? How might you teach about thinking with positivity? How might you instill in children and young people the strength and skills to turn negative group thought into positive group thought?
5. Interdependent thinking is best learned through imitation. As a parent, when you have family meetings or around the dinner table, how might you model the skills of interdependent thinking?
6. As a parent and/or teacher, what one skill would you first invite your family or class to consciously employ to enhance interdependent thought? How would you know it was successful?
7. What commitments will you make to improve your own capacities for interdependent thought and action?

About the Editors and Contributors

Arthur L. Costa, EdD, is a national and international leader in the area of thinking. His *Developing Minds*, *School as a Home for the Mind*, *Cognitive Coaching* (with Bob Garmston) and *Habits of Mind* (with Bena Kallick) have led educators through research and practices that continue to serve as a foundation for cognitive development for adults and children. Author of many books and articles, Art facilitates individuals and groups to become critical, creative, and curious thinkers. He served as president of the Association for Supervision and Curriculum Development from 1988–1989.

Pat Wilson O'Leary, MA, is a consultant and coach in K–12 classrooms and districts across the United States, Canada, and Puerto Rico. She co-authored three editions of *A Guidebook for Cooperative Learning: Techniques for Creating More Effective Schools,* has written numerous articles, and has worked with thousands of teachers and administrators in the areas of cooperative learning, cooperative teacher teams, new teacher induction, mentoring, academic coaching, and teacher development. In recent years, Pat has served on two long-term committees for the Michigan Department of Education to update state policies for school improvement.

Together, Art and Pat have collaborated over the past 32 years co-training cooperative learning, Cognitive Coaching, and Habits of Mind; have co-authored articles on the cooperative development of the intellect; and share a passion for helping groups and individuals learn to function thoughtfully and empathically in collaborative settings.

Marie Alcock, PhD, president of Learning Systems Associates, is a national and international education consultant, and professor at Walden University's School of Education. With 20 years' experience in public and private education as a teacher and administrator, she founded Tomorrow's Education Network to connect the greater community to classrooms in an effort to improve student literacy.

Larry Alper is a former teacher and school administrator with over 35 years' experience leading schools and developing learning communities for students, teachers, and parents. He is currently co-director of Designs for Thinking, an educational consulting group focused on research, cognitive development, literacy, and whole-school improvement through the use of Thinking Maps. He is the author and co-author of books on thinking and leadership.

Elizabeth Baker, violinist and graduate of Oberlin Conservatory and Indiana University School of Music, was a member of the San Francisco Symphony and is now a member of the Los Angeles Philharmonic. She often has played as concertmaster and as soloist at the Oregon Bach Festival in Eugene, Oregon. She performs in chamber groups and has taught violin at Cal Arts in Valencia, California, and helped with youth orchestra projects supported by the Los Angeles Philharmonic.

Virginia V. Baker, a violinist and graduate of the Julliard Graduate School of Music, was concertmaster of the Pasadena Symphony for 15 years and played in regional orchestras in southern California. She was an assistant concertmaster in the San Francisco Symphony for 21 years and played with the Berkeley Symphony. She has taught violin privately and at Long Beach State University, Occidental College, and UC Berkeley, and in the Young Musicians Program, an outreach program of UC Berkeley.

William Baker is a graduate of the University of Missouri and Fuller Theological Seminary. He has been a classroom teacher, school music teacher, elementary school principal, long-time consultant and coordinator at the Alameda County Office of Education in California, and consultant for the Institute for Intelligent Behavior.

Jill Barton currently teaches 4th grade in Michigan and serves as a district academic coach. She holds a master's degree in educational technology from Boise State University.

Sandra Brace holds a master's degree in dance performance choreography from the University of California, Los Angeles, and a degree in secondary education from National University. She has taught drama, dance, language arts, and music at all levels from kindergarten to university. A school and camp consultant and featured artist in a variety of arts festivals, she is also the composer of a rock opera.

Mary Burke, MA, teaches middle school science and serves as a district instructional specialist and academic coach. She also teaches science methods for elementary and middle school preservice teachers at Western Michigan University.

Lauren A. Carner, PhD, is co-author of *Raising Caring Capable Kids with Habits of Mind* (2012). A school psychologist for over 30 years, in workshops, school and in private practice, she is increasingly focused on teaching Habits of Mind as a versatile and powerful approach to parenting.

Sabrina French, MA, is a Michigan instructional consultant with experience as a pre-K–4 teacher and as a Title I interventionist. In 2008, she was one of 12 educators chosen internationally by the Association for Supervision and Curriculum Development (ASCD) to be interviewed for the 2009 Outstanding Young Educator Award program.

Robert J. Garmston, EdD, is an emeritus professor of Educational Administration at California State University, Sacramento, and co-developer, with Dr. Arthur Costa, of *Cognitive Coaching*. Formerly a classroom teacher, principal, director of instruction, and acting superintendent, he works as an educational consultant and is director of Facilitation Associates, a consulting firm specializing in leadership, learning, personal, and organizational development. He is co-developer and founder, with Bruce Wellman, of the Center for Adaptive Schools (adaptiveschools.com). He has made presentations and conducted workshops throughout the United States as well as in Canada, Africa, Asia, Australia, Europe, and the Middle East. Bob has written and co-authored a number of books, including (with Arthur Costa) *Cognitive Coaching: A Foundation for Renaissance Schools*. In 1999, the National Staff Development Council (NSDC) selected his *The Adaptive School: A Sourcebook for Developing Collaborative Groups* as book of the year.

James Heath has taught history and economics and has a master's degree in sports administration from Ohio State University and an MBA from the University of Notre Dame. Jim joined the Stryker Corporation in May 1988. He has held numerous positions within the company and is now president of Stryker Instruments.

Shirley M. Hord, PhD, is scholar laureate with Learning Forward (previously National Staff Development Council), following her retirement as the first scholar emerita at the Southwest Educational Development Laboratory, Austin, Texas. Prior to this work, she served on the faculty in the College of Education, Science Education Center, University of Texas at Austin, and engaged in research on school change and improvement for 10 years in the federally funded R&D Center for Teacher Education, University of Texas at Austin. She authors books on school-based professional development, leadership, school change and improvement, and professional learning communities. Her latest publication (with Edward F. Tobia) is *Reclaiming Our Teaching Profession: The Power of Educators Learning in Community* (Teachers College Press, 2012). In addition to working with educators at all levels across the United States, Canada, and Mexico, she presents and consults in Asia, Europe, Australia, and Africa.

David Hyerle, PhD, is an author, consultant, and researcher whose work focuses on integrating content-learning, thinking-process instruction, and assessment. In his doctoral work at UC Berkeley and Harvard Graduate School of Education, Hyerle refined a practical language of visual tools he created and called Thinking Maps®. He has written and produced professional development resource guides, videos, and software packages based on Thinking Maps as tools for student-centered learning and whole-school change.

Angela Iadavaia-Cox is co-author of *Raising Caring Capable Kids with Habits of Mind* (2012). A former book and magazine editor of parenting materials, she has worked for 20 years in a school district north of New York City, providing information to parents.

Jerry Jennings, EdD, has been an elementary school teacher, principal, deputy superintendent, and superintendent in his 32-year public school career. He served in rural, suburban, and urban school districts in Michigan. Currently, he is a leadership coach for the Great Lakes Leadership Academy at Michigan State University and is assistant director of Courageous Journey (a three-year staff development opportunity for sitting school superintendents) sponsored by the Michigan Association of School Administrators.

Mark Jones earned a degree in life sciences and physical education at California State University, Chico, where he was a pole-vaulter and high jumper. Mark has been a teacher and coach in the Woodland Unified School District since 1975, teaching biology and anatomy/physiology, and coaching track and field, cross country, basketball, and golf.

Bena Kallick, PhD, is a private consultant providing services to school districts, state departments of education, professional organizations, and public agencies throughout the United States and across the world. Kallick received her doctorate in educational evaluation at Union Graduate School. She has authored or co-authored multiple books, including *Changing Schools into Communities for Thinking* and *Assessment in the Learning Organization* (co-authored with Arthur Costa), and is co-founder of Technology Pathways, a company dedicated to providing easy-to-use software that helps integrate and make sense of data from curriculum, instruction, and assessment. Kallick's teaching appointments have included Yale University School of Organization and Management, University of Massachusetts Center for Creative and Critical Thinking, and Union Graduate School.

Laura Lipton, EdD, is co-director of MiraVia, LLC. Laura is an international consultant whose writing, research, and seminars focus on organizational adaptivity and learning through training and development in data-driven dialogue, group development, action research, and learning-focused collaborations. Laura is author or co-author of numerous publications related to organizational and professional development, learning-focused schools, and literacy development.

Jeremy Little is the choral director at Vernon Hills High School in Illinois. He holds degrees from the University of Illinois and the University of Wisconsin–Milwaukee. His choirs have traveled to England, Italy, the Bahamas, and Ireland.

Patricia Reeves, EdD, is an associate professor of educational leadership, research, and technology in the College of Education and Human Development at Western Michigan University. She is a former K–12 superintendent. Prior to that, she was an instructional consultant for gifted and talented programs, a reading specialist, and a classroom teacher, and has worked with the Michigan Department of Education and the Michigan Association of School Administrators on new statutes and credentialing systems for school leaders. Her research focus includes superintendent practice, data-informed school improvement, administrator development and credentialing, and qualitative research methods. She currently runs the Michigan superintendent endorsement program called Courageous Journey and serves on the Learning Centered Leadership grant team through Western Michigan University.

Patricia A. Roy, EdD, is an independent educational consultant based in Virginia. She has worked with schools, districts, and state departments across the United States and internationally, and recently as faculty for the Arizona Department of Education's Professional Development Leadership Academy. She is a former Learning Forward newsletter columnist and, with Shirley M. Hord, co-authored the innovation configuration maps for Learning Forward's standards for professional learning.

Peter Saucerman, AIA, is a partner with Dreyfuss & Blackford Architects, a leading design firm in Sacramento, California. He graduated from UC

Berkeley, College of Environmental Design, and has practiced architecture in Northern California for 35 years. Peter specializes in master planning and urban design for a variety of public and private clients. He has been active with the American Institute of Architects and the U.S. Green Building Council, particularly on environmental and sustainability issues. He is currently chairman of the Sustainability Council for the Urban Land Institute in Sacramento.

William A. Sommers, PhD, retired in 2012 after teaching and serving as a high school principal, former executive director for Secondary Curriculum and Professional Learning for Minneapolis Public Schools, and a senior consultant with Learning Forward. Bill is an adjunct professor of educational policy and administration at the University of Minnesota, where he also served as a senior fellow for the Urban Leadership Academy. He was an adjunct faculty member at Texas State University, Hamline University, University of St. Thomas, St. Mary's University, Union Institute, and Capella University. Bill is a former board member and past president of the National Staff Development Council, now Learning Forward.

Bruce Wellman is co-director of MiraVia, LLC. He consults for school systems, professional groups, and organizations throughout the United States and Canada, and presents workshops and courses for teachers and administrators on interactive/collaborative instruction, thinking skills development, learning-focused conversations for supervisors and mentors, presentation skills, and facilitating collaborative groups. Wellman has served as a classroom teacher, curriculum coordinator, and staff developer in the Oberlin, Ohio, and Concord, Massachusetts, public schools. He holds an MEd from Lesley College.

Judy Willis, MD, a board-certified neurologist, practiced neurology for 15 years and then received a credential and master's degree in education from the University of California, Santa Barbara. She taught elementary and middle school for 10 years. Dr. Willis has written six books for educators and parents, and now consults with education departments and provides professional development presentations and workshops, nationally and internationally, about learning and the brain.

Pat Wolfe, EdD, is a former K–12 teacher, county office administrator, and adjunct university professor. Over the past 25 years, as an educational consultant, she has conducted workshops for thousands of administrators, teachers, boards of education, and parents in schools and districts throughout the United States and in over 50 countries internationally. Her major area of expertise is the application of brain research to educational practice. She is an award-winning author and has appeared on numerous videotape series, satellite broadcasts, radio shows, and television programs. Dr. Wolfe is a native of Missouri. She completed her undergraduate work in Oklahoma and her postgraduate studies in California. She presently resides in Napa, California.

Diane P. Zimmerman, PhD, was superintendent for the Old Adobe Schools in Petaluma, California. She has worked as a teacher and administrator in special education, as an elementary principal, and as assistant superintendent. Her work with job-embedded staff development has been featured in the joint ASCD–NSDC publication, *A New Vision for Staff Development*. She has collaborated for over 25 years with members of the Cognitive Coaching community.

Index

An *f* following a page number refers to a figure.